It Could Happen to Anyone

Second Edition

To battered and formerly battered women
and their children and to the advocates
who work so tirelessly on their behalf

It Could Happen to Anyone

Second Edition

Why Battered Women Stay

Alyce D. LaViolette
Ola W. Barnett

Sage Publications, Inc.
International Educational and Professional Publisher
Thousand Oaks ▪ London ▪ New Delhi

For information:

Sage Publications, Inc.
2455 Teller Road
Thousand Oaks, California 91320
E-mail: order@sagepub.com

Sage Publications Ltd.
6 Bonhill Street
London EC2A 4PU
United Kingdom

Sage Publications India Pvt. Ltd.
M-32 Market
Greater Kailash I
New Delhi 110 048 India

Printed in the United States of America

Library of Congress Cataloging-in-Publication Data

LaViolette, Alyce D.
It could happen to anyone: Why battered women stay / by Alyce D. LaViolette and Ola W. Barnett.—2nd ed.
p. cm.
Barnett's name appears first on the earlier edition.
Includes bibliographical references and index.
ISBN 0-7619-1994-5 (cloth: alk. paper)
ISBN 0-7619-1995-3 (pbk.: alk. paper)
1. Abused women—United States—Case studies. 2. Abused wives—United States—Case studies. I. Title: Why battered women stay. II. Barnett, Ola W. III. Title.
HV6626.2 .B27 2000
362.82′92′0973—dc21 00-008737

05 06 7 6 5

Acquiring Editor: C. Terry Hendrix
Editorial Assistant: Anna Howland
Production Editor: Diana E. Axelsen
Editorial Assistant: Cindy Bear
Typesetter/Designer: Lynn Miyata
Indexer: Jeanne Busemeyer
Cover Designer: Candice Harman

4/07

Contents

Foreword

A couple of years ago, when my husband was away on a business trip and my sons had a day off from school, I slipped while running from the shower to answer the phone. I had been waiting for that call all morning and, as luck would have it, the phone started ringing just as I got the shampoo into a nice lather. In what seemed like an instant, my right foot went out from under me, my body twisted, and my head hit the woodwork on the wall before slamming down on the polished slate floor. Trying hard not to pass out so that my children wouldn't find me and then bring in the neighbors to rescue their naked mother, I realized that the right side of my face was resting in a pool of blood. When I finally looked in the mirror, I saw a deep gash just above my right eye, like the kind of cut a boxer gets when an opponent connects with a left jab. The hospital is within walking distance of our house, but my sons were still too young at the time to leave home alone, so off they went with me. They were feeling guilty for not having answered the phone themselves and they were worried about what would happen to me at the hospital. As I walked hand-in-hand with them and saw the fear on their faces, it suddenly dawned on me: "Damn, I look like a battered wife. This visit to the emergency room is going to take forever. They're going to ask me dozens of questions, and they won't believe me when I tell them how it really happened. Maybe they'll even question the kids separately while my face is being stitched."

Domestic violence—it could happen to anyone? Not in the eyes of the hospital staff who treated me that Friday morning. The intake clerk was more concerned about the kind of insurance I had than about my injury. The nurse asked me rather perfunctorily how I got the injury, but she never made eye contact with me as she busied herself setting out the medical supplies the doctor would be using. As the doctor examined my eye, he chuckled, and with my children sitting right beside me, he asked, "What happened? Did your husband beat you up?" That was the proverbial last straw; the ER doc got an earful. "As a matter of fact," I began, "I really expected you to seriously question me about how I got hurt. Domestic violence isn't funny. Do you know what I do for a living?" Of course, he didn't, but I filled him in. Maybe my lecture will make him think twice before he talks to an injured woman like that again, although I strongly doubt it. I am fairly certain that that experience had a more profound effect on me than on any of the hospital staff I encountered, including the ER physician.

Walking home from the hospital, I remembered my earlier thought—"I look like a battered wife"—and asking myself in light of the ER staff's response, "What does a 'battered wife' look like? What did I need to look like for the staff at that hospital to be concerned about my safety?" In the pages that follow, Alyce LaViolette and Ola Barnett's answer to the first question is, "Any woman." In the diversity of battered women's voices that they present and in their own words, they emphasize that domestic violence can occur in wealthy households as well as poor ones, among couples of any race or ethnicity, among Native Americans and descendents of the Mayflower pilgrams as well as recently arrived immigrants and refugees, among the young and the old, the physically abled and disabled, those who are straight as well as those who are lesbian, gay, bisexual, or transgendered. Nevertheless, one of the things I like most about this book is the authors' simultaneous awareness of the importance of disadvantage and marginalization in the etiology of domestic violence. Yes, it can happen to anyone, but research is increasingly showing that women who are economically and socially disadvantaged—women who are poor, nonwhite, noncitizens or refugees, very young or very old, disabled, and/or not heterosexual—are often at especially high risk of violent victimization and also are often overlooked or neglected by service providers. The irony of the dual effects of disadvantage and marginalization in terms of victimization and service provision are not lost on me in light of my own experience. When I went to the hospital that Friday morning, my statuses were pretty obvious: I am an upper-middle class, white, U.S.-born, forty-something, physically abled, heterosexual woman—I'm not supposed to be battered because that happens to Other women. Yet, had I been one of those Other women—and this book documents this point well—abuse may have been suspected, but I would not necessarily have been asked about it, and I likely would have been treated with disdain or even hostility.

But LaViolette and Barnett do not just cite research studies or their own practice experiences to make these points; instead, they let us hear the pain, the personal conflicts, and the tremendous strength and resilience of the real experts on domestic violence—battered women. Interspersed with statistics and research findings are the stories of battered women from diverse backgrounds, stories usually told in their own words. It is these stories, I think, that do most to shatter the stereotypes of what a battered woman "looks like" and how she's supposed to think, feel, and act. Moreover, these stories document not only the diversity of battered women, but also the diversity of their experiences. They force us to rethink traditional definitions and images of battering. I have long argued that standard measures of physical and psychological abuse, with their long list of horrors, miss the point. Some batterers hit and punch to control and punish their partners, some restrict social contacts or disconnect the telephone, and some tailor the battering to the specific vulnerabilities of the victim—after all, being intimate brings with it knowledge of a partner's otherwise secret fears. Our measures of who did what to whom how many times typically do not identify these very individualized forms of abuse. Instead, we hear them in women's personal accounts, and LaViolette and Barnett must be applauded for including these women's words. As those of us in academia continue to argue over whether it is methodologically more sound to use broad or narrow definitions of abuse, this book reminds us to do what we should have been doing all along: *listen to battered women.*

Let the reader beware: This is not a "fun" or entertaining book to read. It is a powerful, often gut-wrenching book that you may have to read in small pieces, not only to deal with your emotional reactions, especially to some of the women's experiences, but also to think long and hard about the issues it raises. For me, for example, the book brought to the surface many of the conflicts I feel in working to eliminate violence against women and increase women's safety, while at the same time holding batterers accountable for their behavior. We often encourage battered women to leave abusive relationships, but leaving for some women may mean giving up eligibility for public housing, the only housing they can afford. Many of us in the battered women's movement have advocated for mandatory arrest policies only to find following the enactment of such legislation more women being caught in the police net, usually for defending themselves or retaliating against a batterer—behavior that is nonetheless violent in the eyes of the criminal justice system. Mandatory arrest laws have also had a disproportionate impact on communities of color. And do we really want to solve the problem of domestic violence by locking more men away in prisons and jails that have abandoned the goal of rehabilitation?

In *It Could Happen to Anyone,* Alyce LaViolette and Ola Barnett challenge us to think critically about how we *image* battered women and batterers, and about how we *respond* to battered women and batterers. As we embark on a new century, I think that unfortunately *inclusivity* remains an elusive goal of the battered women's movement. LaViolette and Barnett and, most important, the battered women whose voices we hear in these pages remind us that if we exclude any group from our work, we will not succeed in ending violence. This goal of inclusivity remains elusive to some extent because of the current political climate dominated by a "lock 'em up and throw away the key" mentality. However, not all women and men are equally likely to be locked up; it is the disadvantaged and marginalized who, as always, bear the brunt of this burden. As we begin the 21st century, then, we must reevaluate our current policy goals for meeting the needs of battered women and addressing men's violence. And that reevaluation must include a critical analysis of how each policy may impact—for better or for worse—women and men from *all* social groups in our society.

When I sat down to read this book, I certainly didn't think I had all the answers, but I was pretty confident I had a good bit of the puzzle sorted out. This book substantially shook my confidence, and I'm grateful to Alyce LaViolette and Ola Barnett for the wake-up call.

—*Claire M. Renzetti*
St. Joseph's University
Philadelphia, Pennsylvania

Acknowledgments

The authors wish to thank Terry Hendrix for his support and commitment to this book. We especially wish to express our appreciation to Claire M. Renzetti for her dramatic and heartfelt foreword. Thanks are also due Liann Lech and Diana Axelsen for their expertise in book production and for meeting all the deadlines. We wish to give specific thanks to Carol V. Harnish, who critiqued and edited the first edition of this book and persisted in her conscientious endeavor through this second edition. Special appreciation to Paul Mones, Barrie Levy, and Joan Zorza for their feedback. Finally, we offer our most profound thanks to Raquel Bergen, for reviweing this revised edition. She made many invaluable suggestions and helped us refine our comments to better describe the plight of battered women.

Alyce LaViolette wishes to thank her mother, whose life was an inspiration, whose advocacy touched many lives, whose love embraced her children, and whose death has left an incredible void. Alyce wishes to thank her father, who is a role model of courage, dedication to family, friends and community, a man who is a constant source of strength to his children and grandchildren, and a man who is what a Hallmark Father's Day card is all about. Alyce also wishes to acknowledge the best coauthor anyone could wish for. Ola's integrity is exceptional and her friendship invaluable.

Ola Barnett wishes to thank her many professors and colleagues who have motivated her throughout a lifetime of academic pursuits. Because of their efforts, she has had this unique opportunity to contribute to society's efforts to eliminate family violence. She treasures her supportive husband and children and her four grandchildren, Kelley, Lesley, Devin, and Shane. Ola wishes to thank Alyce for her dedication and advocacy on behalf of battered women. Ola prizes her friendship with Alyce that has extended over 20 years. Last, Ola wants to call attention to Alyce's success in making battered women's case histories come alive in this book.

Introduction

CASE STUDY

On May 2, 1982, Michael Connell visited his estranged wife, Karen, and their son, Ward. Karen and Michael had been separated for more than a year, but they were seeing each other again. A friend of Ward's was also visiting, and the four of them were going on a picnic. They never made it.

At around noon, Karen staggered from the house, bleeding profusely from the neck. She collapsed into a neighbor's arms, gasping that her husband had stabbed her and was still in the house with their 5-year-old son and his friend.

The South Pasadena Police arrived on the scene to investigate. After several attempts to make contact with Michael or the children failed, they contacted the Los Angeles Sheriff's SWAT team. The SWAT team, using a bullhorn, requested that anyone inside the house come out.

Two boys walked out of the house with their hands up, pleading "Don't shoot; we're the good guys." The SWAT team forced entry into the house at about 3:00 p.m. They found a man lying on the bathroom floor. He had massive slash wounds to his neck area and a stab wound to his chest. The wounds were self-inflicted. Michael Ward Connell was dead.

At the same time, Karen was undergoing an operation at Huntington Memorial Hospital. She had lost seven pints of blood, and her vocal cords had been severed. Her young son, Ward, had saved her life by jumping on his father's back and hitting him, screaming, "Don't hurt my Mom!"

The coroner reported that the decedent apparently had marital problems with his wife for quite some time. Karen and Ward had been residents of Haven House, a refuge for battered women and their children. At the time of the attack, Karen had been a member of their outreach counseling group.

HISTORY OF THE BATTERED WOMEN'S MOVEMENT

Fortunately for battered women, batterers, and their families, the issue of domestic violence has come out of the closet. In the early 1970s, the women's movement spawned the shelter movement, along with advocacy for women's rights. When media attention focused on issues affecting women, such as jobs, pay equity, and child care, the violence directed at women in their own homes came to public attention. The *New York Times* indicated an increase in articles on wife abuse from zero in 1970 to 44 in 1977. By 1978, battered wives had become a separate topic, distinct from reports on assaults and murders.

Tierney (1982) sums up the issue of public awareness as follows:

> Wife beating has become the object of media attention and government policy, not because of an increase in its frequency, or because the public has become more concerned, but because a social movement developed in the 1970's to help battered women. The growth of the battered women's movement illustrates both successful resource mobilization and the creation of a social problem. (p. 207)

Although the women's movement of the 1970s gave necessary impetus and attention to battered women through media focus and education, the first shelter for battered women and their children was started in 1964. Haven House, in Pasadena, California, was established through the efforts of Al-Anon members, who saw the need to provide safety and shelter for the families of physically abusive alcoholics. These Al-Anon members held bake sales and small fundraisers to pay rent on a house in Pasadena. From 1964 to 1972, there was no more than one paid staff person. All other staff were volunteers, and the only program (until 1974) was Al-Anon. Chiswick Women's Aid, established in London, England, in 1971, was the first widely publicized shelter for battered women. In 1972, Women's Advocates, Inc. established a crisis hotline in St. Paul, Minnesota. Rainbow Retreat opened in 1973 in Phoenix, Arizona. In 1975, NOW formed a national Task Force on Battered Women/Household Violence. Activists lobbied successfully for passage of broader protection laws for battered women in 1976.

DOMESTIC VIOLENCE: THE FACTS

The drama and tragedy of woman abuse will touch most of us, at some time in our lives, in a very personal way. This could happen directly as a result of our own intimate relationships with lovers, or through the experience of other family members and/or friends. Whether or not we have been raised in an abusive family environment, we are almost certainly going to have close contact with, and be affected by, someone who has. And that someone, unless he gets help, will carry the legacy of violence with him into his intimate relationships. Understanding battering becomes a significantly relevant issue when applied to our own personal experience.

> Violent crimes, particularly rape and violence against intimates, are vitally important to understand and to prevent. The debilitating effects of these crimes, most of which are against women, are dramatic and long-lasting for the victims and for society. Yet the very nature of these crimes and the consequences of them mean that victims are often unwilling or even unable to report them to the police or to a National Crime Survey (NCS) interviewer. (Harlow, 1991, p. iii)

VAWA. Under the leadership of Senator Joseph Biden of Delaware, the U.S. Congress passed the Violence Against Women Act (VAWA) in 1994. VAWA includes sweeping changes affecting nearly every aspect of criminal justice responses to battered women. It calls for the expenditure of $1.62 billion in five different areas (or Titles) related to gender-based violence (Klein, 1995). No other set of laws has ever tackled domestic violence so directly or aggressively.

The O.J. Simpson case. Another event occurred on June 12, 1994. Nicole Brown Simpson, the ex-wife of American football hero O.J. Simpson, and her friend, Ron Goldman, were found murdered, their throats slashed, in the entryway of her condominium in exclusive Brentwood, California. A shocked nation had trouble reconciling their picture of O.J., the Heisman Trophy winner, with a man who had previously beaten two ex-wives and now was charged with double murder with special circumstances (Turque et al., 1994). The excessive media coverage turned a painful national spotlight on the tragedy of domestic violence.

The story did not end with the juries' verdicts (not guilty in O.J.'s criminal trial, and liable in his subsequent civil trial). The Simpson case continued to reverberate in family court over the custody of O.J.'s minor children (McGuire, 1999). Judges are increasingly considering domestic violence as a factor in custody decisions, and by 1995, 44 states required them to do so (Hofford, Bailey, Davis, & Hart, 1995).

STATISTICS ON VIOLENCE AGAINST WOMEN

By the mid-1980s, domestic violence had reached such epidemic proportions (e.g., Finkelhor, 1984; Koss, Gidyez, & Wisniewski, 1987) that the U.S. Centers for Disease Control in Atlanta, Georgia began to treat partner abuse like any other epidemic by gathering statistics to include in its measurement section on the epidemiology of homicide and suicide ("Epidemiology of Domestic Violence," 1984). According to data (1979-1987) collected from the Federal Bureau of Investigation's (FBI's) *Uniform Crime Reports* (FBI, 1989), males perpetrated 5.6 million violent attacks on their female partners, an annual average of 626,000 (also see Flanagan & McGarrell, 1986). Saltzman et al. (1990) found that women were more than twice as likely as men to be victims of nonfatal intimate assaults.

Assault data. Murray Straus and his colleagues conducted two national surveys of family violence using the Conflict Tactics Scales (CTS) (Straus, 1979). In the most recent survey, 3,520 currently or previously coupled men and women were asked 18 specific questions about individual acts of verbal, symbolic, and physical aggression that had occurred during the previous year and during their entire relationship. (See Appendix A for estimates of perpetration of assaults based on the Straus and Gelles, 1986, study.)

These data suggested that wives were at least as aggressive as their mates. The researchers did not consider motivation for and outcome of the assaults (or any contextual issues). The gender mutuality asserted by the report sounded a battle cry to battered women's advocates, already embroiled in the controversy over gender bias in society (see Browne, 1990). Recently, the findings of the National Violence Against Women Survey (NVAW), studying only victimization and using a modified version of the CTS, did not support the notion of mutuality (see Appendix A). The researchers randomly sampled 8,000 men and 8,000 women between November 1995 and May 1996. The results indicated that 22.1% of the women interviewed and 7.4% of the men reported being physically assaulted by a current or former intimate (Tjaden & Thoennes, 1998).

The National Crime Victimization Survey (NCVS), using interview data drawn from a large national sample of households, corroborates these findings. This survey includes crimes that are not reported to the police. NCVS data obtained from victim respondents revealed more than 960,000 annual incidents of violence against intimates (current or former spouses, boyfriends, or girlfriends). Almost one third of the assaults were repeat victimizations, and 85% of the victims were women. According to respondents, almost one third of male perpetrators also threatened to kill their female partners. It is important to note that victims had recounted only about one half of the incidents to the police (see Greenfeld et al., 1998). (For statistics on racial and ethnic differences, see Craven, 1997, in Appendix A.)

Injuries. Injury data dispel any notion of gender equivalency. Mercy and Saltzman (1989) determined that the leading cause of injury to women is intimate violence. Toufexis (1987) spells out the statistical drama of spouse abuse in her article, "Home Is Where the Hurt Is": "An estimated two to four million women are beaten [annually] by their husbands or boyfriends, more than are hurt in auto accidents, rapes, or muggings" (p. 68). (See the Bachman & Saltzman, 1995, study in Appendix A; also see Campbell, 1989b; Markward, 1996; Waldner-Haugrud, 1999.)

According to Campbell and Sheridan (1989), approximately 20% to 50% of all female emergency patients (not just trauma victims) are battered women. The NCVS found that about half of female victims of partner aggression claim some sort of injury, and about 20% seek medical assistance (Greenfeld et al., 1998). In the 1994 National Electronic Injury Surveillance System (NEISS) study of hospital emergency room patients, 84% of all individuals treated for injuries inflicted by intimates were women (Rand, 1997; also see Abbott, Johnson, Koziol-McLain, & Lowenstein, 1995). The National Survey of Families and Households found that women were almost three times more likely than men to be injured in intimate victimizations (Zlotnick, Kohn, Peterson, & Pearlstein, 1998). (Appendix A contains additional statistical data relating to injuries.)

Homicide data. Homicide is the least likely outcome of a domestic assault, but it is the most feared and the primary basis for formulating criminal justice policy. Women in America are killed in overwhelming numbers by the men who profess to love them (Bachman & Saltzman, 1995; Campbell, 1992; Crawford & Gartner, 1992). Over the 6-year period from 1983 to 1988, 64% of spousal homicide victims were female, and 36% were male (FBI, 1989). Because the relationship between the perpetrator and victim is known in only about 60% of the deaths, most statistical analyses rely on data that actually undercount the number of domestic homicides (Johnson, Li, & Websdale, 1998). (See Appendix A for recent homicide statistics gathered by the FBI and presented by J. A. Fox [included with Greenfeld et al., 1998].)

In 1997, the New York City Department of Health released a review of coroner records for women (1,156) over the age of 16 who were killed between 1990 and 1994. Of the 484 cases where the killer's relationship to the victim was known, intimate partners murdered 49% of the women. Also of crucial social significance was the fact that in 67% of the cases, at least one child was physically present during the murder.

The rage displayed by the men who killed their loved ones amazed the reviewers. More than half of the women were stabbed, strangled, beaten, kicked, burned, punched, hit, or thrown from windows. In 26% of the incidents, at least one other person was killed, and in 44% of these murders, the other person was a child (see Wilt, Illman, & Field, 1997).

Leaving the relationship. Leaving, which was once thought of as the avenue to safety, is not as safe as once believed. A number of battered women recount episodes of being stalked before, during, and after an intimate relationship (see Burgess et al., 1997; Westrupt & Fremouw, 1998). Stalking often evokes extremely high, if not paralyzing, levels of fear (see Appendix A for statistics on stalking).

Many women also experience violence as they attempt to separate or become "unmarried." Lehnen and Skogan (1981), in analyzing data from the National Crime Survey, found that, contrary to popular beliefs, most victims were divorced or separated at the time the violence occurred. The U.S. Department of Justice (1983, p. 21) revealed that about three fourths of reported spousal assault victims were separated or divorced at the time of the incident. In Harlow's (1991) account, ex-husbands perpetrated 216,000 spousal assault incidents, more than in other categories (current boyfriend or spouse). According to several more recent studies, separated women were victimized about 3 times more often than divorced women and about 25 times more than married women (Bachman & Saltzman, 1995; also see Zlotnick et al., 1998).

SPECIAL POPULATIONS

As research has continued, investigators have found that violence also occurs in populations that have previously been understudied. These groups have nearly all the problems of the majority of battered women, but they also have special challenges that place them outside the mainstream of society's customary support systems. Some of these unique considerations encompass age, legal status, and physical and mental limitations, and others are related to sexual orientation, economic, social, cultural, and religious differences (e.g., Mason, 2000).

Dating populations. Sugarman and Hotaling (1991) have estimated that 9% to 60% of dating relationships include physically abusive encounters. Two studies found that about 20% to 40% of college-age dating couples have experienced courtship violence (Stets & Straus, 1990; White & Koss, 1991; see also Neufeld, McNamara, & Ertl, 1999). NCVS data (1992-1993) established that boyfriends or ex-boyfriends perpetrated approximately 16% of assaults, and current or former girlfriends were responsible for 2% (Bachman & Saltzman, 1995). (This study appears in Appendix A.)

Lesbian populations. Several factors influenced early researchers regarding same-sex relationships. Historically, lesbians had been adversely affected by homophobic prejudice (Herek, Gillis, & Cogan, 1999). Furthermore, many people believe that women will not really hurt each other, and that they are not aggressive or violent. Nonrandom samples indicate that between 17% and 47% of lesbians experience repeated acts of violence in intimate relationships (see Coleman, 1992; Lie, Schlitt, Bush, Montagne, & Reyes, 1991; Lockhart, White, Causby, & Isaac, 1994; Waldner-Haugrud, Gratch, & Magruder, 1997). Renzetti (1992) stated that more than half of the victims of lesbian battering in her study experienced more than 10 abusive incidents during their relationship. (See the Tjaden, Thoennes, and Allison, 1999, study summarized in Appendix A for another statistical estimate of lesbian abuse; for police department studies, see Cook-Daniels, 1998.)

Elder women. Studies of elder abuse have tended to be limited and frequently failed to include the gender or the relationship of the perpetrator to the victim. What few studies are available gather data from vastly different samples of elders. (See Appendix A for data about abuse of elder women from three studies: Bachman and Saltzman, 1995; Pillemer & Finkelhor, 1988; and Tatara & Kuzmeskus, 1997.) Research in several other countries suggests that most elder abuse is spouse abuse (e.g., Halicka, 1995; Johns & Hydle, 1995).

Rural and disabled women. Rates of wife abuse in rural communities (population 2,500 or less) and against women with physical or developmental disabilities are essentially unknown. Nevertheless, there is every reason to believe that the difficulties faced by women in both populations are severe and services much more limited (see Thompson, 1995, and Websdale, 1995a, 1995b, about rural women, and Carlson, 1997, about disabled women). Studies of partner abuse and marital rape in women with a mental illness disclosed rates varying from 21% to 75% (Briere, Woo, McRae, Foltz, & Sitzman, 1997; Carmen, Ricker, & Mills, 1984; Cole, 1988; Lipschitz et al., 1996).

A global perspective. In most countries, wife beating is an acceptable form of control, whether legal or illegal (Schuler, Hashmi, Riley, & Akhter, 1996). Many countries have been slow to identify wife assault as a social problem. On the broadest scale, research has only recently begun to capture the overlap between wife assault, community violence, and violence within and between countries (see Walker, 1999, for a review).

Throughout the world, injury-causing assaults routinely reflect a pattern of male-to-female violence, whether in Austria, Nigeria, Hong Kong, or Japan (see Bernard & Schlaffer, 1992; Kalu, 1993; Tang, 1999; Yoshihama & Sorenson, 1994). Marital assault rates in Canada, Australia, and New Zealand are analogous to those found in the U.S. national family violence surveys (Brinkerhoff & Lupri, 1988; Knight & Hatty, 1992; Moffitt & Caspi, 1999). In countries such as Korea, Nicaragua, and Bangladesh, rates are much higher (Kim & Cho, 1992; Wessel & Campbell, 1997). Russia seems to have one of the highest wife murder rates in the world, with approximately 14,000 to 16,000 female homicides per year (Horne, 1999).

THE REALITIES OF DOMESTIC VIOLENCE

Some of the realities of domestic violence come from statistics. Most of the realities, however, come from the emotional, economic, familial, cultural, and legal burdens placed on battered women as they attempt to make decisions that will greatly affect their lives and the lives of their children.

Battered women face a number of difficult decisions as a result of living in a violent household. The most fundamental of these is the decision to stay or leave. If a woman remains with her abuser, she is criticized and quite often blamed for her own victimization. If she leaves, she is judged as demonstrating a lack of commitment and concern for the welfare of her children and her spouse.

It is not uncommon for theories in behavioral science to portray victims as provocateurs—people who incite the hapless culprit to violence, robbery, rape, or mayhem. We have held people responsible for being burglarized because they did not have better locks or alarm systems. We wonder whether the victim of a drive-by shooting was actually an innocent victim or a gang member. It seems as if the mere act of victimization casts aspersions upon the character of the victim. This is a dilemma that few women can resolve.

As crimes become more "personal or intimate," we question more closely the culpability of the victim. We hold the rape victim accountable for both her whereabouts after dark and her dating practices, and we wonder if her turtleneck sweater was cut too low! Defense attorneys have asked rape victims, "What did you do to indicate that you did not wish to be raped?" By contrast, how frequently did they ask the victim of a burglary, "What did you do to indicate that you did not want to have your house burglarized?"

Similarly, there is a feeling on the part of some people that battered women have "asked for it." Overall, there is little understanding of the reasons that battered women stay, and little empathy for their plight. Several factors compound these problems: (a) the ability of nuclear families to insulate and isolate themselves from neighbors, family members, and societal repercussions; (b) acceptance of sex-role stereotypes and behaviors limited by gender; and (c) the reluctance of the system to interfere in the private sphere of a sacrosanct institution. Nevertheless, spouse abuse parallels the existence of humankind. It has been an unwelcome, yet unchallenged stepchild residing in our families for generations.

PURPOSE OF THE BOOK

The following pages are an attempt to provide understanding and empathy regarding this complex issue and to present an integrated learning theory explanation of the conditioning that culminates in wife abuse, the resulting state of the victim, and the decision to stay with an abuser. We have asked battered women why they stayed in their abusive relationships, or why they left. We have asked about their survival both in and out of the relationship. This book represents, in part, their answers to these and other questions. Information has been gathered from both the scientific and clinical sectors to formulate a comprehensive explanation that is also congruent with grassroots experience. Our work is anchored in empirical data, especially data collected from the battered women themselves.

Finally, actual case histories furnish graphic illustrations of the topics covered. Our case studies represent a range of battering situations. We have heard from a number of battered women who were unable to relate to the severity of abuse described in the case studies. They may be in a state of denial, but battering relationships do vary in degree of injury, types of abuse involved, severity, frequency, and nature of the attachment to the perpetrator. For these reasons, our case studies are diverse. Some may seem lacking in drama if you have seen *The Burning Bed,* but not to the women and children involved. *Fear, both emotional and physical, is present in every case.*

When we describe battering in this book, we are not talking about an isolated instance of aggression. We are talking about an atmosphere that is created by many forms of abuse, and a pattern that may escalate over time in frequency and intensity (Dobash & Dobash, 1979; Pagelow, 1981b; Walker, 1979). One form of abuse does not occur in isolation from all others, and physical abuse does not have to occur frequently in order to create a climate of fear. Adams (1986) defines the battering control pattern as involving intimidation and pressure, withholding of financial or emotional support, issuance of ultimatums and accusations, and employment of children as a confederate against the woman. We are using a definition of battering that includes four areas: *physical* (slapping, pushing, kicking, restraining, using a weapon); *sexual* (raping, beating genitalia, sodomizing, forcing unusual sex acts); *destruction of pets and property* (beating a wall, breaking furniture, destroying valued possessions, misusing pets); and *psychological* (making threats, taking all the money, calling her names, ridiculing). *Violent* relationships are characterized by *fear, oppression,* and *control.*

Men who batter often find it difficult to recognize verbal and psychological abuse as abuse. They do not relate to the fear it can create, and they find it most difficult to change these kinds of behaviors. Much of the work that must be done in effective batterers' programs revolves around recognizing these forms of intimidation and halting nonphysical as well as physical abuse in the relationship.

We will attempt to address some of the myths surrounding domestic violence. There is an old saying: "If there are two stories, the truth is usually somewhere in the middle." Lenore Walker (personal communication, 1985) has created the new, improved version of this saying as it relates to partner abuse: "If there are two stories, the truth is usually worse than either one of them."

We have also found that the truth is closer to her story than to his. Riggs, Murphy, and O'Leary (1989) found that perpetrators of abuse purposefully conceal undesirable interpartner aggression. That revision of reality makes sense. Emotional survival depends upon our ability to look at ourselves and to conclude "I am a decent person." If our deeds are incongruous with that statement, it might be necessary to modify our perceptions and recollections of the deeds. For instance, it is more satisfying to our egos to say: "My partner and I mutually decided we were not compatible," than to say, "I got dumped."

When a man hits, belittles, or bullies someone he loves, he needs to create a framework by which to make that behavior seem reasonable. His emotional well-being depends upon it. Provocation is a great equalizer in this perceptual battle. Minimizing or forgetting details, or the degree of injury, is a tool that can be used to construct this framework. Jouriles and O'Leary (1985) found that the woman's perceptions of her partner's behavior and beliefs may be more accurate than her batterer's self-report.

A couple's report to a therapist:

His story: I have not been really violent. I only hit my wife with a pillow.

Her story: We had an argument. He took a small, hard couch pillow and hit me across the face 'till I almost lost consciousness.

He says: I wouldn't of hit her, but she attacked me with the phone.

She confronts him with a new, revised edition: I wouldn't have thrown the phone at you, but you were very angry and came across the room, ranting and waving your arms. You were on the attack and I was defending myself.

His rebuttal: Oh yes, that's right.

Most of us say that we do not understand people who put up with abuse from a spouse or lover. Most of us say that we would leave if that happened. To understand the battering relationship, it is necessary to understand that most relationships do not start out with one partner seriously injuring the other. Unless you are with someone who has battered several partners, the onset of battering usually is gradual and subtle. Our own theory is that you could live with Jack the Ripper or Ma Barker for at least a year, and if you were in love, you would not figure it out. This could happen because most of us are not looking, we are just feeling, and because Jack and Ma would be on their best behavior.

Let us make this a personal issue. We would ask the reader to think about a time when you were in an important relationship (lover, friend, job) and left that situation, only to look back on it and wonder why you had stayed so long. Did you find yourself asking how you had gotten there in the first place? How did you answer these questions? You might also ask yourself how you felt about your own anger and the ways you express it. What feelings do you usually have after you have gotten angry?

Put yourself in the beginning of your love relationship. Think about the intensity of your feelings and beliefs regarding your partner and the relationship itself. Most of us enter a marriage or important relationship feeling that we will be nurtured, loved, and protected. Let us call our hypothetical couple Sam and Diane (for those of us who have watched *Cheers*).

THE STORY OF A TYPICAL BATTERED WOMAN: DIANE

CASE STUDY

Sam and Diane have dated for more than a year and decide to get married. They know each other's friends and family. They have spent birthdays and holidays together and share many common interests, including religious beliefs. Diane's family and friends like Sam and vice versa, and everyone is excited about their marriage.

They are married and move into an apartment with their cat and two goldfish. They are setting up their home with many of the gifts they have received. Sam and Diane have had a few arguments while they have been together, but nothing serious.

After they have been married about 6 months, Sam comes home from work late again. He has been putting in lots of overtime. Diane is upset because dinner is cold, he has not called, and they have not had time together. Sam is tired and grouchy, and they begin to argue. Sam yells louder than he ever has, calls her a bitch, and throws his glass of water down, breaking a glass that was a wedding gift.

How many of you think you would leave the relationship? Think about it. Diane and Sam do not break up. Sam apologizes. They really talk to each other for the first time in a few weeks. He says he is tired and did not mean to break anything. Diane feels his pain and remorse. He takes her out to dinner, and they feel close again. She understands, and when they get home, they make love. Diane may feel upset, but she puts it aside as she empathizes with Sam. After all, she thinks, people are not perfect. It is important to be tolerant.

They go on a camping vacation that year to celebrate their first anniversary and share time with both families. Sam likes Diane's brother, and they enjoy going to ball games together. Sam and Diane get rid of some hand-me-down furniture and buy a new couch and chair. They even own an electric toothbrush and Seal-a-Meal. It is at the end of their second year of marriage that Diane announces she is pregnant, and it is shortly after that time that they have a major argument. They yell at each other and call each other names; then Sam hits the wall and slaps Diane once. How many of you would leave now? Why or why not?

After the birth of their first child, the families celebrate the baby's baptism at Sam and Diane's new home. There is reminiscing about the past 3 years and enthusiastic anticipation of the next holiday with the first grandchild. There have been several serious arguments during the first pregnancy, but only the one episode of hitting. Diane does find herself feeling apprehensive when Sam gets angry, but she reassures herself that it is only the financial pressure that set him off.

Sam begins to fear his anger and tries not to get mad, but he finds that the harder he pushes anger away, the angrier he gets. He remembers his father's outbursts, the terror on his mother's face, and his own fear. He knows he can control himself, except sometimes, Diane just really pushes his buttons.

When the baby is 1 year old, Diane discovers that she is pregnant again. Everyone is excited. Two days after her announcement, she and Sam argue over finances and her desire to return to work. Sam slaps her twice and pushes her. Then, he leaves the house. Diane cries; she is almost hysterical. She is also afraid that Sam is gone. He calls several hours later, crying and begging for forgiveness. She is not ready to forgive, but she tells him to come home anyway. He returns, they reconcile, and neither of them tells anyone what has happened.

Both Diane and Sam feel embarrassed about the aggression, and they do not want their friends or family to know about it. It has been 3½ years, one broken glass, two holes in the wall, two episodes of slapping, one push, 18 months of increasing fear, one house, many joyous holidays, 1½ children, shared memories, love, religious connections, economic security, and family bonds. How many of you would leave now?

As Diane and Sam develop their own cycle of violence—which includes tension over an indefinite period of time, outbursts, and a honeymoon—they begin to close off emotionally from their friends and families.

The process is subtle. It begins with the first little lie. It continues when Diane and Sam do not go to friends for dinner, because Diane "tripped" and hurt herself, or because she got the "flu," as opposed to she is upset because she has been slapped.

The lies chip away at their integrity and separate them from others. The lies also form a bond between the two people (or more, if there are children) involved. Isolation develops slowly. Can you imagine telling your close friends that you have been slapped and pushed by your husband (whom they like, and whom you still like)? Most of us want shared friends, want others to like our partners, and want others to think we have good taste.

Most of us establish bottom lines about relationships before we become involved. Bottom lines are the lower limits of our basic expectations of a relationship. "If she ever had an affair . . ."; "If he ever hit me . . ."; "If she does not have children . . ." are all examples of bottom lines. These basic expectations remain until they are confronted. Then, for most of us, it is easier to lower or alter them than it is to change our lives.

It is our purpose to demonstrate that battered women have learned to endure abuse and to remain in their unhealthy relationships. Their learning occurs not only through common and "normal" socialization processes, but also through exposure to the abuse itself. We hope to point out convincing analogies between learning in the laboratory using animal subjects, and learning in the lives of battered women. That is, the principles of learning that control behavior discovered by such scientists as Pavlov, Skinner, and Seligman will ultimately be linked to the same principles of learning affecting the behavior of battered women.

Our theory of battering is eclectic. It includes the effects of male-female socialization, sex-role stereotyping, family history, and gender-related power differences. It also rests upon research conducted from behavioristic and cognitive learning perspectives, as well as on social learning research and theory. In general, we assume, as does Kishur (1989), that family violence has multidimensional causes: intrapsychic (individual), interfamilial (family), and environmental (cultural) dynamics. The decision to leave an abusive relationship may be determined by a confluence of individual factors (Frisch & MacKenzie, 1991).

Experiences that cause stress-induced symptoms in other populations (e.g., Vietnam veterans) can be likened to the experiences of a battered woman. She is a human being responding to a crisis brought on by abuse, and her response is like the response of other human beings who experience similar intense and/or prolonged trauma.

A woman cannot know with complete certainty that the man she loves and plans to marry will not eventually abuse her (Avni, 1991a). A battered woman could be any woman or *every* woman. It is truly a case of "There but for the grace of God go I."

Weaving the Fabric of Abuse 1

Learned Hopefulness and Learned Helplessness

Men are taught to apologize for their weaknesses, women for their strengths.

—Lois Wyse

CHAPTER OVERVIEW

The enigma of battering relationships and why women remain in them begins with the long journey of learning to be female in this culture. To cover the topic of sex-role socialization, both in the family and in the world, is to explore the *Wonderful World of Women*. The fundamental principle underlying female sex-role socialization is that female identity rests on a woman's attachment and affiliation with a male partner, chiefly through marriage. The mores of the culture provide a psychosocial foundation for understanding the complexity of abusive relationships.

CASE STUDY

LISA—FOR BETTER OR WORSE

I believe that you stay with your partner for better or for worse. I didn't know what "worse" was when I made that promise, but I promised. I believe my husband loves me, and I'm starting to believe he could kill me. I'm not sure how long I should stay and how "bad" is "too bad." I know I don't believe I should be hit, but I do believe if my relationship is a mess, I should stay to help make it better.

SOCIALIZATION

Berger and Berger (1979) define socialization as the "process through which an individual *learns* to become a member of society" (p. 9). Learning applies not only to observable behaviors, but also to cognitions (thoughts) and attitudes. Learning is strengthened through reward and punishment, as well as through observation of others' behavior (i.e., modeling) (Bandura, 1971). Ideally, an individual learns to discard nonproductive behavior and to retain healthy behaviors and beliefs through reinforcement. (Turn to Appendix B for a description and explanation of technical learning terms such as *reinforcement.*)

Society exposes men and women, boys and girls, to differential expectations as part of learning their gender identity. Sex roles tend to magnify biological disparities. Carol Tavris (1992) believes that male and female behavior is not governed so much by genetic sex (chromosomal variation) as by the social context (see Lorber & Farrell, 1991). In other words, if customs were reversed, men who had sole responsibility for the care of their children would learn to be child-focused and nurturing, and women whose experiences centered on climbing the corporate ladder would learn to be aggressively businesslike. The opportunity to develop these aspects of personality plays an important role in their acquisition. "Practice makes perfect," and gender limits practice (see Draper & Gordon, 1986; Silverstein, 1996).

The culture permits and encourages male aggression, but monitors its form (Cohn, 1991; Maccoby & Jacklin, 1974). Peers exert considerable pressure on males to be masculine, to devalue women, and even to be abusive (DeKeseredy, 1990; Myers, 1995; Price & Byers, 1999; Silverman & Williamson, 1997). Female aggression, on the other hand, is tolerated primarily in defense of a loved one, particularly children (Miller, 1976). Marlo Thomas highlights this point with a bit of sarcasm: "A man has to be Joe McCarthy to be called ruthless. All a woman has to do is put you on hold."

In adulthood, traditional success is governed by gender (Josephs, Markus, & Tafarodi, 1992). Masculinity is characterized by independence and competence, whereas femininity is typified by interdependence. In men, but not women, self-esteem is highly dependent on traditional task or occupational success (Overholser, 1993). Whereas boys are afraid of failing at tasks, girls may actually be afraid of succeeding; furthermore, girls may become anxious about task success because they anticipate or expect negative consequences (Horner, 1972). They are in a double bind (Pipher, 1994). To avoid the conflict between achievement (male-defined) and affiliation (marriage and motherhood), most girls learn to equate achievement with affiliation (see Mickelson, 1989).

Society still values male traits more than female traits. One can go so far as to say that women are actively devalued (see Murphy & Meyer, 1991; Myers, 1995). Television continues to depict masculine characters as much more appealing than feminine characters. This discrepancy reinforces teenage girls' recognition of their subordinate status. One of the most powerful needs expressed by today's teenage girls is their desire to be seen as equal to young men (see Labi, 1998; McDowell & Park, 1998).

AFFILIATION AND SOCIALIZATION

Ferguson (1980) says that "women's identity is forthrightly and consistently defined in terms of the contexts of social relationships. . . . For most women, connection with others is a primary given of their lives, not a secondary option to be contracted at will" (pp. 159-160) (also see Woods, 1999). "A woman's very sense of herself becomes organized around being able to make and then maintain affiliations and relationships" (Miller, 1976, p. 83). To a certain extent, her sense of well-being depends on her marital relationship with her adult partner (Mookherjee, 1997).

In Landenburger's (1989) judgment, a woman's conception of self acts like a filter through which she interprets the world. Girls learn to value themselves as they are esteemed by others. Girls first become defined as daughters or by their relationships with their parents. Daughterhood is a common bond for all women and a beginning step for knowing and learning what it means to be feminine, to be a wife, and to be a mother. The only change in adulthood is that the most important source of esteem is no longer her parents but her romantic partner (Gilbert & Webster, 1982).

The need to develop and retain heterosexual relationships forces girls to abandon some of their selfhood, to actually stifle their own ambitions and personalities (Woods, 1999). The socialization process used to accomplish this goal is called the *silencing of the self.* Whereas *preteen* girls are still able to be honest and authentic about themselves, teenage girls are not. Teens have come to realize that revealing who they really are is not socially desirable. Too much authenticity may lead to affiliation losses (Pipher, 1994).

One thing women learn is that to obtain the prized possession of a harmonious relationship, it is important to be *nice.* Oprah Winfrey ("Learning to Be Assertive," 1992) calls this inclination the *disease to please.* A glance at the titles of some current magazine articles gives an indication of the enormous societal pressure placed on women to find and maintain a relationship with a man.

"Beating the Man Shortage—Cosmo finds the best places to meet them"

"Supporting a Husband Isn't the Worst Idea"

"Three Ways to Learn to Live With Your Husband's Infidelity"

"Sexy Ways to Calm Your Savage Beast"

"Five 'Come-and-Get-Me' Tricks"

"Making Every Minute You Spend Together Spectacular"

CASE STUDY

CINDY

Cindy was abandoned by her parents at an early age and raised by strict, moralistic relatives. She and her sister were taught to be nice girls with traditional values. Disagreement was not tolerated, nor was unladylike behavior. Verbal abuse in the form of put-downs or threats was part of normal life. Slapping and pushing were common forms of discipline for unacceptable behavior.

Cindy decided early in life that the price of breaking family rules was too high. She had very few friends, did not stay out late, got good grades, and did not date often. She married young and quickly learned that her husband's rules were much like her aunt and uncle's. Cindy believed that she had no power to change the situation. Mild abuse was chronic, a familiar pain, endurable. She believed that maintaining her marital relationship was the most important achievement in her life.

Affiliation pressures on battered women are even more intense than those placed on women in general. A battered woman may think that her partner's violence represents a failure in her relationship, rather than an impulsive act by her abuser (Gilligan, 1982). The threat of a rupture in her adult relationship, fear of isolation from her partner, or rejection by her partner may cause her even more apprehension than sporadic physical aggression (see Frisch & MacKenzie, 1991).

As part of fulfilling attachment mandates, women have learned how to support men emotionally. A description of today's woman includes adjectives that have described virtuous women over the centuries: patient, self-sacrificing, and long-suffering. Self-sacrifice for women has a long and noble history (Campbell & Lewandowski, 1997; Koss, Koss, & Woodruff, 1991a; Sansone, Wiederman, & Sansone, 1997). As Anna Quindlen (1992), a columnist for the *New York Times,* wrote in an editorial:

> The fact is that there's still a tacit agreement in American society, despite decades of change, that women support. Like a French word that always takes "la," self-sacrifice remains a feminine noun. It is a deal that works beautifully for men, which is why you hear so much about how natural it is, even that it was God's idea; that there is a theological basis for women's inevitable compromises. (p. 10)

Women who are supportive and self-sacrificing, but are not physically battered, are considered good women; those who are battered are not. Women who are abused are significantly more self-sacrificing than are nonabused women (Woods, 1999). Ascribing traits such as martyrdom or masochism to battered women not only fails to take female socialization into account, but also fails to acknowledge research evidence refuting this myth (Caplan, 1984; Kuhl, 1985; Symonds, 1979).

SEXISM AND POWER

Sexism is a system of combined male controls: physical control, psychological control, derogatory beliefs about women, and institutional policies and regulations that discriminate against women (Adams, 1984) (see also Cook, 1997; Gay, 1997; and Messner, 1997, for other viewpoints). Sexist thinking and political principles were part of the founding of America (Kann, 1998). In a recent newspaper article, Tucker (1999) describes a stunning reversal of fortune for Zimbabwe women. The nation's Supreme Court overruled or challenged nearly every law relating to women's rights. In a 5-0 decision, the Court declared that "women are not equal to men, especially in family relations" (p. 14).

Assaultive men generate higher need-for-power themes than do nonassaultive men (Dutton & Strachan, 1987) (also see Gondolf, 1995). From a behavioral learning perspective, a batterer's ability to gain control, feel powerful, and be sexually aroused through intimidation is reinforcing (as in Dutton, Fehr, & McEwen, 1982), and therefore the aggression will increase (also see Wood, Gove, Wilson, & Cochran, 1997). Perhaps it is fair to say that part of the "job description" for being male is the ability to control women, or as West and Zimmerman (1987) put it: "In doing gender, men are also doing dominance and women are doing deference" (p. 130).

Sexism occurs in the family, media, psychiatry, medicine, language, organized religion, government, and legal system. Acceptance of sexist stereotypes has been used to justify unequal treatment of women. In fact, many observers present evidence for the *feminization of poverty* (Brenner, 1991). "If you are a female, that's one strike against you; if you are either a poor female or a nonwhite female, that's two strikes against you; if you are a poor, nonwhite female, you have struck out" (Julian & Kornblum, 1983, p. 337).

POWER

Webster's (1947, p. 152) definition of power (cited in Murphy & Meyer, 1991) is as follows: "Power is the probability that one actor within a social relationship will be in a position to carry out his own will despite resistance" (p. 152). Interestingly, the definition fails to incorporate personal power and the ability to accomplish goals in a participatory fashion. Other, related concepts are decision making and dominance. Gilbert and Webster (1982) contend that power is the reward for doing masculinity well; powerlessness is the reward for doing femininity well. A girl who becomes the woman she is meant to be receives love, but never power.

Coleman and Straus (1986) examined the relationships between marital power, marital power consensus, conflict, and violence in 2,143 representative American couples. Contrary to the view that the customary model of male head-of-household best preserves the family unit, the research found that an egalitarian, shared-power, marital relationship exhibits the lowest level of conflict and aggression. This finding was true even when both partners agreed that the husband's role should be dominant. In fact, consensus about marital power reduces the level of marital strife. When discord does arise, it is associated with much higher levels of violence in nonegalitarian marriages (also see Anson & Sagy, 1995).

Almost uniformly, professionals in the field have proposed some variation of a control theme to explain male-to-female aggression (e.g., Gondolf, 1995; Tinsley, Critelli, & Ee, 1992). Studies of power, control, and dominance suggest that batterers' violence may stem from men's need to control, or, relatedly, not to feel powerless (see Hamby, 1996, for a review). Violence is a deliberate, chosen behavior that batterers believe is warranted, given the situation (Ptacek, 1988). From the perspective of learning theory, battering is a goal-oriented mechanism that maintains an imbalance of power between the batterer and battered woman (see Barnett, Lee, & Thelen, 1997; Felson, 1992; Hamberger, Lohr, Bonge, & Tolin, 1997). Others conceptualize power needs more within the realm of interpersonal needs (Coan, Gottman, Babcock, & Jacobson, 1997).

From a sociological perspective, battering can be viewed as the extreme end of a continuum of controls meant to reinforce male dominance of women (DeKeseredy, 1990). Murphy and Meyer (1991) state that "there are striking parallels between the use of violence as a means of control in marriage and in the larger culture outside of the family" (p. 97). In sum, a battering relationship is both cause and effect of stereotyped roles and the unequal power relationship between men and women (Smith, 1984).

CULTURAL SUPPORT FOR MALE-TO-FEMALE VIOLENCE

Many experts believe that a focus on individual psychology, such as the psychopathology of some male batterers, cannot end wife abuse. They hold that only by changing the social and cultural institutions that permit wife abuse will a permanent solution be realized (Goodman, Koss, Fitzgerald, Russo, & Puryear-Keita, 1993; Pagelow, 1993).

One example of changing a cultural institution to reduce violence against women occurred in Pakistan. A bank credit program assisted women in obtaining a financial foothold toward independence by channeling economic resources to them that expanded their employment and income-generating opportunities. As one woman told a researcher,

> In the past my father-in-law would never stop my husband from beating me. But after I joined the Grameen Bank he said to my husband, "You had better stop beating and scolding your wife. Now she has contact with many people in society. She brings you loans from Grameen Bank. If you want to you can start a business with the money she brings." (Schuler et al., 1996, p. 1738)

A review of the literature suggests a number of behaviors reflecting male peer support for abusing women: (a) offering information and advice to a male abuser (e.g., "Get an attorney so she can't ruin your career"); (b) keeping silent when told about the abuse (seeming agreement with abuse by failing to support the victim's position); (c) pressuring women for sex as a badge of male prowess, even at a woman's expense; and (d) providing admiration for male dominance and keeping the upper hand (DeKeseredy, 1990; see also Smith, 1990; Tontodonato & Crew, 1992).

Additional empirical evidence shows that patriarchal norms contribute to wife beating. These beliefs include the following: (a) The man has the right to determine if his wife may work; (b) the man has the right to decide if his wife may leave the home at night; (c) it is important to show the wife that he is the head of the household; and (d) a man is entitled to have sex with his wife even if she does not want to do so (the "woman as chattel" theme) (Smith, 1990; see also Myers, 1995; O'Toole & Schiffman, 1997).

The following quotation from *Newsweek* magazine sums up the need to counteract the negative aspects of misogynous male socialization:

> Men's aggressive, powerful, domineering approach, their negative social attitudes toward women, and their belief in rape myths seem to have implicated men as perpetrators, while exonerating women. Perhaps the time has finally come for a new agenda. Women, after all, are not a big problem. Our society does not suffer from burdensome amounts of empathy and altruism, or a plague of nurturance. The problem is men—or more accurately, maleness. ("Guns and Dolls," 1990, p. 62; also see Levant, 1995)

Similarly, Asher (1990) says: "With the recent findings linking testosterone with aggressive behavior, the thought of dumping estrogen in the water supply certainly did come to mind" (p. 7).

CASE STUDY

TRISHA

Trisha called the hotline for information. She wanted to find out whether her marriage was typical in terms of highs and lows. She said that she did not get black eyes; she was just pushed and shoved. Verbal outbursts and threats were just a fact of life. She said, "The kids and I just don't make Daddy mad." Her husband's male psychiatrist had told her that she needed to "take the good with the bad." Her male minister told her to "turn the other cheek and be more loving."

Trisha's husband, the psychiatrist, and the minister are symbols of power. Male authority figures in the community tell women that they must keep their families intact at all costs. The culture encourages women to become chameleons, to adapt to their environments, to camouflage themselves and their feelings.

Battering happens because, somehow, society has given its consent. Married men approve of slapping women for some of the following reasons: (a) She insults him privately, (b) she insults him publicly, (c) she comes home drunk, (d) she hits him first, (e) she has an affair, or (f) she does not do what he tells her to do (Ellis, 1989; see O'Toole & Schiffman, 1997, for a review).

Although society pays lip service to the belief that male-to-female violence is unacceptable, or at least less acceptable than the reverse, reality provides a conflicting norm. There may be a dichotomy between what people say and what they actually believe, and culturally, there may be a state of cognitive dissonance residing in our collective psyche (Harris, 1991; Koski & Mangold, 1988). Marvin Kahn (1980), a professor from the University of Arizona who studied aboriginal islanders, offers a final word on this topic. He commented about the custom of wife beating: "Severe injury or damage . . . cannot be condoned, but to totally condemn the practice [of wife beating] may be to negate an important aspect of island culture" (p. 731). (By the way, we were unable to reach these women for comment!)

A CHANGE OF ATTITUDES

In 1992 and 1995, researchers conducted two different types of public opinion polls, including questions about attitudes toward domestic violence (Klein, Campbell, Soler, & Ghez, 1997). The 1992 poll found that Americans ranked domestic violence fifth on a list of public concerns, with only 34% of the total agreeing with the notion that it is an extremely important topic. By 1995, 79% thought domestic violence was an extremely important social issue. At this time, Americans also thought that public intervention was necessary (82%), especially if an injury occurred (96%). The principal reason that people thought that public intervention was necessary, however, was to protect children, not women.

Sadly, it took the murders of Ronald Goldman and Nicole Simpson in June 1994 to bring domestic abuse into the forefront of the nation's attention. Of respondents replying to questions about information learned from the O.J. Simpson trial, 93% ranked domestic violence as a very serious problem (Klein et al., 1997).

In the 1992 poll, arresting batterers was unpopular. Most respondents chose counseling as the best alternative for intervening in wife abuse. At a minimum, a man would have to hit a woman *hard* (53%) to deserve arrest, but if he punched her, 94% agreed arrest was appropriate. One disturbing and persistent belief among 38% of the participants was that some women provoked men into abusing them (Klein et al., 1997). Even judges have shocked courtrooms by sympathizing with a batterer's justification for assaulting or murdering his wife (Myers, 1995; Schornstein, 1997). On the positive side, research-based educational strategies designed to affect beliefs in schools, clinics, the media, and courtrooms (e.g., speakers, posters, classes, and films) are beginning to diminish acceptance of wife beating (Chalk & King, 1998; Goelman & Valente, 1997; Klein et al., 1997; O'Neal & Dorn, 1998). One study, for example, found that respondents exposed to public service announcements, such as "It *is* your business," were substantially more likely than those not exposed to believe that physical abusers should be arrested and incarcerated (see Klein et al., 1997).

SEXISM AND THERAPY

Sexism seems to flourish even in mental health professionals (see Eisikovits & Buchbinder, 1996; Ross & Glisson, 1991). In a revealing study, Swenson (1984) investigated the judgments of experienced psychotherapists concerning the relationship between sex roles and mental health. Results indicated that the psychotherapists rated a "healthy" person (sex unspecified) as having *masculine* traits. They did not rate as healthy individuals who possessed both favorable masculine and feminine characteristics. These findings coincide with those of early researchers showing that subjects valued masculinity more highly than femininity (Broverman, Vogel, Broverman, Clarkson, & Rosenkrantz, 1972).

Gender bias can also affect a therapist's ability to recognize intimate violence. During a counseling session, a therapist reacts to what he or she believes about the power dynamics in relationships (Petretic-Jackson & Jackson, 1996). Hansen, Harway, and Cervantes (1991) used two hypothetical cases to study the abilities of family therapists to recognize marital violence and recommend appropriate protection strategies. In one of the two test stories, Carol told her therapist privately that she had sought an order of protection because James "grabbed her and threw her on the floor in a violent manner and then struck her." In the other vignette, Beth claimed that Tony "punched her in the back and stomach and caused her to miscarry." Tony asserted that Beth tried to hit him and punched herself in the back.

Of the 362 therapists, 22% correctly identified the problem as violence or battering and 17% as an abusive relationship. Others classified the problem as conflict (8%), anger (5%), a power struggle (4%), lack of control (1%), or other (4%). The remaining participants did not categorize the problem as any type of conflict. Only 45% of the therapists advised crisis intervention; 48% called for further assessment, 60% suggested work on a nonviolent marital problem, and 28% recommended couples counseling. Only 10% addressed the need for protection. Even when psychologists are appropriately involved, they often fail to take domestic violence into account (Ackerman & Ackerman, 1996).

IS IT SAFE TO USE COUPLES OR FAMILY THERAPY WITH ABUSIVE COUPLES?

Although studies rating the effectiveness of couples counseling have been inconclusive (Chalk & King, 1998), many traditional couples and family therapists have not been sensitive to the impact of gender on family relationships, and they have inadvertently imposed a patriarchal view as the standard of "normal" family functioning (Hare-Mustin, 1986; Trute, 1998).

> In my experience, well-coached (metacommunication) patients will not incite a target (abusive spouse) to violence if they attempt to metacommunicate empathetically, no matter how clumsy the initial attempt. This is true even in fami-

> lies where violence is a routinely occurring pattern. The reason is that family violence against adults is invariably cued by the person to whom it is directed. A battered wife, for instance, helps the abuser play the role of abuser. If a victim did not wish to do that, she would leave the relationship as soon as the spouse caused her significant injury, no matter how much financial hardship she had to bear. (Allen, 1988, p. 318)

Counselors, psychotherapists, psychologists, and psychiatrists must give special consideration to the dangers inherent in providing family or couples counseling to violent families. The primary issue is *safety.* A battered woman may be afraid to speak out in front of her abuser about what has happened; or, she may feel safe in the therapist's office, speak out, and pay for it later. A second concern is that an individual issue (e.g., control and violence) may become confused with a family issue (e.g., communication and parenting). It is critical to recognize that a battering problem belongs to the person who batters (Gondolf, 1998a; Hansen et al., 1991).

CASE STUDY

BERNICE—A TALL WOMAN

We are both therapists. Trying to find someone to counsel us without feeling completely exposed was difficult, and I was desperately seeking help. I was afraid and feeling trapped at this point. We finally found a marriage counselor who was well-known; he had written books and articles on relationships.

During the second session, I mentioned the battering. I began to get angry and agitated when the marriage counselor did not address the violence directed at me. Instead, he talked about *my* height and *my* anger. He said I was very tall for a woman, something I was always self-conscious about. He asked my partner if my size, my anger, and my verbal ability (otherwise known as nagging) were intimidating to *him*.

Family therapists can reject the tendency to legitimize a power imbalance in the family. When exploring interpersonal power and control issues, therapists can misperceive too readily a battered woman's attempts at adaptation as a contest over power. From this position, it is a short step to succumb to the familiar victim-blaming routine. Failure to address gender issues minimizes the support that battered women need and deserve (LaViolette, 1991). The rationale for using systemic approaches may be to make violence seem more manageable than it is (Bograd, 1992).

On the other hand, newer studies imply that a one-size-fits-all approach may cast too large a net. Although conjoint therapy remains extremely controversial, it may be appropriate and effective for some couples whose relationships are marred by infrequent, mild, and non-fear-provoking violence (Heyman & Neidig, 1999). Safety concerns are so compelling, however, that therapists undertaking this type of counseling must prescreen couples carefully for suitability (e.g., Hanks, 1992; O'Leary, in press). Poteat, Grossnickle, Cope, and Wynne (1990) have developed a screening device that, taken together with other information, should alert psychotherapists to the potential for relationship abuse. Detection of this risk factor could contribute to the overall therapeutic treatment plan (also see Ackerman & Ackerman, 1996).

FAMILIES

> *One is never finished with the family. It's like the smallpox—it catches you in childhood and marks you for life.*
>
> —Sartre

In families, mothers and fathers struggle with the obligations and restrictions of their sex roles. Although both parents may share the breadwinner role to some degree, they do not equally share the nurturing and domestic duties (Brines, 1994; Hartmann, 1981). Conflict arises not only from daily hassles and workloads, but also from power struggles and the challenge of changing sex-role expectations (Eisler, Skidmore, & Ward, 1988; Levant, 1995). Although times have changed, old stereotypes have remained intact (Snodgrass, 1990). Marital harmony is difficult when one lives in a democratic country *and* in an autocratic home.

It is important to recognize that the family is a powerful cultural transmitter of behavior, both positive and negative (Langley, 1991). Family members might learn unhealthy ways of coping, such as suppressing anger and other emotions, or using drugs, alcohol, and aggression (Belmore & Quinsey, 1994; Burton, Foy, Bwanausi, & Johnson, 1994; MacEwen, 1994). Children tend to accept the family standards, whatever they are, as normal, and they often go on to practice them, regardless of their later usefulness. These skills become internalized responses, and their expression is almost reflexive. When an adult feels pushed against the wall, the old behavior patterns (survival skills) rear up to meet the challenge. People do what they have *learned* to do, and they do it with the rapidity of a knee jerk.

CHILDREN EXPOSED TO MARITAL VIOLENCE

There is no longer any doubt that children exposed to marital violence are learning harmful lessons about interpersonal relationships. Little attention has been devoted to understanding this problem until recently, because intergenerational transmission was not a focus, nor was the link made between random acts of violence and their incubation in a violent family (Barnett, Miller-Perrin, & Perrin, 1997; Holden, Geffner, & Jouriles, 1998b).

A number of factors greatly affect research on children who are exposed to adult spousal violence. These factors include the kinds of samples obtained, where and how they are obtained, how abuse between adults is defined, and how the child's exposure to abuse is defined. For instance, child witnesses may observe a violent act, overhear an abusive exchange, or see the results of assault (e.g., bruises, broken household objects). Most advocates and many authorities consider exposure to marital violence a form of psychological maltreatment or trauma (Kilpatrick, Litt, & Williams, 1997; Somer & Braunstein, 1999; Tomkins et al., 1994). In fact, experts who study acute stress reactions classify exposure to a broad spectrum of situations (e.g., war, killings, seeing dead bodies, listening to horrifying stories) as traumatic (Gore-Felton, Gill, Koopman, & Spiegel, 1999).

Children of battered women are frequently exposed to *recurrent* male-to-female violence (Jaffe, Wolfe, & Wilson, 1990). Murray Straus (1991a) estimates that the number of children in the United States exposed to marital violence every year is nearly 10 million. Estimates vary according to the sample of respondents queried (e.g., mothers, fathers, children), but parents seem to underestimate what their children have seen or heard (O'Brien, John, Margolin, & Erel, 1994; Tomkins et al., 1994). One Memphis medical team accompanying local police on domestic violence calls discovered that most children in these homes had directly witnessed the assaults. A few not only witnessed their mother's assault, but also were assaulted themselves when they tried to intervene (Brookoff, 1997; see Hilton, 1992).

OVERLAP OF SPOUSE ABUSE AND CHILD ABUSE

There is a large volume of available literature that addresses the overlap between the abuse of spouses and the abuse of children. Evidence shows overwhelmingly that in households where women are beaten, children are also abused (McGee, 1998; O'Brien et al., 1994; Peled, 1993; Petchers, 1995; Straus & Gelles, 1990).

Estimates of co-occurrence range from a low of 6.5% (Dobash, 1976-1977) to a high of 97% (Kolbo, 1996). In an article reviewing 35 studies, Edleson (1999) found that in 30% to 60% of families, both were taking place at the same time (also see Magen, Conroy, Hess, Panciera, & Simon, 1995; Straus & Gelles, 1990; Valencia & Van Hoorn, 1999).

Children living in maritally violent homes experience many risk factors simultaneously: direct physical and sexual abuse, neglect, parental alcoholism, low income, stress, and maternal impairment (see Gibson & Gutierrez, 1991; Hughes, Parkinson, & Vargo, 1989; Suh & Abel, 1990).

Empirical data support the notion that exposure to marital violence, coupled with other forms of abuse, increase the severity of adverse consequences experienced by children who live in these families (Holden et al., 1998b; O'Keefe, 1994b). The most severe forms of abuse, of course, lead to the death of a child. Child fatalities are especially likely to occur in families where males abuse their female partners (e.g., Felix & McCarthy, 1994; Pecora, Whitaker, Maluccio, Barth, & Plotnick, 1992). Most families involved in a child's death are two-parent households where a majority of the perpetrators are either the child's father or the mother's boyfriend (see Felix & McCarthy, 1994; Pecora, Whitaker, Maluccio, Barth, & 1992). Investigators identified 119 homicide-suicide cases involving female victims in North Carolina between 1988 and 1992. Male partners or former partners committed 99 of them, and family members or acquaintances committed the other 20. Of the 99 cases, authorities established that 56 children under the age of 18 saw their mother being killed and their father committing suicide, found their parents' bodies, or were killed themselves (Morton, Runyan, Moracco, & Butts, 1998; see also Sharps, Campbell, McFarlane, Sachs, & Xu, 1998; Wilt et al., 1997).

Children exposed to parental violence often present a complex and heterogeneous diagnostic picture that blends elements of trauma symptomatology with features of more traditional disorders (Rossman, 1994). A number of elements of parental violence affect the children exposed: (a) the nature and amount of abuse witnessed; (b) the target of the abuse; (c) the severity and frequency of the abuse; (d) the degree of assumed responsibility for the abuse and its outcome; (e) the age and gender of the children; (f) the mediating factors, such as familial, interpersonal, and community resources; and (g) the suitability and presence of interventions (Fantuzzo et al., 1991; Jaffe et al., 1990; Rossman & Rosenberg, 1992; Sternberg et al., 1993).

The effects of living in a domestic war zone are myriad and fall into several categories. Marital conflict and violence have the potential of making children feel insecure by interfering with parent-child bonding. Insecure attachment, in turn, places children at risk for behavior problems (DeLozier, 1992). On the more extreme end of the continuum, their experiences may fall into Hart and Brassard's (1990) category of "terrorized," manifesting symptoms of PTSD, including dissociation and hypervigilance.

On the less extreme end, exposed children compared with nonexposed children tend to exhibit significantly higher levels of adverse effects: (a) behavioral problems (aggression, delinquency, hyperactivity, substance abuse, promiscuity); (b) mental health problems (anxiety, depression, anger, shyness); (c) health problems (headaches, rashes, stomachaches); (d) learning problems (school failure, absenteeism); and (e) social problems (poor social skills, difficulties in forming relationships) (Gleason, 1995; Klesges et al., 1999; McCloskey, Figueredo, & Koss, 1995; O'Keefe, 1994a; Sternberg et al., 1993).

According to an address by Lynn Loar (1997), a children's advocate,

> Children from violent families sound old, "parentified" (i.e., acting like parents), and flat. These kids are hypervigilant, walking psychotherapists to their parents, who can't tie their own shoes. They know about safety, but don't know how to share a toy. They know what they need to know and are accelerated in certain areas, especially survival. When a child gets a message in a state of arousal and fear, the message tends to stick. (also see Alexander, 1997)

Recent research is connecting violent prenatal familial interactions to in vivo development of fetal brain organization and function. After all, it is not the hand, knife, gun, or penis that ultimately creates the act of violence, it is the brain, the self-talk, the emotional reflex. Experiences that can be tolerated by an older child can destroy an infant. In the developing central nervous system, there are critical periods during which the brain is most sensitive to environmental cues and organizing experiences. The ability to feel remorse, empathy, and sympathy are all experience-based capabilities. The effects of emotional neglect in childhood predispose individuals to violence by decreasing the strength of inhibition and decreasing the capacity to empathize and sympathize (Perry, 1994, 1996; Singer, 1995; Thoenen, 1995).

Factors that increase the reactivity of the lower brain stem (e.g., chronic abuse) and factors that decrease the moderating capacity of the midbrain and cortex (e.g., neglect) will increase an individual's propensity for aggression and impulsivity (Halperin et al., 1995). If, during development, events require the stress response apparatus to be persistently active, the central nervous system will develop special stress-response neural systems. A child growing up in a violent, chaotic environment becomes hypersensitive to external stimuli and ready to respond to what he or she perceives as a threat (see also Haddad & Garralda, 1992; Perry, 1994; Rossman, 1998).

LEARNING TO BE VIOLENT

The majority of children traumatized by family violence do *not* become remorselessly violent, but they have learned to believe that violence and aggression are viable options or solutions to problems. Their first emotional language is a reflection of the environment in which they live.

> Belief systems, in the final analysis, are the major contributors to violence. Racism, sexism, misogyny, children as property, idealization of violent heroes, cultural tolerance of child maltreatment, tribalism, jingoism, nationalism—all unleash, facilitate, encourage and nurture violent individuals. Without these facilitating belief systems and modeling, neglected and abused children would carry their pain forward in less violent ways. (Perry, 1997, p. 131)

Unfortunately, the effects of childhood exposure to parental abuse frequently extend into adulthood (see Choice, Lamke, & Pittman, 1995; Downs & Miller, 1998; Henning, Leitenberg, Coffey, Turner, & Bennett, 1996; McNeal & Amato, 1998; Silvern et al., 1995). Even if a child seems to be functioning adequately when examined, "sleeper effects" (latent effects), such as anxiety, depression, substance abuse, aggression, promiscuity, and self-esteem, often show up later (e.g., Cummings, 1998; Graham-Bermann, 1998).

CHANCES OF HEALTHY FAMILY BACKGROUND

Certainly, not all battered women are from dysfunctional families. Coming from a healthy family is no guarantee that a woman will find a healthy partner (Avni, 1991a). In fact, many battered women come from loving families. The family history of battered women is much less uniform than the histories of men who batter (Hotaling & Sugarman, 1990). Although the women were raised in various societies from all over the world, the common denominator is that each was raised in a patriarchal culture, where women are one-down in terms of actual power, and where the incentive to hope, believe in change, and "stand by your man" is paramount (see Moss, Pitula, Campbell, & Halstead, 1997).

Lenore Walker (1985b) cites several modern myths about battering relationships. One myth is that it is impossible to love someone who hits you. Love and physical force often occur together. The commonly heard phrase, "If he ever lays a hand on me, I'll leave," does not mirror reality. As Lloyd (1988) noted, physical aggression does not herald the demise of a marriage. By and large, battered women do not leave their relationships the first time their partners push, slap, or hit them (Campbell & Sheridan, 1989; Follingstad, Hause, Rutledge, & Poleck, 1992). Actually, most adults have grown up in homes where loving parents spanked them as a form of physical discipline, "for the child's own good" (Flynn,

1996; Graziano, Lindquist, Kunce, & Munjal, 1992). Adults have come to believe that in families, a certain amount of physical force is not a denial of love, but can even be tangible proof of it. (See Appendix C for a review of the Ayllon and Azrin, 1966, study.)

CASE STUDY

BIANCA AND DAMIEN

Bianca had lost her husband after an 11-year marriage. She had two children and a supportive family, but she was depressed and vulnerable. After 18 months, she met a man at work who was understanding, seemed to love children, and was divorced. He had two children of his own. She began to date him.

After Bianca and Damien moved in together, the emotional and verbal abuse began. He became angry when she spent too much time with her family, calling her "Mama's girl." He was jealous of her friends and wondered why he was not enough for her. He got upset when their plans changed because her children were ill. His kids were older and out of the house most of the time. He wanted quiet, romantic dinners alone, sans children, on a routine basis. She gave up what was important to her a little at a time.

Bianca came from a family that was close and enjoyed time together. She had no context for understanding abusive behavior. When she confronted Damien, he told her that she was too sensitive. By the time Damien began to hit her, she was confused about her own perceptions.

Human beings tend to adapt to their situations regardless of the quality of their environment, a sort of "chameleon effect." In the isolation of a battering relationship, the batterer's reality becomes the family's reality. In the words of Claudia Black (personal communication, April 1981), who works with adult children of alcoholics, "When you invite a healthy person into a sick family, you give him or her the opportunity to become sick."

THE ROLE OF LEARNING AND THE CYCLE OF VIOLENCE

A scientific analysis of such processes as socialization and emotional dependency leads inevitably to an inquiry about the common, underlying mechanism: learning. That is, women learn to be feminine, rely on a husband, and follow prescribed religious concepts. The following illustration demonstrates the basic role that learning plays in behavior. (Appendix B presents a brief review of operant conditioning, a type of learning based on the consequences of actions.)

CASE STUDY

HEATHER AND RON

Heather had learned to iron her husband Ron's shirts just the way he wanted them. She had mastered nearly all of his favorite recipes, and she had worked very hard to teach the children to be quiet and pleasant when Ron was at home. She graduated in the top 10% of her "Fascinating Womanhood" (Andelin, 1963) course.

If Heather performed well (e.g., ironed, cooked, and got the children to bed quietly—"operants"), she and Ron often had an enjoyable evening watching TV and just "hanging out" together (reinforcement). At such times, they shared happy, intimate moments and often ended the evening by making love. She had learned that having a pleasant evening with Ron depended on her ability to please him. (Heather had been operantly conditioned.)

WALKER'S CYCLE OF VIOLENCE THEORY

As summarized in the introduction, Walker's cycle of violence theory describes a recurrent sequence of behaviors typical in battering relationships: (a) *Tension-Building*—A phase in which minor incidents of violence may occur along with a build-up of anger; (b) *Acute or Battering*—A phase in which the major violent outburst occurs; and (c) *Honeymoon-Respite Phase*—a phase in which the batterer woos his wife.

Walker's (1979) theory provides a valuable illustration of operant conditioning. The cessation of violence in the third phase can be seen as a reinforcer. At this time, a battered woman receives discernible validation of her identity as the good wife and of her importance to her partner. Here, she recovers from her battle scars. Here, she remembers that abuse is not the only significant aspect of her relationship. She recognizes that she loves him too, that she cares about how he feels, his health, his survival if she leaves, his reputation, and about his life in general. She seems concerned about his relationship with the children and with friends and family. In fact, if she has already left him, she may return because of love (Barnett & Lopez-Real, 1985; Goldner, Penn, Sheinberg, & Walker, 1990; Johnson, 1988).

It is not much of a conceptual leap to consider an abusive male partner's loving behavior, if and when it occurs, as a form of intermittent reinforcement. Intermittent reinforcement has powerful effects on behavior. Laboratory research on many species of animals and on many human populations has documented repeatedly that intermittently reinforced behaviors resist change (Dutton & Painter, 1993a; Wetzel & Ross, 1983). (See Appendix B for information on intermittent reinforcement and other variables controlling reinforcement.)

LEARNED HOPEFULNESS

For many women, the honeymoon stage provides reason to hope. Muldary (1983) called this outcome *learned hopefulness.* Learned hopefulness is a battered woman's ongoing belief that her partner will change his abusive behavior or his personality (also see Moss et al., 1997).

A survey of shelter residents identified the following list of reasons for staying or returning to a battering relationship: "I wanted to save the relationship"; "I thought we could solve our problems"; and, "I loved my partner" (Muldary, 1983). Barnett and Lopez-Real (1985) found "hoped partner would change" to be the number one reason why women remained with their abusive partners ("feared revenge" was number two). Some women in their study made the following comments:

> "That he would change was still a thought in the back of my head."
>
> "I was always hoping since he had gone to A.A."
>
> "I kept making excuses for him."
>
> "After living together for so long without the abuse, I was hoping he would go back to his old self. I don't understand the change in him."

Pagelow (1981b) indicated that 73% of one shelter sample returned home because the batterer repented and the women believed he would change (also see Frieze, 1979; Frisch & MacKenzie, 1991; Johnson, 1988; Pfouts, 1978). Some battered women's remarks emphasize the same feeling with an added twist: "It's not that I really believe the relationship will change, but that I want to believe that it will be different" (Maertz, 1990).

A batterer's participation in psychotherapy also can be a key factor in a battered woman's return (Gondolf, 1988b). Indeed, batterers frequently resort to counseling as a means of manipulating their female partners, and not as a means of changing their own behavior. One of the authors (A.L.), who works with batterers, contends that

> men do not come into therapy because they think personal growth is "far out," and they "can't wait to change." They come in either because their partner left, or they really believe that she will leave, or because God speaks to them through the SWAT team.

In one comparison, 95% of the battered women interviewed believed their partners would complete their court-ordered counseling, despite findings that less than half of these men do (Gondolf, 1998b). In a later survey, almost three fourths of the female partners, 43% of whom were still being threatened, reported feeling "very safe" after their partner's therapy at the 15-month follow-up period (Gondolf, 1998c). What an individual believes about his or her own reality is more important than an outside observer's perception (Swann & Read, 1981).

Hope also springs from the fact that an abusive male is not unidimensional. Women report that their partners can show kindness, romance, and intensity (Dr. Jekyll), and then flip to the other side (Mr. Hyde) (i.e., behavior typifying intermittent reinforcement). Research has validated this two-sided profile of some batterers. Hastings and Hamberger (1988) describe this group of men as follows: "In superficial interactions, for example, batterers may appear entirely 'normal,' appropriate, and even charming. A casual observer might conclude that these are 'typical males'" (p. 43).

Eventually, the honeymoon stage, with all its hope, comes to an end. The batterer's negative behaviors (intimidation and violence) emerge again when his sense of control is threatened. Naturally, when the positive behaviors stop, battered women feel especially frustrated. Their frustration is likely to motivate them to try even harder to make the relationship work. They desperately want Dr. Jekyll to return (see Amsel & Rousel, 1972; Hull, 1952; Spence, 1956, for an analogy to studies of animal learning).

CASE STUDY

SYLVIA AND DAN

Even after Sylvia left Dan, she was torn by mixed feelings. Dan would call and offer support. He sometimes picked up the children and would spend a little time with them. He sounded interested in her and what she was doing for the first time in years. After they talked, he would ask her to consider reconciliation.

Between the bouts of reason, he would call her, screaming and condemning her as a wife and mother. He harassed her at work. He had his mother call Sylvia to implore her to "think of the children." As the holidays approached, they talked less, and Sylvia felt relief. He began to pay the back child support he owed her and saw the children more regularly.

And then, one day, she met Dan in the park. He came to pick up the kids. Instead, he attacked her. He choked and hit her. The children were terrified and crying. A passerby pulled Dan away so that Sylvia and the children could escape. Dan threw himself in front of her car, screaming to his daughters: "Mommy is trying to kill me." He has called her since the incident, alternately asking for forgiveness and blaming her for his rage. He threatens to kill her.

This pattern of hope and caring followed by brutality and fear kept her confused and immobilized for years. His vacillation continues to keep her off balance, even 8 months after their separation.

Relationship hope seems to be an internalized and reinforced notion characteristic of women in general. Families, friends, song lyrics, literature, religion, and the media all encourage women to hope and believe that they can change their male partners, and that they should persevere to see the results of their labor of love—the reward will be great. Is it not true that behind every good man is a woman (who changed him)?

RELATIONSHIP COMMITMENT

Commitment to a relationship is usually seen as a positive attribute. Society urges couples to stay together through thick and thin. There are numerous illustrations of well-known women who have demonstrated marital commitment under very painful and humiliating revelations of their partners' infidelity: Hillary Clinton, Kathie Lee Gifford, Elizabeth Hurley, and Mary Alice Cisneros. So strong is public sentiment about the virtue of marital sacrifices that Hillary Clinton's approval ratings skyrocketed when she remained with Bill (Rogers, Krammer, Podesta, & Sellinger, 1998; Schindehette, 1998).

Commitment is an important issue because keeping a relationship together *no matter what* significantly differentiates women who leave an abusive relationship from those who do not (Frisch & MacKenzie, 1991; Strube & Barbour, 1983; see Bauserman & Arias, 1990). It seems that for battered women, keeping a marriage covenant is a sign of *situational pathology.* Observers tend to judge their commitment as a sign of mental illness. To define seemingly healthy traits as sick because of their context, however, is to pathologize behavior learned through the ordinary socialization process.

Procci (1990) noted that the failure of a marriage to meet one's expectations causes bitter disappointment. Both abusive and nonabusive couples devise plausible reasons for hanging on to unhappy relationships (Vaughn, 1987): (a) belief in commitment, (b) legal bonds, (c) desire not to hurt the partner, (d) fear of not finding a better person who is available, (e) belief in her ability to make the relationship better, (f) avoidance of being a quitter, (g) need to protect children and parents, and (h) religious convictions. In general, couples hide their troubled relationships from others. They develop rationalizations, such as "All relationships have trouble," or "After a while, all couples lose interest in sex" (also see Varvaro, 1991). Regarding rationalizations: A friend of one of the authors (A.L.) asked her whether she would rather give up sex or rationalizations. As she was thinking about her answer, her friend inquired, "Have you even gone a week without a good rationalization?"

MARITAL SATISFACTION

One inquiry compared battered women still involved in abusive relationships with those who were not (Ellard, Herbert, & Thompson, 1991). Similarities existed in regard to psychosocial attributes such as mutual trust, love and respect, satisfaction with sex, and sharing of household chores. The key difference was that enmeshed women assumed that other women had comparable problems (see Anson & Sagy, 1995; Campbell, 1989a, for contrasting findings).

Nevertheless, battered women are aware of the discrepancy between their actual marital relationships and their ideal relationship. On one clinical scale, a large group of battered women rated their actual relationship as *extreme* (rigidly disengaged with excessive emotional separation). In these marriages, one individual is highly controlling, roles are strictly defined and constrained, both partners are likely to be manipulative, and each individual is likely to do his or her own thing. Another group of battered women rated their actual relationship as *chaotic* (characterized by impulsive decision making and unclear, ever-changing role expectations). The type of relationship the battered women desired and idealized was *balanced* (healthy, with normal give and take) (Shir, 1999).

FAILURE TO RECOGNIZE ABUSE

Women who were raised in nonviolent families may not recognize abusive behavior in its early stages because they have no frame of reference. According to McLeer (cited in "The Battered Woman," 1989),

> Early on, she may be trying to figure out how to decrease the violence but keep her relationship intact. It can take a long time for her to recognize that she can't do anything about his violence—he's a violent man—all she can do is get out. (p. 108)

APPROACH-AVOIDANCE CONFLICT

Early psychologists, attempting to understand human conflict through studies using rats, demonstrated all of the following kinds of conflicts (translated below into human examples): approach-approach, avoidance-avoidance, and approach-avoidance (e.g., Miller, 1959). (See Appendix C for a description of this study.)

When an individual has a choice between two desirable options (e.g., going on a vacation to Hawaii or to Alaska), an *approach-approach conflict* arises. That is, the person would like to go to both Hawaii and Alaska. At other times, a choice occurs between two undesirable alternatives (e.g., cleaning the oven or cleaning the garage—caught between a rock and a hard place). This circumstance also gives rise to ambivalence (*avoidance-avoidance conflict*). When one choice includes both desirable and undesirable features (the house you want to buy is affordable, but 60 miles from your job), one may enter an *approach-avoidance conflict.* When two choices each contain both positive and negative elements, the person finds him- or herself in a *multiple approach-avoidance conflict.* People caught in such conflicts vacillate, first going toward one goal and then retreating, and then going toward the other goal and then retreating, and so forth.

Approach-avoidance behavior is relevant to comprehending the reasons why battered women remain. The combination of benefits (learned hopefulness) and costs (fear) inherent in most battering relationships leads to ambivalence, conflict, and frustration. A battered woman becomes trapped in a double approach-avoidance conflict. On one hand, her relationship meets many of her emotional and economic needs, but it is degrading and dangerous. She wants to approach the love that is hopeful and run from the abuse that is frightening. She wants to retain her relationship but move toward safety. For a while, the conflict is reflected by her ambivalence about staying or leaving.

SUMMARY

This chapter has attempted to explain the role that cultural mores and sex-role socialization play in a woman's decision to remain with her abuser. A woman learns gender identity in her family. She learns that affiliation with a man gives her status and worth. Battered women form attachments and become emotionally dependent on their male partner in the same way that other women do, following the same path as their nonbattered sisters.

Society's acceptance of male dominance and aggression, along with its stated disavowal of male-to-female violence, creates a societal dissonance. Battered women also experience this conflict as they recognize the abuse in their own relationships. They may assume, erroneously, that their relationship struggles correspond to those faced by other women in their marriages.

A woman also learns about hope and commitment in her family, qualities continually nourished by cultural messages. Her primary reason for remaining in or returning to a battering relationship is her hope and need to believe that her abuser will stop the violence, a need called *learned hopefulness.* Some of the traits most valued in women, such as commitment and tolerance, may be used to pathologize her behavior and to blame her for staying. Cultural mores, coupled with the likelihood of meeting a dysfunctional mate, support the contention that becoming a battered woman could happen to anyone.

Institutional Battering
The Power of the Patriarchy 2

The thing women have got to learn is that nobody gives you power. You just take it.

—Roseanne Barr

In ancient times, virgins were sacrificed to appease vengeful gods. A virgin was not a high price to pay for rain or a bounteous crop. It was an honor for the parents and the hapless virgin herself to be offered up in this way. As civilization has advanced, the powers that were, and are, no longer sacrifice maidens. They ask only that the maiden agree to sacrifice herself (Roiphe, 1986).

CHAPTER OVERVIEW

This chapter explores some of the practical issues faced by battered women trying to leave their abusive partners. Among these issues are economic dependency; patriarchal, social, and religious practices; and the inadequacies of the medical and criminal justice systems' responses. Battered women find little institutional support for leaving an abusive relationship.

BELOW THE POVERTY LINE AND BELOW THE BELT

"Women often put up with men's violence because they see no acceptable alternative and their lack of alternatives is often part of the larger cultural logic that sanctions the violence" (Schuler, Hashmi, Riley, & Akhter, 1996, p. 1729).

Over the course of their lives, women are at much greater risk than men for an economic loss (Burkhauser & Duncan, 1989). Women represent 57.7% of economically poor adults (U.S. Bureau of the Census, 1997). In 1987, Duncan referred to single women and children as the "new poor" in this country. The feminization of poverty has changed little in the intervening years (Espinal & Grasmuck, 1997; Haberfeld, Semyonov, & Addi, 1998). The Bureau of Labor Statistics (BLS) shows that women make approximately 76.7 cents for every $1 a man makes. The median income of women who work full-time is $24,492 per year, and for men, $31,928 (BLS, 1999). "Though business leaders say they are aware of and deplore sex discrimination, corporate America has yet to make an honest effort toward eradicating it" (Faludi, 1991, p. xiii). Despite the rumor that women have made it to the executive washroom and through the glass ceiling in large numbers, economic realities paint a not-so-vibrant picture.

POVERTY, WELFARE, WORKING, AND BATTERING

Women as a group have much to fear from poverty. Poor women are disproportionately exposed to crime and violence (Byrne, Resnick, Kilpatrick, Best, & Saunders, 1999; DeFronzo, 1997; Kury & Ferdinand, 1997); illness and death of children (Belle, 1990); and inadequate housing (Brown, Bhrolchain, & Harris, 1975; Fitzpatrick, La Gory, & Ritchey, 1993). Women who break away from battering relationships often become vulnerable to poverty and homelessness. For example, a 3-year study of 2,863 women revealed that victimization by interpersonal violence increased women's risk for unemployment (Byrne et al., 1999). Women usually have few financial resources and little social support to help them surmount the host of institutional and social obstacles that impede their progress toward self-sufficiency (see Browne & Bassuk, 1997; Clarke, Pendry, & Kim, 1997).

Whereas unemployment and lack of education are the primary causes of homelessness in general, family violence and other forms of victimization are the major causes of *female* homelessness (e.g., Montgomery, 1994; Virginia Coalition for the Homeless, 1995; Waxman & Trupin, 1997). Domestic violence affects 21% to 64% of homeless shelter clients (e.g., Bassuk et al., 1996; Goodman, 1991; Virginia Coalition for the Homeless, 1995; Waxman & Trupin, 1997). One reason that domestic violence is such a potent contributor to homelessness is that some abusers sabotage or prevent their female partners from working (Tsesis, 1996; Zorza, 1991).

Finding a safe place for a woman alone or a woman with children is a critical early step in ending a battering relationship. Many battered women are unaware of the existence of emergency shelters. Even those who know about them encounter difficulty finding one with space available (Frisch & MacKenzie, 1991; Irvine, 1990; see also Huisman, 1996; Suarez, 1994). A 1994 survey in Los Angeles ascertained that shelters turned down requests by 8,800 families (Burke, 1995). Older women, lesbians, immigrants, and disabled women may find it nearly impossible to obtain refuge (see also Huisman, 1996; Suarez, 1994).

In an article examining low-income women from four different cities, data consistently revealed that high percentages of women on Aid to Families with Dependent Children (AFDC) were currently abused by their partners. The percentage of these abused women reporting interference from their intimate partners with education, training, or work ranged from 15% to almost 50% (Raphael & Tolman, 1997; see Pearson, Thoennes, & Griswold, 1999). It is interesting to note the broad range of ethnicities of the recipients: (a) Caucasian, 5%-45%; (b) Hispanic, 22%-49%; (c) African American, 10%-55%; and (d) ethnicity not specified, 1%-4% (Raphael & Tolman, 1997). Depending on the assessment used and the sample tested, domestic violence (psychological, physical, sexual, etc.) appears to affect 33% to 67% of women on welfare (see Raphael, 1999, and Tolman, 1999, for reviews).

Even when battered women are employed, their abusers have a negative impact on their performance. In a survey of working women, battering resulted in absenteeism from work in more than half of the women, lateness or leaving early in nearly two thirds, job loss in about one fourth, and job harassment in more than half. According to the women's reports, abusers also prohibited (33%) or discouraged (59%) them from working, prohibited (24%) or discouraged (50%) them from attending school, and successfully prevented 21% of them from actually obtaining a job (Shepard & Pence, 1988; also see Browne, Salomon, & Bassuk, 1999; Lloyd & Taluc, 1999).

Ending abuse, however, can enable many women to change their employment situation or school status (Browne & Bassuk, 1997; Frisch & MacKenzie, 1991). Despite the general findings of employment sabotage by batterers and improvement in working when abuse is not present, one federal court recently concluded that the law offered no protection against dismissal from employment because of spousal violence ("Federal Court," 1996).

Ferraro (1981) highlighted the hurdles that battered women living in a shelter face in their attempts to achieve economic independence. Most of them are young mothers of one or more small children. They are high school graduates with relatively few job skills. They also lack a number of essentials: (a) cars, public transportation, or both; (b) timely access to subsidized housing units; and (c) affordable child care. For a moment, stop and imagine yourself in this situation. How would you cope?

LIZ

Liz arrived at the shelter following a 2-week stay in the hospital for a fractured ankle that required surgery. Over the course of her 8-year marriage, she had developed a first-name relationship with several nurses. Staff had stopped believing that she was accident-prone, and on this occasion, medical staff persuaded Liz to call the local shelter.

Liz was an at-home mother with two young sons, 3-year-old Ben and 6-year-old Patrick. She was taking medication to control the occasional seizures she suffered because of head injuries inflicted by her husband. Over the course of the relationship, she had received numerous injuries, such as broken bones, concussions, facial stitches, and torn ligaments, not to mention a myriad of cuts and bruises.

Her case was a complicated one. She was virtually unemployable because of her injuries, and she had an inconsistent job history prior to her stay in the shelter. She was financially dependent on her husband, and although he made a decent living and they owned a home, she had no independent funds. After she entered the shelter, her husband took all of the money from their joint savings account, leaving Liz with no money.

Within a week of their entry into the shelter, her sons, Ben and Patrick, tried to stab another child with a dinner knife. Liz had a difficult time keeping up with the boys because she was on crutches, and discipline was not her strong suit.

Filing for divorce was the only avenue she saw to have access to any money so that she could leave the shelter. She appeared at the initial hearing to obtain a restraining order, which included a kick-out order (her husband would have to leave the home), temporary custody, and child support. Although the judge ordered her husband to pay temporary child support, he determined that she should be restrained from staying in the house, because her husband would know where to find her and she would not be safe.

Liz's husband remained in the house but selectively forgot to pay child support. He filed a counterpetition demanding visitation with his children. That order was granted by the court. Liz had been in the shelter for 5 weeks, still had no money, was dependent on emergency food, and was unable to return to her home. She was also now in contempt of court for failure to allow visitation while living in the shelter. [As a safety precaution, staff may not allow visitation during a shelter stay.] Her husband's refusal to pay child support left her and the children penniless and unable to leave the shelter.

Liz felt discouraged as she watched other women and their children come and go. At the end of 8 weeks, Liz received her first disability payment, which she

CASE STUDY

needed to save for rent on her own apartment. She had just begun to look for a job, but with her injuries and few marketable skills, she was financially better off with disability. Another month passed before she received her second disability payment and her first child support check. Liz and her husband finally put their house up for sale. Liz looked for an apartment and was able to find an affordable one-bedroom in a poor section of town. With the assistance of the shelter staff, she and the boys moved in. The boys had calmed down because they had some consistency and nonviolence in the shelter. Altogether, it took almost 4 months before Liz was able to leave the shelter, and another year before she was able to find a job. Ten years after her stay in the shelter, Liz called to serve as a volunteer.

Much like Liz's husband, other men have penalized their wives and children economically. A 1990 U.S. Census Bureau study (cited in Waldman, 1992) showed that only half of 5 million women received full court-ordered payments; one fourth received partial payment; and the rest received nothing (also see Pearson & Griswold, 1997). One account of women seeking protection orders revealed that the court awarded child support payments to only 13% (Rowe & Lown, 1990).

The Personal Responsibility and Work Opportunity Reconciliation Act (PRWORA) of 1996 transformed welfare from an entitlement program that provided ongoing cash assistance to needy families to a program that grants only temporary assistance (Tolman, 1999). Advocates for battered women have expressed concern that certain provisions of the Act could place battered women and their children in harm's way. For example, requiring paternity identification in order to compel child support payments could be very dangerous. A batterer, enraged over payments, could gain access to public court documents containing information about victims' whereabouts. Because of these fears, federal guidelines demand that victims of domestic violence be given exemptions, as needed, from participating in activities that place victims and their children at risk. Welfare staff charged with qualifying welfare applicants, however, frequently deny exemptions (Raphael, 1999; see Brandwein, 1997, for a review).

ECONOMIC DEPENDENCE AND REMAINING WITH AN ABUSER

Many researchers have observed the economic dependency-failure to leave connection (e.g., Kalmuss & Straus, 1982; Strube & Barbour, 1983; Wilson,

Baglioni, & Downing, 1989). In two surveys of shelter residents, the probability of staying in the violent relationship was highest for women whose husbands were the sole breadwinners (Aguirre, 1985; Johnson, 1992). In a study of 141 shelter residents, researchers found that most of the women interviewed were in need of material goods and services (84%), social support (79%), education (71%), health care (70%), finances (64%), legal assistance (62%), employment (62%), transportation (58%), and child care (57%). A significant number were also in need of housing (39%). The racial distribution of this group of women was as follows: 45% Caucasian, 43% African American, 8% Hispanic, and 1% Asian American. Sixty-eight percent of the women had at least one child (Sullivan, Basta, Tan, & Davidson, 1992).

Marital discord by itself increases the likelihood that married women will seek employment (Rogers, 1999), as well as the likelihood of divorce (Buttell, 1997; Byrne et al., 1999). One investigation determined that women who did not escape, compared to those who did, were significantly more likely to feel unable to make it in the work world because of poor job skills (Frisch & MacKenzie, 1991). It is probable that survivors who decide to return to their abusive relationships perceive their alternatives within the marriage as more rewarding and less costly than their alternatives outside the marriage (Johnson, 1988).

Barnett and Lopez-Real (1985) reported a constellation of reasons for staying given by the battered women that can be labeled as resource and economic dependence (also see Erez & Belknap, 1998). These were some of the comments:

> "I still feel scared of supporting the kids and bringing home enough money because I can't depend on him."

> "I'm facing eviction now. I'm scared."

> "I've never worked and have no high school education."

> "I am disabled because of his battering."

> "I feel one of the keys to this whole thing is for women to be economically independent, so as soon as they find themselves in a destructive relationship, they have the means to get out."

> "I only left once, but I came back because I didn't have any money, but money isn't everything."

"I know I'll eventually get out of this situation, that is, finding a place to live, getting a job, and supporting my children."

Corporate America has only recently begun to look at the effects of spousal abuse on their employees and on their businesses. Victims of intimate violence have higher levels of absenteeism, tardiness, job errors, and apathy, and these cost employers millions of dollars annually (Bryant, Eliach, & Green, 1991). Of the 20,000 workplace crimes actually reported to the police between 1992 and 1996, intimates perpetrated 60.7% (Warchol, 1998). The leading cause of occupational death to women is homicide (Jenkins, 1996).

A survey of 11 Employee Assistance Programs (EAPs) in 1992 (Magee & Hampton, 1993) indicated that none of the EAPs had written policies covering issues relevant to domestic violence victims. Although 9 of the 11 EAPs referred self-identified victims to shelters and women's services, less than half provided victim protection.

A few corporations, such as Liz Claiborne, Marshall's Department Stores, and Polaroid Corporation, have spearheaded efforts to assist victims and educate their own employees. State Farm Insurance Company, motivated by the efforts of K. C. Eynatten, formed the Corporate Alliance to End Partner Violence (CAEPV). The alliance focuses on increasing public awareness of domestic violence through school prevention programs. Some of its members include Archer-Daniels-Midland, American Express, Hewlett-Packard, and the National Football League ("Fighting Discrimination," 1996).

MASLOW'S HIERARCHY

A well-known psychological theory describing human behavior and growth seems to apply to a battered woman's decision making. Maslow's Hierarchy of Needs describes the path to self-actualization, or becoming a whole human being (Maslow, 1970). The scale ascends from basic needs—such as air to breathe, food and water, shelter, and safety—to affiliation, esteem, cognitive or intellectual needs, aesthetic needs, and needs for self-fulfillment. The basic tenet of this theory is that movement up the ladder is contingent upon meeting lower-level needs. It is obvious that a battered woman whose needs for food, shelter, and safety are not met will have little physical or emotional energy to invest in achieving higher-level needs. Social expectations imposed on battered women to move up the ladder usually fail to address survival needs. For many battered women, it may feel like two steps forward, one step back.

CASE STUDY

GLENDA

Glenda attended a woman's group run by the YWCA in her hometown in the Midwest. The group's theme was "Women and Self-Esteem." She had been in the group for several months before she hinted at "not having her needs met" in her marriage. A few weeks later she came to the group with bruises on her face and an Ace bandage on her wrist. After she told the group that her husband had hurt her, the other women comforted her and wanted to help.

The group leader had heard about a shelter for abused women somewhere in California. None of the other women knew of any safe place for Glenda to go. After a 2-day search, the group facilitator obtained the information about the shelter. With the help of other group members and the counselor, Glenda packed up her children and her household belongings, and boarded a bus to California to become one of the first women to enter one of the first shelters in California.

RELIGION

It's hard to fight an enemy who has outposts in your head.

—Sally Kempton

The Judeo-Christian ethic has greatly affected American culture. God and religion are mentioned in the Declaration of Independence, the U.S. Constitution, the Gettysburg Address, and the Pledge of Allegiance. The Judeo-Christian heritage exerts an influence on anyone who lives in this country, whether he or she is denying it, condemning it, actively participating in ascribed religious practices, or somewhere in between.

Marie Fortune (1987), an ordained Christian minister and author of *Keeping the Faith,* made the following claim:

> The majority of women in the United States were raised in Christian homes or as adults have affiliated themselves with a Christian Church. This is a sociological reality. Therefore, when a woman is battered by a member of her family, she will likely bring to her experience her background and values as a Christian woman. Also likely, is that her experience of violence in her family will not only be a physical and emotional crisis, but also a spiritual crisis. (p. 2)

This crisis of faith is not limited to Christian women. Most women of faith struggle with their spiritual principles when confronted with personal violence inflicted by the person whom they have loved and trusted. It is essential to acknowledge the dilemma of those who feel bound to their relationships by the very tenets of their religious beliefs. A woman with deep convictions may look to her minister, rabbi, or priest to interpret God's word and to ensure her eternal consequences. She turns to her spiritual adviser and to other members of her religious community for support. For a battered woman in particular, the quality of the assistance she receives can have life-and-death consequences. At the very least, the advice she is given can alter her life and her children's lives, and perhaps have a significant effect on her batterer.

As Clarke (1986), in her book *Pastoral Care of Battered Women,* states,

> Theological beliefs become an integral part of one's being and these beliefs are very powerful for a religious woman in a battering relationship. If a battered woman's religious convictions lead her to believe that a wife is subordinate to the husband, that marriage is an unalterable lifetime commitment, or that suffering is the lot of the faithful, then those convictions have the sanction of God. (p. 61)

CASE STUDY

CLAUDETTE—A CHRISTIAN WOMAN

Hitting had gone on for a few years before we went for help. We were members of a strict Protestant denomination. They had a counseling center, and we wanted Christian counseling. We talked to the counselor about our marriage, our children, about everything except the violence. Finally, I told him I was afraid of my husband. The counselor told me in front of my husband to be a better wife and mother, to pray harder, to be more submissive. He told my husband he shouldn't hit me. When we got home, my husband only remembered the part about how I should be more submissive.

> *[As long as] God is male, then the male is God.*
>
> —Mary Daly

Nineteenth-century suffragette Mathilda Gage (Stanton, Anthony, & Gage, 1881/1889) asserted that "the church, which should have been the great conservator of morals, dragged women to the lowest depths" (p. 763). Gage went on to explain that "the most grievous wound ever inflicted upon women has been in the teaching that she was not created equal with man, and the consequent denial of her rightful place and position in Church and State" (p. 754).

Many of the writers who assert that a sexist society is the fertile soil that allows for woman abuse also contend that traditional theologies have contributed to the victimization of wives by supplying Biblical evidence that God ordains patriarchy (Dobash & Dobash, 1979; Martin, 1978; Pagelow, 1981a; Star, 1980; Walker, 1979). Stacey and Shupe (1983) conclude that "the overwhelming role played by religion in the lives of the violent couples . . . was a regressive, and unwholesome one" (p. 97).

One example of the strong role that religious beliefs can play in the treatment of women has come to light in the Taliban sect. Since the Taliban militia seized control of Afghanistan, they have instituted severe restrictions on women. The Taliban, a fundamentalist Islamic sect, forces women to wear robes and shawls that totally cover the body. Exposure of any skin is punishable by beating. Taliban men forbid women to work outside the home or to pursue college educations. An egregious regulation prohibits medical doctors from touching female patients (Fields-Meyer & Benet, 1998).

Pamela Cooper-White (1996), who has served as a Priest-Associate in an Episcopal church, concluded that among several possible precipitants, sexual inequality is the overarching cause of violence against women. McDonald (1990) claimed that in systems such as patriarchy, the dominant group uses ideology to force conformity on the subordinate group (also see Lerner, 1986).

Beliefs in sexual inequality have arisen from religious dogma and have spread beyond the confines of specific denominational groups to permeate the entire legal system (Ruether, 1983). "As long as religions continue to create and maintain a patriarchal system paralleled in the secular society which writes the laws, women will be able to advance only as far as the male creators of this system permit" (McDonald, 1990, p. 253).

Alsdurf (1985) believes that his research data show that the clergy's beliefs mirror society's acceptance of patriarchal practices. He mailed a two-page questionnaire to 5,700 ministers from Protestant churches in the United States and Canada. Responses indicated that 26% of the surveyed pastors agreed that a wife should submit to her husband and trust that God would honor her action by either stopping the abuse or giving her the strength to endure it. About 50% of the pastors expressed concern that the husband's aggression not be overemphasized or used as a justification to break up the marriage. About one third of the ministers felt that abuse would have to be severe to justify a Christian wife's leaving her husband. According to 21% of these clergy, no amount of abuse would justify a separation. Only 17% believed that seldomly expressed physical violence was compelling enough to allow a woman to separate from her husband.

JUNE

June was married for 22 years to a mental health professional who battered her and terrified the children. They were both faithful church members, and she prayed daily. Her faith was the fundamental factor in her decision making. She was a devout and very intelligent woman, yet she felt confused and guilty in regard to her own angry feelings, which had recently surfaced.

June's husband broke things around the house, screamed, threatened, and beat her and the children. When he attacked their older son, she tried to stop it, but he hit her and threw her out of the way. Chaos was a way of life in their family. The mood of the family changed when her husband came home from work. June and the kids ate dinner silently. They responded to any quick movement from the head of the household and were ready to duck or run to defend themselves.

When she spoke of her fear and some of the problems at home to her friends in the church women's group, she was advised to submit to her husband and not to even think of leaving him, because leaving would damn her children's souls. Her husband was, after all, a deacon and very well respected. After that first attempt to gain support, June did not risk approaching anyone at her church for a while. Her next attempt was with an assistant minister, who advised her to pray and to endure, and that her husband would eventually change.

Several years later, after a particularly violent argument, June went to the minister in charge. This time, she had evidence. She pulled up her sleeves to show the bruises on her arms, and she pulled down her turtleneck collar, revealing the finger marks on her throat. She explained calmly about hearing her children's screams as she lost consciousness. At that point, the minister decided that the situation was very serious and wanted a conference with June and her husband. After the conference, June's pastor advised her to take the kids and run. And so she did.

CLERGYMEN'S RESPONSES

Although battered women may seek help from clergymen because they do not wish to tell outsiders about being battered, only 14% of women who typify themselves as religious, and 3% of nonreligious women, rated clergy as helpful (Horton, Wilkins, & Wright, 1988; also see Wood & McHugh, 1994). Actual responses of the clergy to victims were limited. They furnished information about treatment programs, provided extended counseling, or suggested that the victim obtain professional therapy. Much less frequently, they advised the women to call the police, obtain a civil protection order, or separate from the abuser. They rarely assisted women to leave, although more than half relayed information about shelters (Martin, 1989). Responses by clergy rated as helpful included validating and supporting women's reports, and emphasizing safety issues even if divorce might result. Unhelpful responses included recommending that battered women remain with the abuser or change their behaviors to be more pleasing to their husbands (Horton et al., 1988).

Some clergy alleged that they do not help because they are seldom asked. Other considerations were the clergy's lack of information about treatment programs or state laws, lack of time to meet the congregation's needs, and lack of training in counseling. Although Johnson and Bondurant (1992) documented an increase in ministerial training (from 30% to more than 50%) about domestic violence from 1982 to 1988, they found that clerics remained ambivalent. Theirs has been an institutional nonresponse.

In July 1997, the California Hospital Medical Center received a grant to provide domestic violence prevention education to community groups. The grant staff selected the faith community as one group that might profit from training. For the first workshop held in October, they invited 21 ministers; 8 attended. Over the next 15 months, volunteers mailed out personalized invitations to 300 clergy, alerting them to the workshop schedule. In response, an average of five or six ministers attended each of the five training programs. During 1998, the staff sent out additional questionnaires to more than 325 clergymen. Of this group, seven expressed interest in domestic violence education (Reyes, 1999).

Guilt is the gift that keeps on giving.

—Erma Bombeck

MORALITY—REASON FOR STAYING

Barnett and Lopez-Real (1985) reported that battered women also identified other reasons of principle or morality for staying with their abusive spouses: (a) "children need both a mother and father" was the most significant of these ethical reasons; (b) "you thought it would be distressing to leave your children";

and (c) "you considered divorce or separation a social disgrace." These comments reflect this conflict of convictions:

> "Divorce is a personal failure."
>
> "I believed you married forever."
>
> "I wanted to make it because of family pressure."
>
> "I have two boys; I'm afraid of them becoming feminine."
>
> "I would never leave my children under any circumstances."

Battered women expressed concern about the negative status of being divorced, and about the social stigma associated with being a divorcée. Many religious precepts, in fact, hold that divorce is a sin. Most spiritual groups extol the virtues of the family unit, a father, mother, and children. Religious groups center most of their activities around family events (not a single parent and her children).

AMANDA AND RAY

Amanda had three children under the age of five. She was the devout Christian wife of a devout Christian batterer. She asked for church counseling after Ray broke her nose. Her husband went with her. He explained that he had been angry, and that she had been "nagging" him. She said she had been pushing him to do some chores around the house. He explained that he had no intention of hurting her, and that he was sorry. She said she believed him. The pastor prayed with them. He admonished Ray and Amanda about the importance of maintaining a Christian home for the children.

By the time Amanda contacted the shelter hotline on the advice of a friend, she had received pastoral counseling on two additional occasions and had appeared before a board of elders. She was also spending three nights a week in her car with her children to avoid an incident. She was very concerned about receiving censure from the church and losing that very significant support group in her life. The church was not only a spiritual and emotional support, but also a possible source of financial assistance for her and the children. Amanda did not believe that she could maintain her resolve to leave the relationship if her wish for peace and safety conflicted with her moral obligations.

CASE STUDY (continued)

Shelter staff agreed to intervene, and they scheduled a meeting with two shelter workers, the board of elders, and Amanda. With reassurance from her advocates, Amanda was able to tell her story in more complete detail. Church members were appalled and agreed that Amanda and her children needed to be at the shelter. Censure was applied to Ray, not to Amanda, and Amanda was able to leave because she had clergy support.

THE FAILURE OF MILITARY RESPONSES

A military institution, ensconced in violence that is not only allowed but encouraged, provides an environment conducive to intimate abuse. Some surveys suggest that the rate of domestic violence in the military is almost five times the rate found in the general population (Radutsky, 1999). In a recent survey, severe violence rates were 3.5% for the military and 0.7% for civilians (Heyman & Neidig, 1999). Within the past 5 years, servicemen have victimized 50,000 spouses. Nevertheless, the military has court-martialed fewer than 5% of the batterers (Radutsky, 1999).

The armed forces spend $150 million per year on family advocacy to support servicemen, their spouses, and families. For the most part, base commanders do not lend their support to these advocacy programs. Authorities seem to routinely disregard threats and evidence of abuse. Soldiers are able to avoid court-ordered counseling by claiming work-related assignments. On one base, the officer in charge of the family advocacy program held this position until he admitted beating his own wife. In reaction to these dangerous oversights, domestic violence victims have filed a class action suit against the military for negligence (Radutsky, 1999).

SEXUAL ASSAULT IN BATTERING RELATIONSHIPS

Two institutions combine forces to maintain the status quo in regard to marital rape: the institution of marriage and the institution of government. Marital rape has a long history of social acceptability and a continuing history of neglect by researchers, service providers, and even battered women's groups (Bergen, 1995; Finkelhor & Yllö, 1982; Russell, 1983; Whatley, 1993). Historically, English law of the 1700s confined legal rape to unmarried individuals because marriage was a legal contract affording husbands nonrevocable sexual access to wives (Hale, 1736/1874). Laws in the United States exempting husbands from wife rape began to change, however, after the first successful prosecution in 1979 (see Barshis, 1983). Thereafter, the evolution in laws was relatively rapid. By 1990, only three states still retained marital exemption laws (Small & Tetreault, 1990), and by 1997, all states criminalized marital rape in at least some situations (see "Wife Rape," 1997).

Although the laws prohibiting marital rape have changed considerably over the decades, public opinion has lagged behind. Convictions about the sanctity of marriage, the need for privacy, and adherence to traditional sex-role beliefs have served to maintain greater social acceptance of wife rape than of stranger rape (Margolin, Moran, & Miller, 1989; Monson, Byrd, & Langhinrichsen-Rohling, 1996; Sullivan & Mosher, 1990; Whatley, 1993). So widespread are such beliefs that married women themselves may not recognize that their experiences qualify as rape (Bergen, 1995; Finkelhor & Yllö, 1982). Nevertheless, marital rape is common. Two studies of battered women in shelters indicated that husbands had sexually abused 44.3% of one group and 32% of a second (see Campbell, 1989b; Markward, 1996; Waldner-Haugrud, 1999).

JUSTICE AND THE SYSTEM

A number of researchers have cited the inadequacy or lack of institutional response as a factor in battered women's decision to stay (Hodson, 1982; Pagelow, 1981b). According to Pope (quoted in Beck, Springer, & Foote, 1992): "In our society, we tend to deny and downplay those types of abuses in which males are the perpetrators" (p. 54). As Hirschel, Hutchison, Dean, and Mills (1992) have asserted, "Spouse abuse is probably the only area of criminal behavior in which it has been considered necessary to justify the arrest of offenders on the grounds that such arrests will serve as a deterrent" (p. 276).

POLICE AND DOMESTIC VIOLENCE

Police departments and social service agencies traditionally have viewed family violence as noncriminal, noninjurious, inconsequential, and primarily verbal (Fields, 1978; Waaland & Keeley, 1985). In general, police have been reluctant to get involved in family problems for reasons rooted in myth, misogyny, and misinformation: (a) If he beats her and she stays, there are no real victims (Waaland & Keeley, 1985); (b) it may be her fault (Home, 1994); (c) it is not the best solution to the problem (Saunders & Size, 1986); and (d) it is too dangerous for police to intervene (Garner & Clemmer, 1986). In one study, police ignored victims' arrest preferences in 75% of the intimate assault cases, but in only 40% of the stranger assault cases (Buzawa, Austin, & Buzawa, 1995).

It is ironic that the police have tended to dismiss domestic disturbances as family spats that women can handle on their own, while feeling gravely endangered themselves when called upon to intervene. Analogously, male police may resent female cops because women are physically weaker than men, but decide that battered women are strong enough to handle assaultive partners.

Studies have varied in their findings and interpretations of the degree of danger faced by police in responding to domestic disturbance calls. FBI statistics for the 10-year period from 1973 to 1982 revealed that responding to disturbance calls was the single most frequent category of felonious assaults on officers (FBI, 1984). A later reclassification of the 1973-1982 data indicated that next to traffic calls, disturbance calls were the least dangerous (see Garner & Clemmer, 1986). In a 3-year study conducted in Charlotte, North Carolina, between 1987 and 1989, police received 1,078,571 calls for service. Domestic disturbance calls accounted for 7.8% of the calls. These calls ranked fifth (of 10 categories) in terms of assaults on police officers and sixth in regard to injuries (see also Hirschel, Dean, & Lumb, 1994).

CASE STUDY

RACHEL AND ABE

Rachel had two children, a temporary restraining order, and an abusive husband who violated it regularly. The order had not been difficult to get, but enforcement was a joke. The first few times Abe violated the order, the police did not arrive until he was long gone. The next few times, the police demanded that he leave the premises. They finally arrested him, but he was out of jail within 24 hours. It was only after four more arrests and court appearances for violating the restraining order that a judge sentenced him to 8 months in jail. The judge was finally persuaded by Abe's continued threats on Rachel's life ("I'll kill the bitch"), despite his demands that Abe "stop threatening her or I will have to incarcerate you."

THE NEED FOR LOGICAL CONSEQUENCES

A synthesis of several different analyses revealed that about one fourth of batterers are arrested, about one third of those arrested are prosecuted, and 1% of those prosecuted receive jail time beyond the time served at arrest (often just a few hours) (see Bourg & Stock, 1994; Hirschel, Hutchison, Dean, & Mills, 1992; Hirschel, Hutchison, Dean, Kelley, & Pesackis, 1991; Holmes, 1993; Yegidis & Renzy, 1994). One review cited 25 studies showing that police typically avoid arresting batterers (Erez & Belknap, 1998). Batterers themselves tend to believe that being arrested or losing their partner is an unlikely outcome of assault (Carmody & Williams, 1987; Williams & Hawkins, 1989).

Some police officers persist in doing exactly what they please despite changes in the law and training (Buzawa et al., 1995). Frequently, police officers simply decide that no crime has been committed (Hirschel et al., 1992). In an ongoing legal dispute, the family of a woman murdered by her husband is suing Los Angeles County on the grounds that 911 dispatchers give a lower priority to domestic violence calls than others ("Court Allows Suit," 1999).

According to Hamberger and Arnold (1991), police in a mid-sized community of 85,000 evidenced a twelvefold increase in arrests of women and a twofold increase in arrests of men over the previous year. Upon further investigation, most of the women arrested (67%) had acted violently, but in self-defense. In another study of police officers in Connecticut, police charged a greater portion of women with assault than men, 34% and 23%, respectively (Martin, 1997).

Police discretionary arrest policies often rest on the relationship between the victim and the perpetrator. The more intimate the relationship, the more blame seems to attach to the victim and the lower the arrest rate of male perpetrators (Buzawa et al., 1995; Fyfe, Klinger, & Flavin, 1997). Police often require higher standards of probable cause for arrest in domestic violence cases compared with acquaintance and stranger arrests (Buzawa et al., 1995; see U.S. Department of Justice, Bureau of Justice Statistics, 1994).

CASE STUDY

DON AND SHAUNA

Don sat in his first group for men who abused their partners, angry and disbelieving. It was not the first time he had pushed his wife around or screamed at her. It was the first time he had choked Shauna, but nobody knew about that. When he finally talked, it was to tell the group about his wife, who was immature and used drugs. He had stopped using a few months before. He was bewildered by his experience with the police and the courts. He had been arrested, and he had to go to a group and spend 200 hours picking up trash on the freeway. "I've hit her before. I've pulled her hair. I know she didn't like it, but this is the first time anybody ever told me I couldn't do it—that I couldn't get away with it."

An analysis of prosecutions established that district attorneys prosecuted women (11%) in dual arrests more often than men (6%). The researchers found that dual arrest rates varied widely by size of the department (and city). In one city, police made only five arrests, four of which were dual arrests. The ramifications of dual arrest policies are unknown, but it is possible that they could deter women from reporting assaults (Martin, 1997).

Dunford, Huizinga, and Elliott (1990) found that the effects of three different police dispositions (mediation, separation, or arrest) did not produce different rates of recidivism 6 months later. In fact, Sherman et al. (1991) maintained that the superiority of arrest lasted only 30 days. On the basis of a Dade County study, Sherman (1992) finally concluded that the deterrent effect was limited to employed offenders. Taken together with previous research, arrest might even escalate violence in unemployed men.

One research team compared three types of police response to domestic violence calls: (a) advising and possibly separating the couple, (b) issuing a citation to the offender, and (c) arresting the offender. Results showed conclusively that arrest was not superior to the other treatments in terms of recidivism or in terms of the victim's evaluations. The researchers concluded that

> the dynamics of domestic violence in general, and the abuse of female spouses in particular, are so complex and intertwined with historical, traditional, psychological, political, and social forces that it may be unreasonable to expect any short-term action by the criminal justice system to have a significant deterrent effect. (Hirschel, Hutchison, & Dean, 1992, p. 31)

Some newer research has shown relatively low rates of arrest in domestic assault, but even lower rates in nondomestic assaults. There were three factors related to police decisions to arrest: (a) belief in the utility of police involvement, (b) less traditional attitudes about women's roles, and (c) knowledge of the department's proarrest policy (Feder, 1997, 1998).

POLICE TRAINING

Eigenberg and Moriarty (1991) examined law enforcement personnel to estimate their "domestic violence I.Q." With training, almost three fourths of the 64 officers knew that Texas law required officers to inform domestic violence victims about social services such as shelters. Most knew that they were legally allowed to make a warrantless arrest of a perpetrator, even if they had not witnessed the assault and even if they saw no visible injuries. Shelters in major metropolitan areas (Austin, Houston, San Antonio) noted a greater support and responsiveness to their clients. Police officers had instituted a more aggressive arrest policy if there was some sign of injury or a woman reported feeling pain as the result of a domestic assault. Unfortunately, the training that is mandated or encouraged for police officers has not been imposed on attorneys and judges.

MANDATORY ARREST

Experts holding contrasting assumptions about mandatory arrest have continued to debate whether such policies merit implementation. Some of the following positions have emerged about when police should arrest: (a) to protect the victim; (b) only after screening indicates that the specific offender is dangerous (e.g., under the influence of drugs); (c) upon request of the victim, in order to produce consumer satisfaction with the police; (d) on every call in order to control police behavior and to avoid civil suits; (e) with great discretion to avoid racial bias; (f) to indicate that society condemns battering as a crime, in contrast to nonintervention, which suggests that battering is acceptable; (g) only in extreme cases so that the family unit can be preserved; (h) when needed to compel the offender to obtain treatment; (i) only with great caution to avoid an escalation of violence directed at the victim; (j) to remove victims from isolation and to empower them; (k) to motivate women to call again, especially when they feel gravely endangered; and (l) because battering violates women's civil rights (Stark, 1993; see Erez & Belknap, 1998; Mills, 1998).

The most influential criminologist on the topic of mandatory arrest operated under the premise that the value of mandatory arrest should be considered in terms of its effects on violent behavior. If mandatory arrest reduced future violence (deterrence), it should be continued; if not, it should be abandoned (Sherman et al., 1991). Davis (1998), however, rejected this logic because it would lead to a policy of arresting no one. Why? Convincing evidence supporting the deterrent effect of mandatory arrest on *any* criminal behavior (e.g., child abuse, burglary) is nonexistent (Sigler & Lamb, 1995). Regrettably, mandatory arrest of batterers may not decrease battering any more than arrest deters other crimes (Davis, 1998).

Mandatory arrest laws, in particular, have led to a large number of arrests of women who were violent in self-defense. Kevin Hamberger stated that the new Wisconsin laws on mandatory arrest have created a new criminal, the *battering wife*. His research has revealed that two thirds of the women arrested were actually battered women fighting back. Hamberger does not believe that the women arrested are true batterers (Hamberger & Arnold, 1991). Asher (1990) says that the police do not always know whom to arrest, that is, who the violent party is.

In support of our one-size-does-*not*-fit-all hypothesis, several researchers and women's advocates have noted serious problems flowing from mandatory arrest policies. Some of these complications include failure to identify the primary perpetrator; failure to recognize women's self-defensive violence; and further hardships for women, such as loss of economic resources (Hamberger & Arnold, 1991; Martin, 1997; Youngstrom, 1992). Mandatory penalties may not uniformly have the desired effect either.

In an Iowa study, individuals convicted of domestic assault did receive greater penalties, but other problems arose. Because fewer wife abusers were willing to plead guilty, and because victim cooperation was more problematic, conviction rates actually declined (Carlson & Nidey, 1995). Other findings suggested that although battered women might call police to terminate a current violent episode, they might balk at taking further action. They often feared giving evidence against their partners or did not want their partners to go to jail (Sirles, Lipchik, & Kowalski, 1993).

According to the New York State Committee on Investigations, Taxations, and Governmental Operations, the police made 12,724 domestic violence arrests at an average cost of $3,241 per arrest. Including these police costs and those for the court and detention, the city paid at least $41 million (see Zorza, 1994).

In light of this critical controversy, a number of spouse abuse experts collaborated on devising an integrated approach to batterer interventions and criminal justice strategies. This group recommended that law enforcement officers should comply with four major guidelines: (a) they should identify the primary aggressor, (b) they should execute a proarrest or mandatory arrest policy, (c) they should gather evidence at the scene for use in prosecutions, and (d) they should arrange for a temporary restraining or no-contact order (Healey, Smith, & O'Sullivan, 1998).

POLICE AS BATTERERS

A modification to the Gun Control Act of 1968, known as the Lautenberg amendment (after Senator Frank Lautenberg), took effect in January 1997. It bans individuals convicted of domestic assault from carrying weapons. Unlike many previous laws, it does not exempt law enforcement officers or any government employees ("Domestic Violence Conviction," 1997). The Lautenberg amendment, however, is under appeal ("Court of Appeals," 1999).

Throughout 1997, the Lautenberg amendment sparked investigations of law enforcement officers across the nation. In December 1996, even before the law went into effect, Sheriff Block of Los Angeles County announced that he intended to comply with the law and that he would reassign convicted officers to desk jobs ("Sheriff Won't Contest," 1996). Within the Los Angeles area, police chiefs in Glendale and Burbank asserted that none of their men had been convicted. In the 9,300-member LAPD, approximately 150 officers may have had arrest records ("Three Deputies," 1997).

Various inquiries suggested that the LAPD's handling of officers convicted of domestic violence was insufficient (Braidbill, 1997; McGreevy, 1997). Under public pressure to comply with the law, the Los Angeles City Council hired additional investigators to check the conviction records of all LAPD personnel. The Investigator General, Katherine Mader, reached several conclusions: (a) The LAPD made arrests in only 6% of cases involving LAPD officers within its jurisdiction, whereas outside agencies made arrests in 16% of incidents in other jurisdictions; (b) by gender, almost 90% of the allegations were against male employees; (c) the Internal Affairs Department (IAD), charged with evaluating these accusations, judged only 38% of the male employees guilty and 58% of the women; (d) reports turned in to IAD were often flawed by inappropriate language describing and blaming victims; and (e) the IAD often took almost a year to investigate domestic violence charges.

A review of 84 IAD incident reports disclosed that the LAPD did not make a single arrest of an officer between 1991 and 1993, even though 48 of the victims had multiple, visible injuries. Reports often described female victims as suffering from "fatal attraction" or as being overly possessive, while describing the accused male officers as productive and hard-working. One report concluded that "there is no fury like a woman scorned" (Braidbill, 1997).

In the final analysis, investigators identified 7 convicted domestic violence abusers from the list of 150 officers, relieved them of their weapons, and assigned them to other duties (Orlov, 1997). Police union officers point out that some convictions are more than 10 years old and no longer relevant. A loophole in the laws has allowed some convicted police officers to expunge their records, and it is expected that other officers will attempt to do so as quickly as possible ("Domestic Violence Conviction," 1997).

THE COURTS

"The attitudes of the public, the court, and even many helping professionals condone a certain level of abuse in the home, and support the patriarchal structure of the family which perpetuates the abuse from generation to generation" (Maertz, 1990, pp. 48-49).

The primary directive for child protection service (CPS) workers is to safeguard children. From their perspective, it is obligatory to take action if a mother is unwilling or unable to protect (i.e., remove) her children from her violent male partner (Berliner, 1998). The law may simultaneously classify a battered woman as an assault victim and hold her criminally responsible for her male partner's child abuse (see Davidson, 1995; Sierra, 1997)! The assumption that a woman can protect her children by simply leaving her batterer is not born out by the facts and tends to ignore the deleterious effects that victimization has had on her (Ellis, 1992; McMurray, 1997; O'Sullivan & Carper, 1998).

Some judges continue to rule in favor of male perpetrators and against battered victims (Stone & Fialk, 1999). The fact that a father who fails to protect his children from a child-abusing mother is rarely, if ever, held responsible appears to reflect yet another gender bias in the judicial system (National Council of Juvenile and Family Court Judges, 1994).

When battered wives ask the court for protection, the criminal justice process often victimizes them ("California Panel Urges Reforms," 1990). The following is an excerpted quotation from the Maryland Special Joint Committee on Gender Bias in the Courts ("Domestic Violence in the Courts," 1989):

> The thing that has never left my mind from that point to now is what the judge said to me. He took a few minutes and he looked at me and he said, "I don't believe anything that you're saying.
>
> "The reason I don't believe it is because I don't believe that anything like this could happen to me. If I were you and someone had threatened me with a gun, there is no way that I would continue to stay with them. There is no way that I could take that kind of abuse from them. Therefore, since I would not let that happen to me, I can't believe that it happened to you."
>
> I have just never forgotten those words. . . . When I left the courtroom that day, I felt very defeated, and very powerless and very hopeless, because not only had I gone through an experience which I found to be very overwhelming, very trying and almost cost me my life, but to sit up in court and make myself open up and recount all my feelings and fear and then have it thrown back in my face as being totally untrue just because this big man would not allow anyone to do this to him, placed me in a state of shock which probably hasn't left me yet. (p. 3)

Under the leadership of Los Angeles Superior Court Judge David M. Rothman, the gender bias committee forwarded a number of recommendations to the court that revolved around the handling of domestic violence cases. Courts handling these cases should have metal detectors, secure waiting areas, and parking lot escort programs to protect victims. The panel further pointed out the need for two types of curative legislation: (a) to find better ways of maintaining court protection of domestic violence victims when emergency protective orders expire, and (b) to exempt domestic violence cases from mandatory mediation in child custody and visitation disputes. In addition, legislation could mandate domestic violence training for judges and attorneys.

Gender bias in the criminal justice system continues to reflect male privilege and lend credence to the argument that wife abuse is an outgrowth of patriarchy. Karen Winner, a policy analyst for New York City, documented widespread overcharging, misrepresenting, and failing to litigate diligently for female clients. Many of these deceptive practices are exacerbated by judges. For instance, judges rarely punish husbands who hide their assets during the discovery phase of the trial.

In 1997, the American Bar Association's (ABA's) Commission on Domestic Violence convened to assess the bar's response to victims of domestic violence (Goelman, Lehrman, & Valente, 1996). So generally flawed was the legal profession's representation of victims that the commission issued a series of recommendations concerning legal education. Interestingly, the commission also reemphasized the necessity of disciplinary committees to include professional consequences for lawyers who abuse their own partners and children (see Goelman & Valente, 1997, for a review).

An antiwoman bias in family court included finding mothers less fit as the custodial parent if they worked, especially if the fathers had remarried and had a stay-at-home wife (Winner, 1996). Such findings occur in the absence of any research on children's relationships with their violent father (Holden, Geffner, & Jouriles, 1998a). According to a report by Taylor in 1992 (cited in Jaffe & Geffner, 1998), some judges believe that a child's estrangement from his or her father is more traumatic than the child's exposure to the father's battering.

Some lawyers have succeeded in attributing two syndromes to mothers that have undermined their attempts to gain custody (see Jaffe & Geffner, 1998, for a review). Malicious mother syndrome (Turkat, 1995), recently updated to divorce-related malicious parent syndrome (Turkat, 1999), ascribes behaviors such as unjustified attempts to punish a parent and deny him or her access to the couple's children. By the author's own admission, the syndrome has no supportive empirical evidence. Parental alienation syndrome (Gardner, 1987) covers false allegations of child sexual abuse. However, several empirical investigations have shown that false allegations are rarely made (see Barnett, Miller-Perrin, & Perrin, 1997, for a review).

Some good news: The Court Statistics Project gathered caseload information from more than 16,000 trial courts in the United States on topics such as torts and contracts, domestic relations, and drugs. The number of domestic violence filings varied widely among the states because of differences in definitions of domestic abuse, police arrest policies, and access to protection orders. Overall, domestic violence filings increased more than 200% from 1985 to 1995 and then leveled off during 1996 (Ostrom & Kauder, 1997).

Under Title II, crossing a state line to violate a protection order is now a federal crime. A valid protection order based on due process issued in one state must be treated and enforced as if it were an order originating in the new state. Some previous state laws and practices concerning protection orders, however, conflict with the new federal law and require modification. As one example, an individual who obtains a valid protection order against a same-sex partner in one state is entitled to have the order enforced in a different state that does not recognize same-sex relationships (also see "Model Police Protocol," 1999; Wilson & Daly, 1993).

In some cases, judges have issued restraining orders against both spouses, giving the false impression that the victim has been violent as well. Brygger (quoted in Youngstrom, 1992) says that restraining orders are effective "only if the batterer has had no contact with the criminal justice system and 'fears the consequences' of violating the order" (p. 45). Fortunately, a number of perpetrators of intimate violence fall into that category.

Another favorable change in protection order laws appended to the Violence Against Women Act (VAWA) addresses the issuance of mutual protection orders and their mandatory enforcement by other states. Congress acknowledged the problems with mutual orders and put a limit on their uses. Generally, they affect battered women negatively in other court proceedings, such as divorce and child custody determinations.

CASE STUDY

OMAR

Omar's wife obtained a restraining order. What she did not know, however, was that Omar was violating it on a regular basis "after hours," usually between midnight and 2:00 a.m. He would "just check up on her" by driving around the house or by stopping and looking through her windows. One night at about midnight, as Omar was peeking through her bedroom window, the police pulled up and arrested him. He spent the night in jail, where his shoelaces were stolen at night. Omar had a "religious" experience; he did not violate the order again.

A research project conducted by the National Center for State Courts assessed battered women's views on the effectiveness of civil protection orders. Interview data from 285 women indicated that 72% thought their lives had improved 1 month after receiving a protection order. At a 6-month follow-up of 177 women, 85% reported improved lives, 90% felt better about themselves, and 80% felt safer. Although 72% experienced no continuing problems at 1 month, the percentage dropped even further to 65% at follow-up. Among the batterers,

65% had an arrest history. Results suggested that judges use abusers' criminal records to craft even more effective protection orders (Keilitz, Davis, & Eikeman, 1998). These findings fit with evidence that the probability of re-abuse declines significantly following issuance of protective orders (Carlson, Harris, & Holden, 1999). Researchers also concluded that protection orders are only one element of many services needed by battered women (Keilitz et al., 1998).

Bennett, Goodman, and Dutton (1999) found a number of factors within the court system itself that contributed to victims' reluctance to prosecute: (a) confusion about the court system (e.g., lack of knowledge about differences between the civil and criminal courts); (b) frustration with the criminal justice system (e.g., slowness, fear triggered by lack of action, lack of contact with the court); and (c) conflict over incarceration (e.g., lack of child support or help in taking care of children, lack of a father in the home, views of the criminal justice system as racist and oppressive).

Despite the increasing number of jurisdictions with vigorous prosecution policies, court resources are so minimal that court personnel are unable to guide battered women through the court system in a way that meets their needs. There is little follow-up. Victims concerned about their abuser's incarceration, for example, may have no information about alternatives such as mandatory counseling or community service for convicted batterers (Healey & Smith, 1998). With better court services, there is reason to believe that many more battered women would choose to cooperate with a decision to prosecute than currently do (Henning & Klesges, 1999).

Syers and Edleson (1992) pinpointed two crucial variables affecting recidivism: number of previous arrests and duration of court-ordered counseling. In this inquiry, men arrested the first time the police visited the residence and who were mandated into counseling programs for a relatively longer period of time were significantly less likely to violently revictimize their female partners than were their counterparts. Gamache, Edleson, and Schock (1988) also called attention to lowered recidivism rates brought about by community intervention projects that coordinated the components within the criminal justice system.

VICTIM COMPENSATION

Availability of victim compensation, especially for victims of domestic violence, has been problematic ("Victim Agencies," 1992). Regulators have used statutes intended to exclude participants in a fight (e.g., a barroom brawl) as a rationale to exempt battered women victims whose behavior was "provocative." The laws also require that victims cooperate with law enforcement agencies (i.e., make an official complaint). A battered woman, however, may choose not to prosecute for a variety of reasons, such as fear. If the battered victim does get financial compensation and the money might somehow assist her batterer, regulators could deny her application based on the principle of "unjust enrichment" of a perpetrator. Recently, the Office for Victims and Crimes has made some headway by publishing newer guidelines that more clearly identify populations in need of such services and by specifying the combination of services most needed by victims (Tomz & McGillis, 1997).

THE IMPACT OF LEGAL REFORMS—VAWA

New spouse abuse laws have been written and older laws modified. In this country, every state has at least one statute pertaining to battered women (Myers, Tikosh, & Paxson, 1992). The Urban Institute in Washington, DC issued a report in March 1997 on implementation of the VAWA (Burt, Newmark, Olson, Aron, & Harrell, 1997). The report primarily included information on how the new laws affect law enforcement and prosecution, victim services, data collection, and supports to Indian tribal governments.

SUMMARY

A number of institutional forces have routinely erected barriers that prevent battered women from obtaining sufficient help. Patriarchal practices within society, the church, and the criminal justice system have created a gender imbalance and removed power from the hands of women. Ordinarily, women do not have a level playing field to compete in the marketplace. They cannot usually find equal employment opportunities even with equivalent educational backgrounds and, as a rule, do not receive comparable pay. Although there has been change, much more must be done to create a safe environment for those who have not traditionally had institutional power.

Following a divorce, the legal system does not uniformly enforce existing laws or compel men to assume financial responsibility for their children. The financial and caretaking burdens placed on women create havoc in their lives and in the lives of their children. On the whole, society allows men to vent their anger and frustration on wives, ex-wives, other intimates, and their own children without fear of reprisal. If a battered woman tries to escape, there may be no place for her to go. She may even become homeless. Despite newer mandates to police departments to protect her, she cannot count on being safe.

What would you do if you had several young children and no job? Would you call your clergyman? The police? Your congressman?

3 Victimization
Why Does It Happen to Her?

Experiencing violence transforms people into victims and changes their lives forever. Once victimized, one can never again feel quite as invulnerable.

—Koss (1990, p. 374)

CHAPTER OVERVIEW

It is important to address the question of whether victims are different from other people. Researchers who study female victims (battered women, adult survivors of incest, survivors of rape) have often attempted to describe them in terms of their presumed deviance, that is, the characteristics that distinguish them from "normal" people. The underlying assumption seemed to be that victims are to blame for their own victimization, and that they are inherently provocative by nature or behavior. The concept of victim provocation formed a framework for understanding all victims. Observation of victimization phenomena brought on by captivity and extreme trauma, however, began to challenge earlier beliefs. This chapter explores victims, the myths surrounding them, and some of the forms and consequences of victimization.

CASE STUDY

ZARI AND AHMED

Zari sat in the office, shaking and confused. She had nothing left. She had given up her friends and family, a Fifth Avenue apartment, and a lucrative job as a media consultant to help Ahmed start his business. She had been in other relationships and had maintained friendships with those other men. Ahmed was different. At first, he did everything she liked to do. They jogged and worked out together,

CASE STUDY (continued)

went to plays, and socialized with her friends. He said that he wanted children, and that was very attractive to her.

"Mr. Hyde" did not appear for some time. The negative behavior started with criticism of her appearance and her friends. Over time, he began to follow her and read her diary. For a long time, she did not notice that cash was missing from her drawer. When she saw Ahmed searching through her dresser, she told him to leave. Ahmed, however, hung on, trying to get her to take him back. He called her friends and family, and he had his therapist call her to plead his case. She took him back.

Criticisms and put-downs began again after they had gotten back together and moved across the country. He began to break her things. She had not realized the extent of her dependence, isolation, and humiliation until most of her furniture had been destroyed. She realized that in helping him start his business, she had lost her independent source of income and her support group. Although he did not pay her a salary, he did pay her expenses. She felt like a child dependent on her parents for her allowance. She felt imprisoned.

He started pushing her around, and he accused her of being crazy and breaking his things. It was only when he choked her and threw her into his glass coffee table, which shattered and cut her leg, that Zari escaped.

The police took pictures of her injuries and wanted her to press charges. She found out that Ahmed had previous charges against him for stalking and terrorizing a business associate. Although he was gone, her freedom did not restore her self-confidence and security. She had escaped from her captor, but she had not stopped feeling controlled and intimidated. She wondered if she would look in her rearview mirror one day and see Ahmed's eyes staring at her. She wondered if he would ever stop following her.

ARE BATTERED WOMEN DIFFERENT?

People still want to know if battered women like Zari are somehow different from other people. The real, underlying questions appear to be whether battered women come from poor, nonwhite families with no education or have some psychological maladjustments that predispose them to provoke their mates, behave in "sick" ways, or choose men who will eventually batter them (e.g., Harrison & Esqueda, 1999; Shainess, 1979). Finding something wrong with battered women makes it possible for the rest of us to distance ourselves from them: "If I am different from battered women, I will not be battered." "If she is different from other women, I do not have to do anything to help her."

VICTIM CHARACTERISTICS

Many researchers have gathered racial and ethnic data to search for possible differences between women abused by their male intimates and those who are not abused (e.g., Harrison & Esqueda, 1999; Krishnan, Hilbert, VanLeeuwen, & Kolia, 1997). For the most part, investigations have not found substantial racial disparities (Gondolf, Fisher, & McFerron, 1988; Rouse, 1988; Sorenson & Telles, 1991). Self-report data from the 1994 National Crime Victimization Survey (NCVS) (Bachman, 1994) and from the redesigned 1995 NCVS also failed to find significant ethnic/racial differences (Bachman & Saltzman, 1995).

In contrast, self-report data from the National Family Violence Surveys revealed a disproportionate amount of violence in Black and Hispanic families compared to Whites (Hampton & Gelles, 1994; Straus & Smith, 1990). The National Violence Against Women (NVAW) survey, which included 8,000 women, also uncovered two interesting racial disparities. American Alaskan Indian women reported significantly more victimizations, and Asian/Pacific Islander women reported significantly fewer victimizations, than did White and African American women (Tjaden & Thoennes, 1998). Other studies of calls to police departments or shelters revealed that African American women are more likely than Anglo-American women to seek help (see Goodman, Bennett, & Dutton, in press; Hutchison & Hirschel, 1998; Murty & Roebuck, 1992; Tjaden & Thoennes, 1998). African American women, however, are troubled by the prospect of contributing to negative racial stereotyping of Black men as criminals by reporting them (see Campbell, 1993; Moss et al., 1997).

Very little is known about battered women who live in rural areas or who have special needs. Women living in nonurban areas often lack access to transportation and service providers. They are often isolated in the most literal way, and their tight communities and local law enforcement can exacerbate rather than expose the secret. American Indian women and migrant women share the plight of rural women. Their situation is complicated further by language barriers (Burt et al., 1997; also see Krishnan et al., 1997; Websdale, 1995a, 1995b).

In an NCVS special report, Bachman and Saltzman (1995) stated that women with a family income under $10,000 were four times more likely to be victims of battering by an intimate than were other women. In a review article of most studies published before 1990, however, Hotaling and Sugarman (1990) judged socioeconomic status to be relevant for only the most severely assaulted. As

Hirschel, Hutchison, Dean, and Mills (1992) have asserted, "It is clear that spouse abuse is not characteristic of any particular group. It is less clear whether all groups are truly equal in both prevalence and incidence of abusive behavior" (p. 256). Whereas some women face unique challenges in addition to confronting the abuse in their relationships, poor women struggle with their survival at a very practical level (see also Byrne et al., 1999; Cucio, 1997).

Nevertheless, prevalence rates detailing socioeconomic status remain controversial for two main reasons. First, many family violence studies employ small samples from shelters and funded community-based programs that generally serve people with the fewest resources (finances, family, friends). Women with more resources usually have more options. Second, statistics based on police calls and arrest records seem to overrepresent minorities and the poor because of differential arrest policies (Bachman & Coker, 1995). In other words, fewer people from Beverly Hills and Scarsdale may be included in arrest and prosecution data (see also Bowker, 1984; Schuller & Vidmar, 1992).

POPULATION COVERAGE

Teenage violence. Levy (1990) suggests that several factors exacerbate teen dating violence: (a) pressures, insecurities, and romanticism of adolescence; (b) misperceptions about jealousy and control as loving behaviors rather than unhealthy behaviors; (c) conformity to traditional gender roles; and (d) lack of experience (also see Lloyd, 1991). Generally, teenagers do not recognize dating violence as a problem (Levy, 1993; Parrot & Bechhofer, 1991). One investigation found that whereas both male and female high school victims of dating violence judged female-to-male violence as more acceptable, more male victims than female victims thought that male-to-female violence was justifiable (O'Keefe & Treister, 1998; also see Bethke & De Joy, 1993; Silverman & Williamson, 1997). For the most part, domestic violence laws do not cover teens. The major stumbling blocks are the legal requirements for adult and marital status (Brustin, 1995; Kuehl, 1991; Suarez, 1994).

In a recent study of 635 high school students ages 13 to 18, 36.4% of girls who dated and 37.1% of boys who dated experienced physical violence (Molidor & Tolman, 1998; O'Keefe & Treister, 1998). A Canadian study of 1,307 male and 1,835 female college students yielded dating violence rates that were somewhat lower than those obtained in the United States. Using the CTS, 17.8% of the males reported acts of aggression against a partner, and 35% of the females admitted to having been victimized (DeKeseredy & Kelly, 1993). In a review of published articles, Jackson (1998) suggests that violence rates range from 10% to 50% of dating couples.

Several college-based studies have characterized courtship violence as largely reciprocal (e.g., Bookwala, Frieze, Smith, & Ryan, 1992; Worth, Matthews, & Coleman, 1990). In a newer study, 145 students had experienced severe physical violence; 57% of the boys and 46% of the girls had also been offenders (Bennett & Fineran, 1997). Another sign of the reciprocal nature of dating violence was the finding that "inflicting dating violence" by either sex was the greatest predictor of becoming its recipient (O'Keefe & Treister, 1998). It is essential to bear in mind that whereas many studies based on self-report perpetration reflect mutuality of gender violence, other studies do not. Self-report victimization studies, hospital-based injury studies, and official police reports all indicate much greater male-to-female violence than the reverse.

Elder battered women. Prior to 1985, researchers paid little attention to older women who experienced domestic violence, and even now, most research on elder abuse focuses on elders living in nursing homes. The etiology of abuse of older women is unclear in many cases, as is the reason why some women leave and some do not. Women abused throughout a marriage may leave in old age as they recognize that their inability to withstand abuse places them at even greater risk for injury and stress-related conditions such as heart attacks. Others believe that older women remain because of real or assumed financial and physical dependence (Pillemer & Finkelhor, 1989).

Domestically abused elders are most often mistreated by people with whom they live, and they more often live with a spouse than with an adult child (Vinton, 1992, 1998). At least some, and possibly most, domestic elder abuse is actually *spouse abuse grown old.* It is unclear to what extent abuse of elders by their adult children is similar to abuse of elders by spouses (Anetzberger, 1987). Service providers tend not to view older women as victims of spousal violence but as victims of elder abuse. Their typical response consists of in-home services to reduce dependency on the abuser and caregiver stress (Vinton, 1991).

Currently, too many older abused women are falling through the cracks between different service providers. Experts in the field of elder abuse have begun to call for broader awareness of abuse across all subfields. For example, domestic violence workers need to know more about the domain of Adult Protective Services, and vice versa (see Nerenberg, 1996, for a review).

Professional women. Financial reasons have always been at the top of the list in explaining why battered women do not leave their partners (Strube & Barbour,

1984). But what about women who do have financial resources and the support of family and friends? Since 1984, the first author (A.L.) has been working with a much broader base of battered women—women with jobs, careers, and the money to leave. In the setting of a private practice and in a training environment, she has met with hundreds of women who judge themselves very harshly for staying with abusive men (and women, in lesbian relationships) because they see themselves as fully able to leave. It has been a challenge to work with these women over time and to develop with them explanations—theories, if you will—that assist them in the process of problem solving, self-forgiveness, healing, and, for many, leaving or staying away from their batterers.

Of course, "there ain't nothing new under the sun," so the ideas anchoring this fresh rationale are a reframing of the work done by earlier pioneers in this field and early feminists such as Del Martin, Lenore Walker, and Barrie Levy. One restructured theoretical rationale for why professional women do not leave their batterers appears in the theme of self-blame for emotional responding that may be termed *spiraling reactivity:* "I am smart enough to have figured this out." "Why didn't I or why can't I leave?"

A better question might be the following: "How does a woman think clearly when she is operating at a level of emotional reflex?" When a woman lives with abuse, the batterer becomes the linchpin of her existence. It is necessary for peace and survival to respond promptly and accurately to perceptions of the batterer's needs and wants. Over time, these reactions metamorphize into a response pattern that is emotionally based, not cognitively based. These battered women are too busy reacting reflexively at a gut level to enter the world of objective and clear thinking (see Lazarus & Folkman, 1984; MacNair & Elliott, 1992).

Most often, the problem solving that is done has a relatively nonproductive focus. These battered women are trying to stop the violence or change the batterer. They are not focused directly on their own escape. They become caught in a pattern of reactions that, over time, spirals out of control. For many battered women, "out of control" is the description they have for their own lives and feelings. When the focus begins to shift to what they can control, the cycle of reaction changes.

Another issue, often left unexamined by women in general, focuses on gender and socialization. It is often useful to ask women about their experiences with fairy tales, a circuitous route for examining some of the influences of socialization. ("Prevention Skills For Violence-Free Relationships," written by Barrie Levy and distributed by the State Coalition on Battered Women, has a very good section on fairy tales.)

It has been thought-provoking to ask women about the characters in fairy tales with whom they identified. Who did you want to be when you grew up? In the story of Snow White, for example, almost every woman wants to be Snow White. For obvious reasons, it is rare for women to choose the Evil Queen/Wicked Witch as their role model.

What is known about Snow White? She was very pretty, fairly passive, extremely sweet, overly indulgent (with the Seven Dwarfs), incredibly nurturing, and exceedingly helpless, and she had a mediocre singing voice. Women's role models (even in the 21st century) have not strayed too far from the characterizations in fairy tales. Snow White, for example, was prepared to meet Prince Charming, to be cared for and rescued. She was not prepared to meet Attila the Hun. She was not prepared to be decisive, assertive, and heroic.

What is known about the Wicked Witch? She was beautiful, aggressive, evil, manipulative, calculating, strong, interesting, and egotistical. She took care of herself and of anyone who got in her way. She controlled Snow White's father, and she was prepared not only to meet but to do battle with Attila the Hun. Not much of a choice, is it? When a woman gets involved with an individual she perceives initially as a handsome Prince and he later takes on characteristics of the Hun, she is often unprepared to handle the new and unsafe situation.

Traits she has grown up believing are valuable, traits that make her a worthwhile woman, such as empathy, compassion, gentleness, and forgiveness, don't protect her. In fact, they may disempower her. Those very attributes she may have spent a lifetime developing are seen as negative, even pathological, in the context of an abusive relationship.

Her friends, her family, her therapist, her advocate may all be telling her that these priorities no longer work. She needs to take charge of her life, channel her anger (or depression) into action, and save herself and her children. Most battered women feel they are being asked to make the Snow White to Wicked Witch conversion. They are asked to become a person they never liked. They are being asked to deny and change their socialization—and to do it rather quickly.

From the perspective of battering relationships, women are in an economic and emotional no-win position. Hornung, McCullough, and Sugimoto (1981) provided evidence linking educational and occupational differences in couples with an increased risk of psychological abuse, physical aggression, and life-threatening violence (also see Anderson, 1997; McCloskey, 1996). Other investigators have also judged a woman's higher economic status relative to a man's to be a risk factor for male-perpetrated homicide in the United States (Gartner, Baker, & Pampel, 1990; Gauthier & Bankston, 1997) and Russia (Gondolf & Shestakov, 1997). Smith (1988) summed up this status conflict for women as follows:

> In the case of lower status husbands, resource theory explains how traditional values of male dominance can lead to violence against higher status wives. Conversely in the case of higher status husbands, the distributive justice hypothesis explains how more contemporary values of status advancement may lead to violence against lower status wives. (p. 15)

Lesbians. Battered lesbians have a history of being both underserved and marginalized by researchers, advocates, and the criminal justice system (Levy, 1997). "The violence in a lesbian relationship takes place between two social outlaws, both of whom may experience discrimination in employment, housing and at the hands of social agencies" (Margolies & Leeder, 1995, p. 141).

Many people assume that it is easier for gay men and lesbians than for heterosexuals to leave their violent relationships. After all, there are no legal contracts, and often no social contracts, and gay and lesbian relationships do not last. The latter assumption is not true. Lesbian couples are as committed and involved in each other's lives as heterosexual couples are. In fact, lesbians may have a particularly difficult time leaving their partners because they have so little social support and may be alienated from family (Renzetti, 1988). Isolation appears to be the major reason that lesbians stay in battering relationships (Renzetti, 1989). Growing up gay, lesbian, or bisexual predisposes an individual to isolation, harassment, and violence from family and peers (Jerome et al., 1998; Martin & Hetrick, 1988).

Significant numbers of lesbian, gay, and bisexual youths report that they have been verbally, physically, or sexually assaulted by family members and peers (D'Augelli, 1992; De Stafano, 1988; Rotheram-Bokes, Rosario, & Koopman, 1991; also see Boxer, Cook, & Herdt, 1991; D'Augelli, 1991; Gonsiorek, 1988). Anti-gay and -lesbian attitudes also permeate communities, causing gays and lesbians involved in battering relationships to face special hostilities. Lesbians experience layers of oppression; they live in a culture that is not only sexist and racist, but also homophobic. Fewer resources are available to gay and lesbian survivors and perpetrators. Of the 143 batterers' programs approved by the 1998 Los Angeles County Department of Probation, only 5 are listed as sensitive to gay and lesbian issues (Los Angeles Department of Probation, 1998). Accessing these services is synonymous with coming out. Coming out for many gays and lesbians is synonymous with isolation and rejection.

The sense of isolation can be compounded by feelings of shame and guilt. Seeking help is frightening for the lesbian victim, particularly if she is closeted (Levy, 1997).

SANDY AND LINDA

Sandy and Linda had been best friends for 3 years before they became lovers. No friends, classmates, or coworkers knew about their relationship, and they had certainly kept it hidden from family members who were deeply religious. When the violence started, it was verbal and was precipitated by Sandy's jealousy. They pulled closer together.

Their love for each other grew, as did their dependency, isolation, and fear—fear not only of physical violence and abandonment, but also of exposure. Sandy often threatened to tell Linda's family about their relationship.

They risked calling a battered women's hotline after Sandy broke Linda's eardrum. Linda made the calls and eventually found a counselor who would see them. They were eager for help. Neither of them talked about Sandy's threats to kill herself if Linda tried to stand up for herself or talked about leaving. To everyone in their lives (except the therapist), they continued to play at being straight friends.

The physical violence virtually disappeared, but the threats and verbal abuse continued. Sandy's fear of losing Linda, who was quite literally everything to her, became even greater as she began to look at what she was doing to her partner. Their hope of being able to live together had been rekindled, and their need to look good for the therapist, who was the only intrusion into their isolation, also increased.

One night, after a particularly violent verbal phone argument, Sandy made good on her threat; she took her own life. Linda was the only person privy to Sandy's plan. She carried it out in every detail. Linda found the music that Sandy had in her tape deck that she had always said would accompany her suicide. She found a note and a scrawled will. She saw the writing drift off and the ink form a wavering line to the bottom of the page. She saw her lover's blood on the bed. And, apart from the therapist, she had never been able to share her grief with anyone. In fact, one of her friends from the church said to her, "I hope you're not going to tell me that you and Sandy had anything more than a friendship. I would never be able to speak to you again."

The system has become more responsive to domestic violence in the gay and lesbian community. In an interesting twist, gay men and lesbians cannot legally marry, but they can be treated similarly to spouses in a court of law when they are involved in domestic disputes. As of 1995, 35 states had domestic violence laws covering same-sex relationships (National Center on Women and Family Law, 1995). In 1997, the Ohio Court of Appeals held that the definition of cohabitation in the context of domestic violence covered same-sex couples (Zorza, 1997).

IMMIGRATION

It seems obvious that language barriers, racism, employment stress, cultural beliefs, isolation, and immigration status compound a woman's vulnerability (Chin, 1994; Huisman, 1996; see Perilla, Bakeman, & Norris, 1994; Rimonte, 1989).

An immigrant woman may be completely dependent on her husband to maintain her status. Her ability to remain in the United States may rest on an application filed by her husband in which she is included as a *derivative* applicant. If her spouse becomes abusive, she may be afraid to leave him or to seek protection for fear that he will withdraw a pending petition or remove her name from a pending asylum application. Until recently, immigrant women had little success in pursuing such claims when they needed protection against gender-based violence.

Two important developments have provided hope for women seeking lawful and independent immigration status. The first is the Violence Against Women Act, which contains provisions that allow battered immigrant women to assert their rights more independently. The second is a memorandum by the INS calling for consideration of political asylum claims for women seeking protection against gender-specific persecution (Orloff & Kelly, 1995; Sue & Sue, 1990). According to a 1997 review of the impact of U.S. immigration laws on battered immigrant women by Tien-Li Loke (cited in Lemon, 1999), many problems remain unresolved. As one example, battered immigrant women married to lawful permanent residents need to be allowed to work, even if their husbands are subsequently deported for criminal acts (e.g., violating a restraining order).

CROSS-CULTURAL ISSUES

> *The men say: So he beat her up? Yes he did. Well, let that be a lesson to her. The women say: Why was she so arrogant? A woman should learn to be cautious and calm. Men like a quiet woman.*
>
> —Rosemary Ofeibea Ofei-Aboagye, in Ghana (1994).

An analysis of cultural practices across the globe makes clear why the plight of women is still a human rights issue (e.g., Heise, 1989; Meyer, 1998). In too many nations, females are third-class, dispensable citizens who can be beaten, raped, burned, mutilated, enslaved, sold, tortured, and murdered with impunity. Some societies still follow traditions, such as selective malnourishment, selective abortion, infanticide, forced prostitution, genital mutilation, dowry deaths, honor killings, denial of education, and rigid codes of dress and conduct that target women (e.g., Counts, Brown, & Campbell, 1992; Heise, 1989; O'Toole & Schiffman, 1997). Illustrations such as these, where women are so routinely the targets of male aggression, helped foster patriarchal explanations of wife abuse (Heise, 1998; Holloway, 1994).

INTERNATIONAL WOMEN

Marital violence seems to occur in nearly every nation. Most societies accept wife abuse as part of the culture and do not define it as criminal (e.g., Chester, Robin, Koss, Lopez, & Goldman, 1994; Walker, 1999). One survey in New Guinea reported that 18% of married women had gone to a hospital for injuries sustained during a beating. In Bombay, one out of every four deaths in women between the ages of 15 and 24 is caused by "accidental" burning, also known as dowry death (a means of murdering a wife in order to get another dowry through another marriage). Most victims had been married less than 5 years (Prasad, 1994; see Heise, 1989, and Holloway, 1994, for reviews).

Surveys of practices in other cultures indicate that wife assault is more likely to be permitted in societies where men control family economic resources, where conflicts are solved by means of physical force, and where women do not have an equal option to divorce (Brown, 1992; Meyer, 1998; see Gartner, 1993, for an opposing view). Examples of ongoing, current abuses of women are not difficult to find. Potentially deadly customs such as female circumcision illustrate the powerlessness of women in many cultures.

When Afghanistan's Taliban sect came to power in the mid-1990s, leaders forbade education of girls past the age of 8 and prohibited all women from working outside the home except in medical professions (Power, 1998). Honor killings in countries like Jordan are a special form of regulating women's sexual behavior. With self-righteous persistence, male family members slaughter female family members guilty of disobedience or infidelity, or even for being a rape victim, to save the family from unbearable disgrace (Baker, Gregware, & Cassidy, 1999). These killings represent a cultural belief that a "man's honor lies between the legs of a woman" (Beyer, 1999). Kosovar women who are raped by Serbian soldiers during ethnic cleansing find it necessary to hide or deny the assaults, or never to return home. Even under the circumstances of brutal war crimes, Kosovar men reject rape victims and find them guilty of bringing shame on the family (Williams, 1999).

Responses of Arab Palestinian husbands in one survey revealed that 41% thought that "it would do some wives good to be beaten by their husbands." Another study showed that even a substantial percentage of women (66%) still considered wife beating justified under certain circumstances, such as when a wife is sexually unfaithful or when she challenges her husband's manhood (see Haj-Yahia, 1998a, 1998b).

In 17th-century Russia, it was lawful for men to murder their wives. A manual, the Domostroi, instructed peasant men how to whip their wives according to legal guidelines (e.g., with their blouses removed). Upper-class men, in contrast, were to banish their recalcitrant wives to *terems* (segregated rooms), allowing them to leave only rarely. In today's Russia, police have the statutory right to refuse service to women who claim that their husbands have beaten them (Horne, 1999). In fact, women find it useless, if not dangerous, in a number of countries to report to police victimization by an intimate (Heise, 1996). In Peru or Pakistan, for instance, an assaulted woman's visit to a police station puts her at risk for being raped by the police (Human Rights Watch, 1992; Kirk, 1992)!

An analysis of 770 calls made to a hotline in Belgrade revealed that 83% of the perpetrators of assaults against women were husbands, former husbands, or partners. When fathers and sons were included, the percentage of family perpetrators rose to 94% (Mrsevic & Hughes, 1997).

In the United States, feminism has been denounced as antifamily, anticapitalist, and philosophically socialist or communistic. In socialist or communist countries, feminism has been labeled procapitalist, Western, and an enemy of the state (Mladjenovic & Librienin, 1993; Mrsevic & Hughes, 1997). It appears that when women get together for other than a Tupperware party, insurgency is in the air. In a survey of 1,700 Thai households, approximately 20% of the men admitted to having hit, slapped, or kicked their wives at least once in their marriage (Edwards, Fuller, Vorakitphokatom, & Sermsi, 1994; Hoffman, Demo, & Edwards, 1994).

In summary, racial, economic, and cultural parameters do not commonly differentiate female abuse victims from nonvictims. Therefore, the question remains: What characteristics, if any, *do* distinguish battered women?

CHILDHOOD ABUSE

It is logical, from an intergenerational perspective, to expect that women who have experienced or witnessed abuse during childhood would have a tendency to accept violence in their own adult relationships as normative (Kalmuss, 1984; Owens & Straus, 1975). Even if such a relationship were found, however, one must question the logic of blaming and typifying battered women as deviant because they grew up in such homes. Currently available empirical evidence does not provide a clear picture.

Some investigations have yielded evidence suggesting that battered women were more abused during childhood than were nonbattered women (e.g., Doumas, Margolin, & John, 1994; Nurius, Furrey, & Berliner, 1992). Others demonstrated a modest relationship between exposure to violence as a child and teenage or adult victimization (Giordano, Millhollin, Cernkovich, Pugh, & Rudolph, 1999; Kalmuss, 1984; Rosenbaum & O'Leary, 1981; Sappington, Pharr, Tunstall, & Rickert, 1997; Sedlak, 1988b). However, a progression from childhood abuse to adult involvement is not inevitable (e.g., Smith & Williams, 1992). A number of analyses judged battered women as no more likely to have been exposed to violence as children than nonbattered women (Astin, Lawrence, & Foy, 1993; Bergman, Larsson, Brismar, & Klang, 1988; Hamberger, 1991; Hotaling & Sugarman, 1990). The fact is that many adults grow up in abusive or dysfunctional families, so the odds of marrying an unhealthy person are really quite high.

Some surveys of sheltered women have revealed very high percentages of sexual abuse during their childhoods, ranging from 49% to 66% (Dutton, Burghardt, Perrin, Chrestman, & Halle, 1994; Johnson, 1988; Kemp, Rawlings, & Green, 1991). Others arrived at rates that were much lower (see Bergman et al., 1988; Hamberger, 1991; Landenburger, 1989), equivalent to those found in general population surveys.

Susan Burnett (cited in "Sex Abuse," 1990) asserts that 25% to 33% of women in the general population have been molested as children (see Wurtele & Miller-Perrin, 1992, for a review). Furthermore, when women in shelters are compared with nonsheltered women, rates vary only slightly (e.g., Astin, Ogland-Hand, Coleman, & Foy, 1991; Landenburger, 1989). Taken together, the incidence of childhood sexual abuse in battered women does not differentiate them consistently from women in the general population (Holtzworth-Munroe, Smutzler, & Sandin, 1997).

A newer line of research has focused on the effects of repeat victimizations. Results indicate that individuals victimized earlier in life develop higher levels of fear than do those who are victimized later (see Kury & Ferdinand, 1997). Also, research has increasingly suggested that the effects of trauma are cumulative (Follette, Polusny, Bechtle, & Naugle, 1996). Revictimization studies imply that childhood sexual abuse seems to place any adult woman at greater risk for a variety of revictimization experiences by partners and other males. Several reviews found that, over a lifetime, sexually abused girls suffer comparatively more sexual assaults, rapes, and physical violence by males than do girls who were not sexually abused (e.g., Kingma, 1999; Nurius et al., 1992; Sanders & Moore, 1999; Wyatt, Guthrie, & Notgrass, 1992).

PERSONALITY TRAITS

While some researchers focused on race, socioeconomics, and child abuse as precursors to adult battering, other social scientists explored individual differences in personality traits. Some searched for personality problems that would indicate battered women were "abnormal." It is possible, however, that battered women do not fit a particular personality profile or fall within a singular diagnostic category (Walker & Browne, 1985).

The Minnesota Multiphasic Personality Inventory (MMPI) (Hathaway & McKinley, 1967) provides a comprehensive assessment of abnormal personality. Using MMPI scale scores, Douglas and Colantuono (1987) detected no *typical* personality profiles of battered women. However, Rhodes's (1992) study, which used a comparison group of nonbattered women from a clinical population, found that battered women scored substantially higher on the Psychopathic Deviate score of the MMPI. Using the MMPI-2 (Green, 1991), Khan, Welch, and Zillmer (1993) found elevations in scales associated with depression, anxiety, and subjective distress. Taken together with findings from other victimization studies (e.g., Scott & Stone, 1986), elevations such as these most probably represent the effects of victimization. In fact, a recent synthesis (meta-analysis) of relevant studies showed that battering was a risk factor (associated factor) for mental disorders, especially depression and PTSD (Golding, 1999).

One historically held contention is that low self-esteem is a precursor to being abused (see Mills, 1985). Early investigations found few differences between battered and nonbattered groups of women (Campbell, 1989a; Russell, Lipov, Phillips, & White, 1989; Walker, 1983). The majority of newer studies, however, do suggest that battered women have lower self-esteem than do nonbattered women (Aguilar & Nightingale, 1994; Cascardi & O'Leary, 1992; Mitchell & Hodson, 1983; Woods, 1999; also see Campbell & Soeken, 1999; Tuel & Russell, 1998).

In a sample of severely battered women, Cascardi and O'Leary (1992) ascertained that as the frequency, form, and consequences of physical aggression increased, the level of self-esteem decreased (also see Woods, 1999). Abuse can lower self-esteem by creating a sense of personal defectiveness (Stark et al., 1981). All in all, the general consensus today is that battered women's low self-esteem, when exhibited, is the result of the battering, and certainly not the cause of it (Aguilar & Nightingale, 1994; Hartik, 1978; see Holtzworth-Munroe et al., 1997, for a review).

There can be little doubt that battered women are depressed (Campbell, Kub, Belknap, & Templin, 1997; Cascardi & O'Leary, 1992; Christian, O'Leary, & Vivian, 1994; Sato & Heiby, 1992). Depression is the primary emotional response to abuse (McCauley et al., 1995; Saunders, Hamberger, & Hovey, 1993). Women who have been abused severely suffer four times the rate of depression, psychosomatic complaints, and suicide attempts of nonbattered women (Kaslow et al., 1998; Stets & Straus, 1990). Such symptoms are often more situational than they are characteristic of a personality type. In fact, physical victimization by an intimate partner is positively related to levels of depression both in men and women (Zlotnick et al., 1998) and in lesbian and heterosexual victims (Tuel & Russell, 1998).

Previous studies have also established an association between a battered woman's self-esteem and depression. The daily impact of living in a context of fear, as well as the abuse itself, is directly related to depression (Campbell, 1989a; Cascardi & O'Leary, 1992; Sato & Heiby, 1992). One longitudinal study found that psychological attitudes, such as depression, had less to do with remaining with a violent partner than did relationship and economic factors (e.g., marital satisfaction, dependent children) (Phillips, 1993). Factors such as greater marital satisfaction (i.e., less severe abuse) and higher levels of commitment and investment in the relationship (e.g., married for a longer period, fewer financial alternatives) are especially likely to be significantly related to battered women's decision to stay with their partners (Rusbult & Martz, 1995; see also Mitchell & Hodson, 1983; Straus, 1987; Sullivan, 1991b).

VICTIM BLAMING

Most early writers who described battered women failed to ascribe the violence to the perpetrator. Frequently, they said or implied that the battered woman was to blame; it was something about her that caused him to be violent. Quite often, members of society blame the victim without regard for the context. They blame people who are robbed for leaving their doors unlocked, and they blame battered women for nagging. Golda Meir, former prime minister of Israel, highlighted this lopsided point of view. When her male cabinet members concluded that they should impose a 10:00 p.m. curfew on women to reduce the incidence of rape, she opposed them. Because men did the raping, why not subject them to the curfew? She was overruled.

Ewing and Aubrey (1987) demonstrated that public opinion about battered women rests on widely held and false assumptions. A random selection of 216 community members completed a questionnaire after reading a scenario about a violent couple. More than 60% of the respondents agreed that if a battered woman were really afraid, she would simply leave. More than 40% decided that she must have been at least partly to blame for her husband's assaults, even though the story provided no rationale for such a belief. There was some tendency for respondents to believe that the woman must have been masochistic or emotionally disturbed if she stayed, that the couple had serious marital problems, and that the woman could avoid the beatings if she entered counseling. By and large, people seemed reluctant to place the blame on the perpetrator.

Beliefs defining the victims of spousal violence in stereotypical detail create a battered woman that society loves to blame. Excerpts from Hotaling and Sugarman's (1990) review of research on battered women emphasize the misplaced focus on women as the provocateurs of marital violence: "Very little heuristic value can be gained by focusing primarily on the victim in the assessment of risk to wife assault" (p. 12). "What is surprising is the enormous effort to explain male behavior by examining the characteristics of women" (p. 120). There does not seem to be a psychological profile that predicts a woman's likelihood of developing a relationship with an abuser (see Rhodes, 1992, for a review). Overall, research lends credence to a "just like anybody else" viewpoint (Harway, 1993).

SOCIAL SUPPORT

Social support theory assumes that exposure to environmental duress leads to personal stress, and that social support may act as a buffer after the event occurs (Thoits, 1982). In one comparison, social support was extremely important to recovery, but gender differences occurred in the kinds and levels of support offered to victims. Whereas the male victims generally found their bosses sympathetic and their colleagues jokingly accepting, battered women experienced pay suspensions and bosses who were characteristically unsympathetic and victim-blaming (Shepherd, 1990). Lack of support, both personal and social, creates a dilemma for battered women that ensnares them in their relationships (Ellsberg, Caldera, Herrera, Winkvist, & Kullgren, 1999; Gelles & Harrop, 1989).

One large national survey of both men and women disclosed that victims of partner abuse received as much actual social support as did nonvictimized individuals (Zlotnick et al., 1998). In a comparison of battered women's *perceptions* contrasted with those of two nonbattered groups, battered women reported receiving less social support than the other groups (Barnett, Martinez, & Keyson, 1996). Apparently, judgments about receiving social support rely somewhat on subjective perceptions, rather than objective reality. Furthermore, social support may occur unevenly within different areas of a person's life (Davis & Morris, 1998). Some dissimilarities between the findings, of course, undoubtedly reflect differences between community and clinic samples and differences inherent in including males in one survey.

On the other hand, victims of family crimes may not be very open to support when offered. Gondolf (1998b) found that very few battered women involved in court cases were willing to accept support services from a shelter outreach program. Of the 1,012 reached by phone from a group of 1,895 women, 644 refused all services for themselves (e.g., 12-session support group, individual counseling, weekly phone counseling). No members of this group had ever been in touch with a shelter before. Almost half of those who refused help did so because they "did not need it." Some women were already in counseling, some had scheduling problems, some had left their abusers, and a few had no transportation. Some expressed worry about triggering a child protective agency referral if they accepted help.

Analogous results emerged from a criminology study in which law enforcement-social service teams provided follow-up visits to households reporting a domestic violence incident, 40% of which involved romantic intimates. When follow-up visits were possible, the team tried to educate victims and perpetrators about the escalating nature of family violence. The team also provided victims with referrals for help (e.g., court advocacy, counseling, public housing, programs dealing with drugs and alcohol, and emergency financial assistance). The one favorable result of the program to visit victims was an increase in calls to police for further service. Apparently, victims had greater confidence that the police would respond (Davis & Taylor, 1997).

It is interesting to note that in another analysis, level of social support did not predict whether battered women whose batterers had been arrested and charged with misdemeanor assault would cooperate with prosecution efforts. The lack of tangible support (e.g., baby-sitting, transportation), however, was a predictor of noncooperation (Goodman et al., in press).

It is probable that even in a troubled marriage, people tend to isolate themselves from friends, family, or both, and to focus on repairing the relationship. Although support is often offered, individuals may be so humiliated or stressed that they ignore or pull away from such aid. In fact, a qualitative study of homeless battered women revealed a phase in their abusive relationships that the researchers labeled isolation/shame and harassment/humiliation (Clarke et al., 1997).

BLAMING ALCOHOL

Most people seem to be looking for someone or something to blame in their attempts to explain wife beating. Violent couples and observers alike are prone to allege that alcohol is the major factor precipitating a violent episode (e.g., Flanzer, 1993; Kaufman & Straus, 1987). Battered women, in particular, have clung to the demon rum hypothesis (LaBell, 1979; Sapiente, 1988). The aggression-enhancing effects of alcohol, however, occur only in conjunction with other factors, such as one's expectations about alcohol's effects; the setting (e.g., bar, home); and whether one has already developed a pattern of drinking (Abram, 1990; Bushman & Cooper, 1990; Cadoret, Leve, & Devor, 1997; Ellis, 1998; Roth, 1994).

In one analysis of arrested spouse abusers in Memphis, 92% had used alcohol or drugs the day of the arrest (Brookoff, 1997). The amount of alcohol consumed during abusive incidents often is minimal. Furthermore, most men who batter when they are drinking also batter when they are not (Bennett, Tolman, Rogalski, & Srinivasaraghavan, 1994). Some evidence suggests that batterers and their victims are more likely to drink after a violent episode than before it (Barnett & Fagan, 1993).

Processes of denial and minimization constitute a basis for both batterers and battered women to blame some agent other than the abuser for the aggression (Katz, Arias, Beach, & Roman, 1995; Ragg, Sultana, & Miller, 1999). For an alcoholic, getting drunk is the goal. For a spouse abuser, getting drunk is the mechanism; hitting is the goal. Research does not support the notion that batterers are out of control when they assault their partners, or that drug-induced disinhibition prompts battering (see Bennett, 1998; Bennett et al., 1994). Nevertheless, the role of alcohol in family violence is complex.

ATTRIBUTIONS IN VIOLENT RELATIONSHIPS

Victims of aggression usually search for explanations to the question, "Why me?" A common attribution (an idea or thought generated to explain the source or cause of behavior) made by battered women is that they somehow provoke the violence. Therefore, they can or should be able to prevent or eliminate it by changing their own behavior (Prange, 1985). Painter and Dutton (1985) speculated that this belief, along with the contradictory belief that they are powerless, leads to enmeshment in the relationship. When a woman falsely believes that she is responsible for the abuse and that changing *her* behavior will probably stop recurrence of the violence, she will remain entrapped in the battering relationship. When battered women no longer believe that they provoked it, they can begin to blame themselves for staying. Alfred Adler (1927), in a discussion about causalistic thinking, asserted that one of the major outcomes of victim blaming is that it excuses the perpetrator from responsibility. For instance, when people blame social conditions for criminal behavior, offenders lose accountability for their actions (and victims seem to acquire it).

Battered women need to explain the very existence and cause of the violence, not just its occurrence. Some common rationalizations given by battered women are that his aggression happened when he was "not himself" and was "temporarily out of control"; and that he was a "victim of child abuse," "an alcoholic," or "unemployed" (see Ragg et al., 1999). When a battered woman says "it is my fault," she is simultaneously absolving or partially absolving her assailant.

Victims of negative events often exaggerate or misconstrue the extent to which they are responsible for their own victimization (Miller & Porter, 1983). Gilbert and Webster (1982) detected a common theme emerging from interviews with women who had experienced assaults at the hands of men (rape, incest, battering): They (a) blamed themselves; (b) denied the magnitude of the events; (c) denied their anger and wish to retaliate; (d) felt unable to set limits or fight back; and (e) found it difficult to indict the men who injured them, wanting instead to protect them. The inability of women to condemn the aggression directed at them by a loved partner seems directly proportional to their level of involvement in the relationship. Prange (1985) found that women who returned to their abusers made internal attributions about their physical abuse—that something was wrong with them. Attributions made by battered women about being assaulted are important determinants of the degree of blame they personally accept (also see Moss et al., 1997).

LAURA

Laura did not want to argue with her husband anymore. They fought about everything, from religion to his job. He said that he was tired of her nagging, and that he would not have to hit her if she would just shut up. Laura began to see her behavior as provocative and tried to change it. She even began to believe that it must be her responsibility to change his behavior. At that point, her husband told her that she was a sick woman and was making him crazy; and at that point, she was convinced.

CASE STUDY

In one comparison of 31 battered women and two groups of 62 nonabused women, battered women had significantly higher levels of self-blame. Battered women blamed themselves more on the behavioral questions than on the item about their own characters. Especially poignant were the feelings of self-blame regardless of their actions (Barnett, Haney-Martindale, Modzelewski, & Sheltra, 1991).

In the Barnett and Lopez-Real (1985) investigation, battered women reported that they were to blame more than any other option listed (e.g., anxious, angry, powerful). They blamed themselves for behaviors such as "not being strong enough" or "not helping effectively." The women also reported an increase in blame correlated with the belief that their "efforts to escape were unsuccessful."

Although most family violence experts have speculated that battered women feel to blame (i.e., responsible) for being victimized (e.g., Andrews & Brewin, 1990), some disagree. Holtzworth-Munroe (1988), for example, states that "abused women generally do not blame themselves for their husband's violence" (p. 331), and Campbell (1990) found that only 20% of the battered women reported feeling to blame. Also, a number of investigators found that battered women blamed their husbands more than themselves for the violence (e.g., Cantos, Neidig, & O'Leary, 1994; McClennan, Joseph, & Lewis, 1994).

Landenburger (1989) proposed that battered women may either blame themselves for causing the abuse, or blame themselves for tolerating it. In either case, blame is the end result, and blame tends to produce guilt. As Erica Jong so cleverly phrased it, "Show me a woman who doesn't feel guilty and I'll show you a man."

Current theories of depression contend that self-blame both causes and maintains depression (Peterson & Seligman, 1984). Andrews and Brewin (1990) studied depression in 286 British victims of violence. Of the women who had suffered partner assault, 53% currently involved with the perpetrator experienced self-blame for causing the violence, compared to 35% of those who were no longer in the relationship. Within the self-blaming group, 68% blamed their behavior, whereas 32% blamed their character.

> *In passing, also I would like to say that the first time Adam had a chance he laid the blame on women.*
>
> —Nancy Astor, British politician

According to Finkelhor (1983), the literature on domestic violence consistently portrays abuse as occurring in the context of psychological exploitation.

Batterers use their power to manipulate victims' perceptions of reality. Battering coupled with self-blame diminishes a battered woman's belief in herself, erodes her self-esteem, and reduces her integrity. She feels demeaned as she responds to the demands of her batterer. She may jeopardize her relationships with her children, other family members, friends, and community contacts. The more extensive her compromise, the greater the erosion of her self-respect.

EFFECTS OF CAPTIVITY

People not only attribute negative traits to battered women, but they also fail to understand the processes in a battering relationship that might contribute to the very traits deemed unfavorable. As one example, battered women exhibit hostage-like behaviors such as praising their abuser, denying the battering, and blaming themselves. These behaviors are similar to those of captives and may actually represent a struggle for survival ("Abusive Relationships," 1991).

Many victims of violent crimes or impending violence identify with the person or people who seem to have control over their well-being. As perceived power differences intensify, the person with less authority generally forms a more negative self-appraisal and feels less capable of taking care of him- or herself. Thus, the person with less power becomes more dependent on the person with greater power (Freud, 1942). This phenomenon is called *identification* with the aggressor and became manifest in brainwashing and in the Stockholm and POW syndromes.

The term *brainwashing* came into being during the Korean War, when imprisoned American soldiers denounced the United States or supplied information to the enemy. Patty Hearst, a wealthy socialite-turned-bank-robber, provided another alleged example of this phenomenon. People condemned the Korean prisoners of war as traitors, and the courts sent Patty Hearst to prison. It seems that those who sat in judgment went on with their lives, believing that the brainwashed were innately weak and completely culpable.

STOCKHOLM SYNDROME

One of the most dramatic examples of identification with the aggressor occurred in 1974 in Stockholm during a bank robbery. Three tellers were held hostage for a period of 10 days. For the first few days, the robbers intermittently threatened them, held them at gunpoint, and pushed them around. At first, the robbers also denied food and bathroom privileges to the tellers. After the initial intimidation, a period of normalcy ensued. The robbers-turned-kidnappers were *kind* to the hostages, letting them go to the bathroom and walk around. Captors and hostages had conversations with each other and began the process of getting acquainted. Think about what you might do to survive in this situation. Forming a bond, becoming a real person to your captors, could save your life.

After 10 days, the ordeal ended with the release of the hostages and the incarceration of the hostage takers. During the trial, two of the three tellers testified in defense of their assailants. Indeed, one of the tellers married her former captor after he was released from prison. In other rare cases, hostages have been known to post bail or to have emotional relationships with their captors (Strentz, 1979). These seemingly strange occurrences have become known as the Stockholm Syndrome (Lang, 1974) and have come to represent a specific combination of emotional responses and behaviors that can occur when someone is held hostage (Kuleshnyk, 1984).

Graham, Rawlings, and Rimini (1988) have successfully applied the Stockholm Syndrome to the psychological victimization processes undergone by battered women. There are five hypothesized precursors to the development of the syndrome: (a) perceived threat to one's physical or psychological survival, (b) belief that the captor (abuser) could carry out the threat, (c) perceived kindness from captor to victim, (d) perceived inability to escape, and (e) captor-controlled perceptions (monopolization of victim's perceptions resulting from isolation) (Graham, Rawlings, & Rigsby, 1994; Rawlings, Allen, Graham, & Peters, 1994). Threat to survival and isolation are the most powerful antecedents for predicting development of the Stockholm Syndrome (Ott, Graham, & Rawlings, 1990; also see Nielsen, Endo, & Ellington, 1992).

Graham et al. (1994) have postulated characteristics of the Stockholm Syndrome typically found in battered women. The following are a condensation of these aspects: (a) a bond between the victim and abuser, (b) intense gratitude for kindnesses shown by abuser, (c) denial or rationalization of violence and anger toward abuser, (d) hypervigilance to abuser's needs, (e) adoption of the abuser's perspective of the world, (f) a view of authorities as bad guys and the abuser as a good guy, (g) difficulty in leaving the abuser after release from the hostage situation, (h) fear of the abuser's revenge even if the abuser is dead or in prison, and (i) experiences of posttraumatic stress disorder (see also Graham et al., 1995).

The Stockholm Syndrome explains the paradoxical behavior of hostages who profess to love their captors. The theory appears to overlap attachment theory in terms of explaining reactions to abuse, but differs in terms of the groups of individuals involved. Whereas attachment theory developed from observations of relationships within families (e.g., mother/child, husband/wife, boyfriend/girlfriend), hostage theory developed from observations of captor/hostage relationships.

JANE AND LEWIS

Jane and Lewis have been married for 9 years. Both are professionals working in the same field. They share many of the same interests, own a home together, are involved with their families, participate in the same organizations, and share an abusive relationship.

Lewis is a soft-spoken and shy man. Rage does not appear to fit him well; it is confusing. His temper tantrums are usually verbal in form. He rants, raves, threatens, and demeans. Sporadically, there is an accompanying physical outburst.

Over time, Lewis's verbal outbursts have diminished Jane's sense of self-worth. Some of the attacks were subtle, questioning her decision making at work, wondering if this or that person really liked her, commenting on the quality of her performance, and then jumping to her defense if her family insulted her or her boss did not appreciate her. He was concurrently her best friend and her biggest critic.

Jane became focused on obtaining Lewis's approval and obtaining his emotional support. She poured her emotional energy into analyzing their relationship, leaving her with little energy to maintain other emotional attachments. Her job performance nose-dived, and she questioned her abilities, even her abilities to contribute to her profession. As her self-confidence waned, her conduct as friend, family member, co-worker, and wife suffered. The feedback she received began to support her diminished self-appraisal, but Lewis remained steadfast, her loyal friend and her avowed enemy.

Currently, Jane's emotional dependence on the relationship has increased. She supports her own negative self-view with quotes from her husband. She fears that without Lewis, she is nothing. She has been brainwashed.

TREBLINKA

In Steiner's (1966) book, *Treblinka,* he describes the victimization of inmates existing in the extermination camp. He asks and tries to answer a number of questions: (a) How do inmates in a death camp stay alive at all? (b) What did living under such conditions do to their souls and to their sense of themselves as humans? (c) Why did they go on when it was easier to die?

At Treblinka, the commanding officers of the SS morally disarmed the camp inhabitants by creating an environment replete with panic and uncertainty. Moral disarmament forces a victim to make minor concessions that lead to others, and eventually leads to humiliation, self-hatred, and submission. The strategy was to make victims accomplices in their own victimization.

The SS removed vestiges of humanity by dividing families and removing social life. The notion of time and space were lost. The commandant of Treblinka committed random acts of violence, including verbal threats, beatings, and executions. This intermittent punishment caused fear and helplessness. The unpredictability of his attacks made his authority seem mystical. Prisoners felt the exaggerated presence of a permanent menace. With a gun and a few guards, the SS controlled 600 captives and created a psychosis of fear.

CASE STUDY

MELINDA AND JASON

As the headlights made a path into the driveway, the three children and their mother in the house stopped laughing. By the time the key turned and the door was pushed open, the children were quietly doing their homework, and Melinda was ladling soup into bowls. As Jason came in the front door and went upstairs, he did not say anything except, "Hi." No one could read his mood. The atmosphere screamed with tension, but the house was silent.

The older boy was afraid that Dad had had a bad day; he worried about what would happen when Dad found out that his report card was not good. The younger boy sat in a corner and tried to make himself invisible. The little girl was afraid that Dad could read her mind and would know that she hated him. She knew that he would hurt her when he figured out what she was thinking.

Melinda did not do much outside of the home. It was almost as if Jason knew when she saw family or friends during the day. She wondered if he had friends around who told on her, because his anger seemed to intensify in direct proportion to her happiness. Two weeks before, he had chased the boys around the house, screaming about the need for discipline, and had finally beaten them with a belt. She used to intervene, but it never worked; she could not even protect herself, much less the children. She felt confused, paralyzed, and disoriented.

Jason came down to dinner. His mood seemed calm. He began to talk. Everyone listened. In a while, the whole group was talking and were more relaxed. They eased into laughter, but they wondered when everything would change. Melinda never quite joined in. Her eyes were a little dull. You never saw much excitement or change of emotion from Melinda. In time, the four prisoners finished their meals and went to bed.

> Until someone is physically abused, they could never know: the humiliation—the damage that is done to your self-respect. To become diminished—to feel less than a human being. To be debased—to be lowered in character, dignity, and value. Emotional scars that never heal. (hearing transcript, cited in Nerney, 1987, p. 9)

As a battering relationship continues, there is an exaggerated belief on the part of a battered woman that her batterer is omnipresent. She becomes less able to see the connection between her behavior and the nature or rationale behind her batterer's aggression. Although his violence may occur randomly, the odds are better than 600 to 1 that she will be the target of his abuse (also see Kandel-Englander, 1992).

TRAUMATIC BONDING—ATTACHMENT

Some features of imbalanced relationships resemble the experiences of captivity. In all cases, the maltreated person is dominated by the other person, and abuse is intermittent. The process of forming strong emotional ties in a relationship where one person intermittently abuses, harasses, threatens, beats, or intimidates the other is what Dutton and Painter (1981) termed *traumatic bonding*. Researchers have increasingly expanded and applied attachment theory to help explain the behavior of individuals involved in abusive relationships. One important aspect of attachment formulations is that they help clarify the finding that love and violence do not seem to be opposite forces as one might expect, but may co-exist (e.g., Dutton & Painter, 1993b; Dutton, Saunders, Starzomski, & Bartholomew, 1994; Kesner, Julian, & McKenry, 1997; Vazquez, 1996).

FORCED INSTITUTIONALIZATION

Examination of data gathered from battered women living in an Israeli shelter convinced Avni (1991b) to apply the concept of institutionalization to circumstances in a battering relationship. Her deduction rested on several comparisons: (a) In an institution, the staff makes all the rules and punishes noncompliance; in the home, the batterer makes all the rules and punishes noncompliance. (b) In an institution, the inmates suffer from constant exposure to the staff; in the violent home, the battered woman suffers from constant exposure to her husband's surveillance. and (c) In an institution, mortification of the self occurs by such procedures as strip searches and shaving the head; in the violent home, mortification occurs as a result of the husband's suspicion and humiliating attacks. Battered women in Avni's study said that they felt like prisoners. Indeed, a number of the women reported being locked in their homes. In one case, a spouse plastered the door shut before he left for work. In another, a batterer locked his wife inside the house, even though she was 9 months pregnant. The isolation experienced by these women led to greater dependence on their abusers. The suspicious climate in their homes led to hypervigilance, and, for at least one woman, who was repeatedly interrrogated about alleged infidelity, total self-doubt about her sanity: "Maybe I really did it without being aware of it. I was going crazy" (Avni, 1991b, p. 145).

CASE STUDY

SANDY AND JIM

Jim: My wife, Sandy, is a teacher and I'm self-employed. I don't fit in with her friends at work, and I don't like to go to her parties. One night, I let her go with a friend, and I'll never do that again. Two guys took their clothes off and jumped into a hot tub. They were drunk and acting crazy. When my wife told me what happened, I went off. I threw her against the wall and grilled her about what she did. Then I beat her up like she was a man. I don't tolerate infidelity. I've only had sex with prostitutes, never an affair.

Sandy: Jim never trusts me. He thinks I'm flirting with everyone, and that I dress up for other men. I was surprised when he said I could go to the party and relieved at his attitude. Sometimes, he literally questions me for hours. It feels like a police interrogation. Sometimes, I wonder if he's right. Am I trying to attract other men? When he beat me up after the party, I wondered what I had done to encourage these guys to strip and jump into the hot tub.

CONFORMITY AND OBEDIENCE

Syndromes do not describe the behavior of all individuals subjected to terror or captivity, but they do portray what happens for most. Even under circumstances less catastrophic than life at Treblinka or institutionalization, individuals exhibit a propensity to conform to authority. In one of the most influential studies ever conducted by a psychologist, Stanley Milgram (1963) explored the extent to which people will obey an authority figure. Before conducting his research, Milgram asked psychiatrists to predict the percentage of individuals who would shock another person simply at the request of an authority figure. Psychiatrists estimated an obedience rate of under 1%.

In this experiment, the investigator requested the teacher-subjects to shock learner-subjects whenever they made a mistake in a verbal learning experiment, and to increase the shock level with every successive error. The experiment was designed so that the learner, who was sitting behind a screen out of sight, appeared to cry out in pain and to beg the teacher to stop. Most teachers stopped at the request of the learner and informed the experimenter that they did not wish to continue. Amazingly, however, the experimenter had only to issue a directive phrase, such as "You have no other choice" or "The experiment must go on," to encourage them to continue. Every teacher conformed to some degree. The unexpected result was that 65% of the participants were willing to administer shocks at a level marked "dangerous" to obviously suffering human subjects.

The outcome of this research was so startling that other scientists tended to doubt its authenticity. Replications, however, demonstrated its validity. For example, Hofling, Brotzman, Darlymple, Graves, and Pierce (1966) devised a real-life experiment in which a doctor, unfamiliar to a nurse, ordered her to give an extremely large dose of an unusual medicine to a hospitalized patient without the required written prescription. Even though the doctor ordered administration of an amount of medicine that was twice the maximum dosage printed on the label, 95% of the nurses tried to obey the order before being interrupted by a confederate of the experimenter.

SUMMARY

Women entering relationships that eventually become abusive do not appear to differ from their nonbattered counterparts in terms of demographic variables, histories of childhood abuse, and other psychological attributes. Nevertheless, society is inclined to place the blame on them rather than on the perpetrators. This proclivity, along with a batterer's tendency to manipulate his partner's feelings, add to the probability that a battered woman will blame herself for being beaten or for her failure to escape.

Victimization is a profoundly negative experience with long-lasting effects. Phenomena like the Stockholm Syndrome and the events at Treblinka demonstrate how individuals who are seemingly normal can become psychologically entrapped. An extrapolation of these processes to battering relationships helps clarify a battered woman's emotional quandary. Compliance with the demands of individuals in positions of authority is well understood by anyone with a parent or boss, or by anyone who has suffered past consequences. Although conformity is an everyday occurrence, the effects of conformity, as evidenced by Milgram's (1963) research, are no less significant than the behaviors resulting from captivity. Conformity experiments reflect these dramatic effects on people in general, and on battered women in particular. Given the nature of victim blame and the victimization process, becoming trapped in a battering relationship could happen to anyone.

4 Living With Fear
The Force That Holds, Molds, and Controls

911

Woman: I'm Robin Prunty calling on Donald Prunty. I'm at work at Smitty's, and he's stalking the parking lot at Smitty's. He's supposed to be wanted in Chandler, and they haven't picked him up yet, and he's breaking the order. I have an order of protection.

Dispatcher: You said your name is Donna?

Woman: My name is Robin Prunty, P-R-U-N-T-Y.

Dispatcher: Has he already been served?

Woman: Yes he has. It's been a good month now.

(Pause . . . 16 seconds of confusion, muffled sound.)

Dispatcher: Is he there shooting?

Woman: I'm supposed to be safe. . . . Oh my God . . .

Man's Voice: Get over here, get up, get up right now. C'mere. C'mon out here.

(Loud bang)

Dispatcher: I think there's a shooting going on . . . ("I'm Supposed to Be Safe," 1992, p. A6).

CASE STUDY

Robin's call was the prelude to a shooting spree. Her estranged husband burst into the coffee shop where she worked. Before he shot himself, he had killed Robin's pregnant friend, who had given her refuge, and a stranger who was having his morning coffee. Robin was seriously wounded, but she survived.

CHAPTER OVERVIEW

Fear, both emotional and physical, is a significant feature in battering families. Its functions include control and entrapment. A discussion of male-to-female injury and homicide clarifies the tangible nature of men's threats of aggression. Laboratory research, clinical impressions, and case studies substantiate the development of fear as a learned response. Denial and minimization are consequences of escalating fear that allow a woman to remain in her violent home and make it difficult to "see the forest for the trees." Gender dissimilarities in the motivations for aggression as well as the experience of fear provide a context for understanding why she stays. The pervasive nature of fear affects not only the family who experiences it, but also those involved peripherally.

RECOGNIZING INTIMATE VIOLENCE

To a certain extent, violence is in the eye of the beholder. For example, Sedlak's (1988a) study demonstrated that perceptions of intimate abuse depended on the nature of the observer's own personal history with aggression. Both male and female subjects who had experienced violence in their own relationships did not recognize battering in the test cases. Perpetrators are prone to describe their own violent behavior as comprehensible and as isolated events, whereas victims portray the perpetrators' behavior as arbitrary, incomprehensible, and as the last in a series of provocations (Baumeister, Stillwell, & Wotman, 1990). Males may be more likely than females to perceive aggression as mutual (Laner & Thompson, 1982). Laner (1990) noted that students seem to believe that becoming jealous, upset, and subsequently violent is not unusual in dating relationships (also see Caulfield, Riggs, & Street, 1999). Similarly, society has generally regarded hitting a wife as acceptable and a private matter, even though the same actions perpetrated by strangers would be termed violent, if not criminal (Dobash & Dobash, 1991). As one woman said, "If you are afraid, then whether it is a tickle or a smack, it's abusive. If you are afraid that you are going to be hurt, that's abuse" (Klein et al., 1997, p. 55).

THE SUBJECTIVE AND OBJECTIVE NATURE OF FEAR

Fear is a powerful element in producing behaviors that are characteristic of victims in general, and battered women in particular. Fear is also the most common response to dating violence in women, with emotional hurt ranked second (O'Keefe & Treister, 1998). Safety issues are a primary concern for both battered women and the individuals who work with them. In a 1998 study of calls to the National Domestic Violence Hotline, telephone operators and advocates tallied comments and requests. More than half of the callers cited "apprehension about retaliation" as their principal reason for remaining with an abusive partner (Danis, Lewis, Trapp, Reid, & Fisher, 1998; also see Campbell & Soeken, 1999; Jacobson, Gottman, Gortner, Berns, & Shortt, 1996).

The findings of the survey of 43 battered women by Barnett and Lopez-Real (1985) were congruent with those from the hotline calls. Fear, specifically "fear of revenge," was the second most frequently given reason by women for remaining in their violent relationships. ("Hoped partner would change" was first.) Women in this study listed some of the following concerns:

> "He kept seeking me out and finding me."
>
> "I felt other people would die if I left."
>
> "He was suicidal; I feared he would come after me."
>
> "I have left and still have trouble getting out from under abuse and fears and threats. My ex-partner is continuing abuse any way he can. I now see why it truly is hard to get out and why it took me so long."
>
> "I remember feeling many times afraid to go and afraid to stay. That very real fear of revenge is so powerful a deterrent to doing anything constructive."
>
> "I think that police protection should be questioned a lot."

Painter and Dutton (1985) believe that a combination of hope and fear entraps battered women. Attachment to an abusive mate reinforced by socialization produces a very powerful connection described as *traumatic bonding* (Dutton & Painter, 1993b). There is a significant link between a style of attachment to a batterer and an abused woman's ability to leave (Dutton & Haring, 1999; Henderson, Bartholomew, & Dutton, 1997). For instance, if a woman believed that she was not a good person, but that her partner was wonderful (*preoccupied attachment*), she was inclined to separate from and return to the relationship very frequently. Furthermore, she maintained her emotional involvement with her abuser even after leaving (Hazan & Zeifman, 1994; Vazquez, 1996). Conversely, a batterer's attachment style to his adult partner can make it impossible for him to let her leave (D. G. Dutton et al., 1994).

CASE STUDY

BETTY AND HENRY

Betty and Henry were married and had a 14-month-old daughter, Melissa. Henry was self-employed but unmotivated. He was also possessive, controlling, and insecure. When Betty's independence got the better of him, he became abusive. Betty had gone to work on numerous occasions with bruises on her face and arms. For the most part, nobody talked about what was happening. (It is often easiest for friends and family to deny abuse, minimize the severity of discord, and ignore evidence.)

Betty's friends and financial security were a threat to Henry. He became more controlling, and he threatened to kill her if she tried to leave. His obsession culminated in Betty's 2-week confinement. He stayed at home to watch her. Eventually, he needed money and took her to the bank to make a withdrawal from her savings account. Betty and Melissa escaped to the Long Beach Battered Women's Shelter.

Henry threatened to sue Betty for custody of the baby unless he was allowed to visit her. A third-party visitation was set up by the shelter through her attorney. No one at the shelter felt good about this arrangement, but everyone felt compelled to go ahead with the plan because of the legal ramifications of noncompliance. Betty and the baby were to go to her attorney's office accompanied by a male friend of Betty's (the father of one of her friends). While they were in the parking lot, Henry grabbed the baby and told Betty to get into his car or she would never see Melissa again.

Betty's body was not discovered for several months. Henry was charged with murder. He had taken Betty to an isolated spot in the desert, where he beat and shot her. Melissa was in the car while her mother was fighting for her life. Her body had to be identified by her dental records.

At Henry's trial, one of his previous wives admitted to the abuse she had experienced at his hands. She was still afraid of him. Henry was eventually convicted of second-degree murder. Betty's last words to one of the authors (A.L.) as she left to meet Henry were, "If I don't come back, it is because he killed me."

Battered women in the Barnett and Lopez-Real (1985) study reported that in addition to being physically assaulted, they were threatened. Of the 43 women in the study, 41 reported that their husbands had threatened to kill or injure them.

The men also threatened to harm other family members and coworkers, take the children, destroy property, or take all the money (see also Nicole, 1997; Pearson et al., 1999; Stahly, Ousler, & Tanako, 1988).

In a subsequent study, Barnett (1990) analyzed the responses of 87 men who confessed to intimidating their wives. Relative to comparison groups of nonviolent men who were either happily or unhappily married, the abusive men more often threatened their wives with various actions. They threatened to (a) destroy property, (b) hurt a child, (c) lock their wives in or out of the house or room, (d) take all the money in the house, (e) leave their wives, (f) hurt or kill their wives, and (h) kill themselves (also see Barnett, Lee, & Thelen, 1997).

It is commonplace to hear battering men talk about their behavior as occurring in the past. Over the course of the relationship, most men expect their partners to ignore the threats and not take them seriously. Abusive men also expect their wives to believe that the men will never really hurt them, that they will know when to stop. For the victims, in contrast, threats typically engender terror and have a long-term effect (see O'Leary, 1999). Strong differences in perceptions of fear emerged in a review of experiences related to sexual aggression. Whereas women reported significantly higher levels of intimidation, men were unaware or unconvinced by these reactions. They either ignored or discounted women's fear (Tinsley et al., 1992).

CASE STUDY

JACK

Jack was mandated to an abuser's program because he had made terrorist threats to his ex-wife. Jack was a former officer in the special forces. He had been trained to use force, even lethal force, when the situation called for it. When he called his wife and told her that unless he saw his son, he would take her on a one-way trip to Mexico in the trunk of his car, she believed him.

Jack, on the other hand, did not believe her. He thought his ex-wife was exaggerating her fright. He had not ever hit her. He thought the therapist was overreacting when she said she understood his ex-wife's terror. He minimized and denied the intent and the outcome of his threat.

After the session, two of the biggest and most volatile men in the group came to the therapist and expressed their apprehension regarding Jack's future behavior: "We think that guy will come back to group next week and shoot all of us. He's one of those quiet, dangerous guys." The therapist encouraged the two men to confront Jack the following week, and they did. It was the first time that he realized his wife could really be afraid.

In battering relationships, it seems as if nothing is really left in the past. The past keeps happening over and over again. Despite the promises of change, change rarely happens, and if it does, it does not seem to last. Moreover, leaving and safety are not synonymous. Some abusive men will continue to harass and intimidate their intimates even after they leave, as is evidenced by a comprehensive study of family and intimate assaults in Atlanta, Georgia (Saltzman et al., 1990). In 1992, the victimization rate of women separated from their husbands was about three times higher than that of divorced women and about 25 times higher than that of married women (Bachman & Saltzman, 1995).

Separation offered no protection against rape, either. One study revealed that 55% of wives who were raped were no longer living with their husbands (Hanneke, Shields, & McCall, 1986). Family, friends, and associates almost uniformly advise battered women to just leave, as if leaving will afford them safety. However, such well-meaning advice can be fatal. An in-depth analysis of 57 women killed by their male partners indicated that 43 (75%) of the women were separated or trying to terminate their relationships at the time the murder occurred (cited in New York Commission, 1998). An examination of 119 women killed in North Carolina between 1988 and 1992 determined that current or former male partners killed 99 of them and then killed themselves. In 29% of the murder-suicides, there was documentation of prior domestic violence. The impetus for 41% of these murders was victim separation from the perpetrator (Morton et al., 1998). For some abusers, "till death do us part" is taken quite literally.

CASE STUDY

ROSA AND PONCHO

Leaving Poncho became the most dangerous action Rosa could take. Her husband had threatened to hunt her down if she ever left. He told her repeatedly that no other man could ever have her, and that if she ever left, he would kill her or "mess up her face" so that no man would ever look at her again. He also threatened to kidnap the children if she did not stay.

Rosa knew that he was not making idle threats. The judge awarded him visitation, and Poncho was always able to find her. Rosa reasoned that if she stayed, she would at least know what he was doing and have some control over what would happen. Her "paranoia" was really an accurate perception of reality.

It is common to hear threats made by men who either do not follow through with them or follow through at a lesser level. No one really knows, however, which violent partner will make good on his threat.

LEARNING TO FEAR

Fear is a powerful emotion capable of creating behavioral and psychological change. To clarify how emotions such as fear are learned, Watson and Raynor (1920) applied Pavlov's conditioning procedure to an infant named Baby Albert. (The mental health of Albert's parents remains questionable at best, because they consented to this research.) Watson showed Albert a white rat (that Albert previously liked and did not fear) and then made a loud sound behind the baby's head. After Watson repeated the process a number of times, Baby Albert began to cry and act startled whenever he saw the white rat, whether or not the sound occurred. It did not take long for Albert to demonstrate a fear response. Albert had learned to anticipate a noxious event when he caught sight of the rat, and the anticipation created fear.

Advances in the neurological sciences and brain imaging processes (e.g., positron emission tomography, PET scans) have revealed a wealth of new information about emotional learning. One section of the brain (the amygdala) is highly involved during fear conditioning. Changes in this area of the brain are enduring and offer an explanation for repeated responses to specific stimuli and recurrence of trauma symptoms (Killcross, Robbins, & Everitt, 1997; McKernan & Shinnick-Gallagher, 1997; Rausch, van der Kolk, Fisler, & Alpert, 1996; Rogan, 1997).

Nearly all studies indicate that men and women are affected very differently by interpersonal violence. In Molidor and Tolman's (1998) survey of dating adolescents, about 90% of the girls reported being hurt, whereas about 90% of boys said that they were not hurt. Boys typified the abuse as something to "laugh" at about 50% of the time, whereas girls "laughed" at the incidents only 10% of the time. In another study, men's most common reaction to interpersonal violence was to find it "funny," and their second was to be "angry." Women's most frequent reaction was "fear," and their second was "emotional hurt" (O'Keefe & Treister, 1998). Such gender differences in fear reactions are consistent across a number of investigations (see Barnett et al., 1997; O'Leary, 1999). Not only do men and women experience fear somewhat differently, but they also tend to be afraid of different things (Rabasca, 1999). For instance, a man walking alone down an empty street at night is unlikely to experience fear at the sight of three unarmed women walking toward him (unless they are Mary Kay Commandos). The reverse is probably not true.

Society readily acknowledges the reality of women's greater vulnerability to victimization and socializes girls to take self-protective measures (Stanko, 1988). Most women experience a chronic low-level apprehension about being victimized (see Kury & Ferdinand, 1997; Smith, 1988). An analysis of 37 professional women recognized that women routinely took a number of precautions to protect themselves. Respondents reported walking to their cars with someone else whenever possible, keeping their keys between their fingers, and carefully checking the back seat of their cars before they got in. Half of the women had taken self-defense classes, and more than three fourths had mentally planned rape prevention strategies. This pilot study also indicated that women tend to cope with fear in one of three ways: denial, flooding (overexposure to fear cues or thinking), or reasoning (Rozee-Koker, Wynne, & Mizrahi, 1989).

Theoretical explanations of avoidance behavior have brought further attention to the role that environmental cues play in maintaining fear. When rats in an experimental group were able to eliminate tones associated with shock, they learned to escape faster than rats who had not learned to fear the same stimuli. In fact, getting rid of the fear cues was very rewarding to the animals (Brown & Jacobs, 1949; Crawford & Masterson, 1978). A critical problem faced by battered women is that they often cannot leave the scene after a traumatic incident. As long as the batterer is nearby, his presence can serve as a cue to produce fear.

Abused women are even more afraid than other women (Russell et al., 1989; also see Nurius et al., 1992). Battered women learn that their spouses may be quiescent for a time (like the Kilauea volcano), but sooner or later, there will be an eruption. For women trapped in a battering cycle, there may be a nonviolent time, but not necessarily a time of feeling safe. Battered women learn to anticipate abuse (i.e., punishment), much as the subject of experimental conditioning learns to anticipate shock. The implied construct in both situations is fear (Healey, 1995; Wirtz & Harrell, 1987).

Several important factors become apparent given the content, quality, and quantity of violence-elicited fear in most battering relationships. First and foremost, there is the apprehension about another beating. Aversive cues such as yelling, breaking things, and particular facial expressions can precede an attack. Even though a physical assault is less common, the possibility of its appearance is always present (Langford, 1996). Although a batterer may believe that his mate should feel safe because he says he won't really hurt her, she does not.

EMOTIONAL/PSYCHOLOGICAL ABUSE

Psychological abuse can stand alone as a stimulus that induces fear. Newer research is beginning to show that psychological abuse generates fear even more definitively than physical abuse (Arias & Pape, 1999). Despite several commentaries on the extreme harm caused by psychological abuse (e.g., Follingstad, Rutledge, Berg, Hause, & Polek, 1990; Marshall, 1992; Straus & Sweet, 1992), society tends to denigrate its significance in comparison with physical abuse. Instead, society has legally channeled (probably reasonably) its efforts in responding toward coping with physical abuse (O'Leary, 1999).

Definitions of psychological abuse are emerging in recognition of its significance in creating an environment characterized by fear: "acts of recurring criticism and/or verbal aggression toward a partner, and/or acts of isolation and domination of a partner" (O'Leary, 1999, p. 19). Psychological/emotional abuse is extremely common, and it exacts a higher toll on women than on men (Vivian & Langhinrichsen-Rohling, 1994). A review of empirical evidence ascertained that psychological abuse increases depression, lowers self-esteem, and nearly always precedes physical aggression (see O'Leary, 1999).

BECKY AND ANNIE

CASE STUDY

Becky: He used to smile at me in this funny kind of way when he was really angry, and then all hell would break loose. I still get scared when I see that smile, and I stop whatever I am doing.

Annie: I'd go home and he'd be quiet. It was a very loud quiet. I'd always say, "Are you okay? Is anything wrong?" He'd always say everything was okay, but I knew I was in trouble. Sometimes, the quiet would last awhile—2, 3 days, a week. And sometimes, it would end quickly, with an ugly remark or yelling or worse. But that quiet was like the "quiet before the storm," a signal telling me I had been bad and would be punished.

Cues associated with an assault become conditioned (discriminative) stimuli that bring about terror when encountered again (Wirtz & Harrell, 1987). Learned fear has a way of mushrooming and spreading into new areas (generalization). Because stimulus generalization occurs, events that are similar to the punished situations may come to trigger a negative anticipation. As a result, cues that seem totally nonthreatening to most people may come to elicit self-defensive responses in battered women. When safety depends on reading significant cues accurately, people become speed readers.

Back to Baby Albert: After he became permanently traumatized by the sight of the white rat, similar objects, such as a fur coat or Santa Claus's beard, also evoked a fear reaction. Baby Albert had learned to generalize (Watson & Raynor, 1920).

CASE STUDY

CHERYL

Cheryl did not risk much anymore. She knew that her husband got angry when she visited friends and family. She knew he did not like her to change plans. She also knew that even though he said she was crazy, he would not like her going to therapy for help.

Cheryl visited her family sometimes, and she took one night class, but her misgivings about her husband's response restricted her activities. She was afraid to make new friends, get a job, or go out after class with other students. Her fear had generalized to almost everything.

Even though her husband told her she needed a "shrink," she was afraid to contact a counselor. Cheryl's sister called a therapist specializing in wife abuse and drove Cheryl to her first few appointments. Cheryl was never able to tell her husband that she was going to therapy, and she paid for it in cash so that her check register could not give her away.

PUNISHMENT EFFECTS AND FEAR

The effects of abuse (i.e., punishment) on battered women are quite variable. Several investigators found a relationship between severity of abuse and the decision to leave. According to many researchers, women who returned to their violent mates reported less intense violence than did women who did not return (Butehorn, 1985; Frisch & MacKenzie, 1991; Gondolf, 1988a). A review of data from 293 shelter residents, however, contradicted these findings. The more severe a woman's injuries, the longer she remained in the relationship. This was true even though severity, frequency, and degree of pain suffered from the beatings increased over the duration of the relationship (Pagelow, 1981a). Finally, Schwartz's (1988) results did not agree with any of the others. He found that tolerance for injury in married, divorced, or separated women varied individually and was unrelated to women's decisions to stay or leave.

Some people think that leaving is easy, and that abused women must like to be hit or else they would not stay. There is no indication that abused women enjoy a good beating. There was nothing about laboratory experiments that indicated that animals liked to be punished in order to obtain food. They just liked to eat! (See Appendix C, Sections 1 and 3, for relevant experiments.)

Laboratory research can provide a model for understanding learned responses brought on by aggression. Violence in an abusive home is analogous to punishment in a Skinner box (Skinner, 1938). Punishment is the presentation of an event that reduces (suppresses) responses. Commonly used punishers are shocks for animals or spankings for children. Experiments demonstrate that a number of variables, such as intensity and timing of punishers, modify their effectiveness. Severe punishment can greatly suppress behavior. (See Appendix B, Section 3, Part 1C and 1D.) The following case history illustrates the long-term effects of intense punishment.

JULIE AND MICKEY

CASE STUDY

Julie and Mickey were high school sweethearts. He was a popular football star. Although she also was well-liked, she thought she was lucky to have Mickey. They married because she was pregnant. Julie believed that her love would mold Mickey into the perfect husband.

He did not hit her until after they got married. Julie says she will never forget the incident. "He balled up his fist and hit me in the mouth. My lip and chin opened up and there was blood all over my face. I remember seeing stars and thinking, 'This is what happens to Popeye in the cartoons.' I went numb. You never forget it when someone hits you that hard, and you never have to be hit that hard again to continue to be afraid. In fact, I don't think he ever hit me that hard again. But in the following years that we were together, I was always afraid that he would, and it kept me in line."

Punishment variables other than intensity affect battered women's decision making. Findings on the effects of intermittent punishment and punishment plus reinforcement (i.e., rewards) form a foundation to explain battered women's persistence in the relationship (see Azrin, Holz, & Hake, 1963; Long & McNamara, 1989). Interpreting battering followed by contrition as punishment followed by reinforcement, Long and McNamara (1989) theorized that the cyclical nature of battering actually increases the female partner's love and dependency. The battering cycle, in conjunction with imbalances in marital power, bond the woman to her abuser, diminishing her resolve to leave (Dutton & Painter, 1981). The effects of this traumatic bonding are resistant to change (Dutton & Painter, 1993b). See Dinsmoor (1952) and Holz and Azrin (1961) (in Appendix C, Section 3); Rosenblum and Harlow (1963) (in Appendix C, Section 4); and Azrin et al. (1963) (in Appendix C, Section 5).

Animal research has established that the gradual escalation of punishment leads to continued responses rather than to suppression. Along the same lines, an initial intense shock followed by shocks of decreasing intensity will continue to suppress behavior (Sandler, Davidson, Greene, & Holzschuh, 1966). (See Appendix C, Section 6 for a summary of this experiment.) Extrapolation of these findings to humans suggests that battered women subjected to escalation of abuse will adapt and will remain in the relationship.

The significance of a gradual build-up of violence came to light primarily from anecdotal reports offered by shelter workers and Walker's (1979) Cycle of Violence theory. Although scientific evidence supporting a pattern of escalating abuse has been a routine finding, it is not inevitable (Keilitz et al., 1998; Pagelow, 1981b; Roy, 1977; Walker, 1979). Other patterns have occurred (see Aldarondo, 1996; Dutton, 1998; Follingstad et al., 1992; Lloyd, 1989; O'Leary et al., 1989). Differences in the participants tested and the data collection methods employed may have caused these disparities.

There are, however, other credible interpretations for the inconsistent findings: (a) Severe abuse early in a relationship may make later abuse unnecessary to obtain the same effects (see Church, 1969; Larkin & Popaleni, 1994); (b) abuse is triggered sporadically by factors such as unemployment and stress (Barling & Rosenbaum, 1986; Margolin, John, & Foo, 1998); (c) victims have perfected their denial and minimization (Adams, 1986; Graham et al., 1988); and (d) escalation may characterize one pattern of abusive relationships while not precluding others (Aldarondo, 1996).

Another supposition that seems likely is that the batterer is also affected by the gradual escalation of so-called punishment (the battered woman's reactions) directed back at him. The responsive punishments that he receives for his violent behavior probably start out mildly as well. Her initial reaction to his abuse may include anger, shock, and withdrawal. Over time, she may add depression, silent suffering, her own angry outbursts, and leaving temporarily. Her behavior will probably occur along a continuum of increasing intensity over a period of time. With gradual, subtle changes in his aggression and her response, adjustments and adaptations in thinking occur. (See Appendix C, Section 6 for an explanatory animal study by Sandler et al., 1966). Couples in which one partner batters the other stop believing each other. They begin to accept as facts that he is not going to stop and that she is not going to leave.

These couples tend to think of the aggression in their relationship as an aberration and the noncrisis period as the norm and true state of their marriage (Douglas, 1991). The gradual build-up of intermittent punishment allows the partners (and children) in a violent family the opportunity to recuperate. With subtle adjustments, individuals may change their standards for judging the violence. What they previously thought of as severe punishment may now seem mild. The once-severe punishment may become the new baseline.

CASE STUDY

KATHY

"The first time I heard him say he felt like cutting my heart out with a knife, I was stunned. Nobody had ever said anything like that to me before. I had never been threatened before this relationship. I guess it just stopped meaning anything after I heard it over and over. It fell into the category of 'That's just the way he talks,' and then he beat me up. As I look back on it, the physical threats should have taken on new meaning, a greater significance, but they didn't. I couldn't sort it out or make sense of it. It was just one more thing."

THE NATURE OF GENDER VIOLENCE

The role that gender plays in intimate violence has fueled a passionate controversy within the field of domestic violence. The primary point of debate revolves around the apparent mutuality of marital violence (i.e., comparable frequency rates) obtained with research based on the Conflict Tactics Scales (CTS) (Straus, 1979). The results of surveys of aggression using the CTS revealed that both men and women admit to initiating violent acts—including slapping, pushing, grabbing, kicking, and punching—at commensurate rates (Straus & Gelles, 1990; Straus, Gelles, & Steinmetz, 1980). "The number of assaults by itself, however, ignores the context, meaning, and consequences of those assaults. The fact that women produce less injury than men is a critical difference" (Straus, 1991b, p. 11).

It is interesting to note that canvasses of the public using scales other than the CTS (i.e., NCVS and National Survey of Families and Households [NSFH]), as well as one using the CTS (NVAW), have not exhibited gender uniformity (Bachman & Saltzman, 1995; Tjaden & Thoennes, 1998; Zlotnick et al., 1998). Further disparities in findings have originated from research conducted in shelters, emergency rooms, and police departments. Frequency data provided by women in these settings diverge dramatically from responses of women in the general population. Family violence experts have ordinarily attributed these inconsistencies to the vast variations between the samples of women interviewed and to the variations in the methods of collecting data (see Koss et al., 1994; Straus, 1993).

Against the historical backdrop of male privilege, a number of experts, most women, and women's advocates, in particular, perceive women to be the true victims of marital violence. Conversely, some experts, some men, and most batterers assign a much more prominent role to women's actions in domestic violence (see Dobash, Dobash, Wilson, & Daly, 1992; Flynn, 1990; Saunders, 1988; Straus, 1997). Steinmetz's (1977) postulation of a Battered Husband Syndrome, in particular, rankled feminists and helped spark a backlash leading to articles such as "The Myth of Sexual Symmetry in Marital Violence" (Dobash, Wilson, & Daly, 1992) and "Return of the Battered Husband Syndrome" (Schwartz & DeKeseredy, 1993). Despite dissension, it is important to note that no one is proposing that violent females do not exist, and that there are no men assaulted by women (Cook, 1997). However, it is rare for a man to be truly battered (by a female) in the physical sense (Campbell & Humphreys, 1984).

Opponents of the gender equivalence viewpoint looked for and found a number of rationales for rejecting the conclusion that women are as maritally violent as men:

- *False assumptions about the context of abuse.* The CTS asks only about abuse during arguments.
- *Flaws in self-report data,* such as issues of honesty and completeness of respondents' reports for each sex (e.g., Dobash, Cavanagh, & Lewis, 1998; Riggs et al., 1989; Szinovacz, 1983)
- *Selection of questions* used in the CTS and other scales. Some test items can be user *unfriendly* because of their dependence on legal terminology (Koss, 1989). Merely redesigning the items for the National Crime Victimization Survey to inquire about more specific behaviors radically altered the results (Bachman & Taylor, 1994)
- *Lack of information on motivations* for the violent act (self-defense, control, and intent to injure) (e.g., Barnett et al., 1997; Browne, 1990; Saunders, 1986)
- *Little information about outcomes* (e.g., fear, end of argument, escape, injuries)

- *Inadequate measures of chronicity of violence* prior to or after the study's time line
- *Insufficient measures of the victim's fear, isolation, and levels of control*
- *False presumptions about gender equivalence of violent acts,* such as the ability to frighten others through aggression (Barnett et al., 1997; Hamberger, Lohr, Bonge, & Tolin, 1997; Koss et al., 1994; Saunders, 1986; Vivian & Langhinrichsen-Rohling, 1994)
- *False assumptions about the parity of an occasional act of aggression and a battering relationship*

Several investigators examined possible distinctions in the initiation and severity of abuse. Although debatable, a number of reports, but not all, found that wives less frequently use severe violence (Browning & Dutton, 1986; Brush, 1990; Harris, 1991; Langhinrichsen-Rohling, Neidig, & Thorn, 1995; Makepeace, 1986; Margolin, 1987; Morse, 1995; Saunders, 1989; Szinovacz, 1983; Tjaden & Thoennes, 1998). Furthermore, some comparisons have disclosed that men usually start the violence and are more likely than women to engage in multiple acts of assault (Emery, Lloyd, & Castleton, 1989; Saunders, 1989). In contrast, teenage girls made the following estimates of violence initiation: (a) 39% reported starting the violence themselves; (b) 20% said boys initiated the violence; and (c) 41% said that both parties equally initiated the violence. Analogous male estimates were as follows: (a) 28% said that they were the first to abuse; (b) 24% said their girlfriends were the first to abuse; and (c) 48% said both parties initiated the abuse equally (O'Keefe & Treister, 1998).

A number of investigators contend that when women react violently, it is more likely to be a product of the situation than when men react violently (e.g., Koss et al., 1994; Laner & Thompson, 1982; Marshall & Rose, 1990). Saunders (1986) asked 56 battered women whether they used violence and, if so, under what circumstances. The women judged the percentage of time (0% to 100%) that their violent responses were self-defensive, retaliatory, and the first strike. Results revealed that self-defense was the most common motive for both severe and nonsevere violence.

Another evaluation of 482 battered women disclosed that 66% said that their violence was self-defensive, and an additional 22% said that it was motivated by fear (Gondolf, 1998a; also see Barnett, Keyson, & Thelen, 1992; Browne, 1987; Cascardi, Vivian, & Meyer, 1991; Hamberger et al., 1997). Collectively, research strongly corroborates the judgment of Marshall and Rose (1990) that "the actions by a person of one sex cannot be considered the equivalent of the other sex engaging in the behavior" (p. 60).

In animal research, punishment leads to increased aggression, a phenomenon termed *elicited aggression.* A punished monkey will attack objects, other organisms not involved in the punishment, or even itself (Ulrich, Wolff, & Azrin,

1964). Humans also will become aggressive toward noninvolved individuals when shocked (Berkowitz & LePage, 1967). This finding helps explain battered women's self-defensive aggression, and it predicts outbursts of aggression toward others. Surprisingly, an extrapolation of the phenomenon of elicited aggression suggests that battered women's aggression toward their children may occur as one outcome of being battered themselves. Another possibility is Freudian displacement of aggression—the *trickle-down* theory—or that women themselves are violent.

Anger and fear emerge as the two predominant reactions to assault (Gore-Felton et al., 1999). Anger can be, and often is, a buffer against fear. In one English study, 62% of crime victims reported feeling angry because of their victimization (Shepherd, 1990; Stuckless, 1998). Similarly, battered women and those in shelters are significantly angrier than are comparison groups of nonbattered women (see also Edleson & Brygger, 1986; Feindler, 1988; Russell et al., 1989).

Several experts have recognized this combination of anger and fear in victims (Blackman, 1988; Walker, 1984). Very likely, the motives of self-defense (fear-motivated) and retaliation (anger-motivated) become blended together for some battered women (Saunders, 1986). Legally, self-defense pleas in homicide cases do not become nullified when extreme terror becomes mixed with extreme rage, because it is reasonable to combine anger and fear when attacked (Schneider & Jordan, 1978).

THE MULTIDIMENSIONALITY OF VIOLENCE

It is important to note that physical abuse is more often in the less severe range (Holtzworth-Munroe & Stuart, 1994; Straus & Gelles, 1986), and it occurs less often than psychological and verbal abuse (Follingstad et al., 1990; O'Leary, Malone, & Tyree, 1994; Stets, 1990; Vitanzas, Vogel, & Marshall, 1995). Episodes of marital violence usually include hitting, throwing things, slapping, and pushing. Ordinarily, the injuries are cuts and bruises that rarely require hospitalization (Rand, 1997; Tjaden & Thoennes, 1998). The level of fright engendered during a battering episode, however, does not parallel the degree of violence used or the seriousness of an injury inflicted (see Cohen, Forjuoh, & Gondolf, 1999; Muelleman, Lenaghan, & Pakieser, 1996). Even a nonphysical form of abuse can create a high level of foreboding (Jacobson et al., 1996).

Battering, abuse, domestic violence, and intimidation have often been used synonymously as descriptors and definitions of the aggression that occurs in intimate relationships. Isolated acts of aggression have not been distinguished from patterns of chronic abuse that weave a web, a context, in which partners live and function. Too often, research and policy are based on a one-dimensional view of a one-dimensional batterer and his one-dimensional family. Researchers and advocates seek to describe batterers in profiles, descriptive lists, or personality traits.

One of the authors (A.L.) participated in a clandestine conversation with staff from a well-respected battered women's shelter. They were having trouble with the concept of women as batterers. They had interviewed women who had initiated acts of aggression that were not self-defensive. They had worked in batterers' groups with many men who did not fit the profile. The saddest part of this meeting was the reluctance of advocates to reexamine notions that had been formulated 20 years ago. The women were afraid to challenge the political rhetoric and factoids (i.e., assertions unsupported by data or experience) (Gelles, 1995) that had spawned the movement. The synthesis of opinion after the discussion was that the term *battering* should be redefined, and that the distinguishing feature of battering might be level of fear, not just the perpetration of aggressive acts.

As stated previously, there continues to be something of a battle of the sexes in terms of the role of women's behavior in domestic violence. Some view women's aggression as more aggravating than intimidating and more limit-setting than controlling. Others think women's violence is as intimidating and controlling as men's. When the debate gets noisy and angry, the result is the creation of something akin to a battering relationship between experts.

It is helpful to keep in mind that people on both sides of this argument do not believe that women are entitled to act out physically whenever they feel like it. Some women are abusive, and some are downright violent. There is no research, however, that can say that the cost of women's violence—emotionally, physically, or in regard to property damage—in any way matches that same violence perpetrated by men. The body of evidence suggests that there should be no argument. Diffusing energy into an ongoing gender war takes away from the critical task of developing effective prevention and intervention strategies.

These issues call attention to the role of patriarchy in marital violence. We believe that male-dominated societies create a type of "patriarchal pollution." Patriarchy is the smog we breathe, the pesticides we ingest, and the toxins that find a home in our bodies. We cannot necessarily taste it or feel it. Its effects may be subtle, but they are cumulative. The patriarchal structure of a society creates a mood that allows, encourages, or normalizes violence, particularly violence directed at the least powerful, *safest* targets (see Kandel-Englander, 1992).

A "single-bullet" theory, in which patriarchy is the single bullet, however, does not adequately explain the existence of wife beating (Dutton, 1994). If patriarchy were the only factor contributing to wife assault, then a large percentage of men raised in that system should exhibit assaultive behavior (see also Julian & McKenry, 1993). Furthermore, patriarchy does not explain female violence in either heterosexual or lesbian relationships in which self-defense is not the impetus (Coleman & Straus, 1986; Kasian & Painter, 1992; Lie & Gentlewarrior, 1991; Renzetti, 1992). A broader rationale for intimate violence that accounts for these more diverse types of violence is needed. One such theory, attachment theory, posits that intimacy generates dependency, jealousy, and anger, all of which are sometimes expressed violently (D. G. Dutton et al., 1994). Some other theories highlight childhood exposure to violence and psychopathology (see Hamberger & Hastings, 1991; Hotaling & Sugarman, 1986).

Any single-answer interpretation of the complex problem of spousal violence would fail to do justice to the men and women for whom causation affects staying, leaving, and the nature of the assistance they receive. Yet of 10 possible factors, patriarchy is most often cited as the underlying and most important factor accounting for men's abuse of women (Adams, 1988; Dobash et al., 1998; Yllö, 1993).

To define partner abuse accurately, all sides of the argument must be considered. One way of conceptualizing spousal abuse is to place it on a continuum. A continuum emphasizes the fact that anyone can, and many people do, commit an act or limited acts of aggression, whereas very few become involved in an escalating and/or chronic pattern of physical abuse and coercive control. A continuum also incorporates the notion that interpersonal violence normally occurring at a low level may erupt suddenly into severe violence with perilous repercussions.

A distinction can be made between *common couple aggression* and *patriarchal terrorism* (Johnston, 1995). These two levels can serve as anchors at opposite ends of the continuum of spousal abuse. At the low end of the continuum, common couple aggression, abuse may include relatively infrequent, noninjurious behavior that may occur in many intimate relationships. It may be mutual, does not tend to victimize the partners, and does not create fear. At the high end, patriarchal terrorism, abuse may cluster around a pattern of assaultive, fear-producing, controlling behaviors that are both criminal (e.g., physical assaults, terrorist threats, stalking) and often noncriminal (e.g., isolating the partner, jealous monitoring of partner's friends and activities, humiliating the partner).

Patriarchal terrorism is rooted in historical and cultural notions of male ownership and domination of female partners. It is simultaneously a mechanism of men's control over women and an escalating pattern of coercive violence. Patriarchal terrorism is most clearly typified by concomitant factors such as chronic foreboding. As Gordon (1988) posits, "One assault does not make a battered woman; she becomes that because of her socially determined inability to resist or escape" (p. 285). Battering includes both physically violent acts and their political framework (the pattern of social, institutional, and interpersonal controls that entrap women and prevent them from determining their own destinies) (Stark, 1993).

Common couple aggression is associated with conflict that inevitably arises in relationships. It is less gendered than patriarchal terrorism and extremely prevalent. It is this type of interpersonal violence that population surveys tend to detect. Although it often includes an element of partner control, it does not engender an alarm reaction. The terminology is meant to infer actions like yelling—a near-universal behavior—that partners use during an argument when things get out of hand. Although this conflict may include psychological abuse or even an occasional push or shove, it rarely escalates into serious violence (see Johnston, 1995; Lupri, Grandin, & Brinkerhoff, 1994; O'Leary, 1999).

Dichotomizing the endpoints of the continuum into common couple aggression and patriarchal terrorism has some advantages. Differentiating the two forms of abuse not only recognizes the validity of different kinds of findings, but also sets the stage for different theoretical formulations and different types of interventions (Johnston, 1995; see also Adams, 1988; Emery & Laumann-Billings, 1998; Hamberger et al., 1997; Marshall, 1996; O'Leary, in press).

Presumably, types of assaultive acts (physical, sexual, emotional) can interact with varying levels of apprehension, oppression, and control to designate different points on a continuum of abuse. *Fear is the most critical emotional element in defining marital violence:* "the presence of at least two acts of physical aggression within a year (or one severe act) and/or physical aggression that leads the partner to be *fearful* of the other or that results in injury requiring medical attention" (O'Leary, 1999, p. 19; see Larkin & Popaleni, 1994). Once fear becomes part of the relationship, the relationship changes.

Emotional abuse (e.g., verbal outbursts, withdrawal, jealousy), rather than physical abuse, generates much of the apprehension in a battering relationship (Follingstad et al., 1990). Because emotional abuse seems objectively less potent and less tangible, it is difficult for a victim to justify making major life changes because of it. Giving up a home, financial security, intimacy, social support, and a job may seem disproportionate in view of the enormity of dread generated by the unknown.

Men in abusive relationships do not ordinarily respond the same way women do. In the Carmody and Williams (1987) study, men predicted that retaliatory physical assault by their wives was very unlikely, and they further judged the severity of their assaults as very low. Men also reported that they could easily protect themselves against physical assaults: "She was easy to stop"; "I just pushed her away"; or "I restrained her." One important reason that few men fit into the category of battered is that unless their mates have used an equalizer, such as a weapon, the men just are not afraid. This does not mean they are not assaulted or cannot be battered.

The combination of sporadic violence interspersed with kindness (as in the Stockholm Syndrome) contributes to the development of hope and allows the battered woman to deny the side of the abuser that terrifies her (Graham et al., 1988). If she denies his violent side, she can deny that she is in danger. That is, battered women deny that their mates either intend to or actually do harm them. In fact, sometimes, they deny being victimized altogether (Hebbert, Silver, & Ellard, 1991). Batterers deny the abusive nature of their behavior as well (Dutton, 1998; Edleson & Brygger, 1986). One of the authors (O.B.) encountered a man who characterized himself as unhappily married, but nonviolent. Later inspection of his test data uncovered that he admitted to having choked his wife "several times a year"!

Professionals working with survivors may be fearful themselves and in danger of developing long-lasting anxiety reactions known as secondary traumas (Gore-Felton et al., 1999; also see Bower, 1999). According to Mary Ann Dutton (1992), work with victims of trauma is the most demanding of professional experiences, and it may have enduring psychological consequences (also see Herman, 1992).

Several authors have described the effects of secondary trauma on therapists (as well as advocates and others working with survivors of violence) (Gore-Felton et al., 1999). Judith Herman (1992) warns that repeated exposure to stories of human cruelty will eventually challenge a counselor's basic faith and trust in other people. Perhaps even more terrifying is identifying with the perpetrator, which can happen to any advocate for battered women. Empathy for a batterer feels like the ultimate betrayal to one's values and beliefs.

CASE STUDY

KEITH

Keith called his counselor early in the morning. She was already gone, but he talked to another therapist in the office. She had no previous connection with Keith, but the conversation made her anxious. When Keith's counselor returned, she got an urgent message from her associate to call Keith. Her previous experience with Keith and his impulsive anger created a strong emotional response of uneasiness and apprehension.

Keith was furious when his counselor called. He sarcastically thanked her for her help, and then said that he was "leaving to kill his wife." Needless to say, the counselor was hooked; she believed that Keith would carry out his threat.

The therapist worried that, as in the past, the criminal justice system would be unable to protect Keith's wife. He had successfully violated a temporary restraining order at least three times and had physically assaulted his wife during several of these incidents. The counselor also hoped that Keith had called so that he would not harm his wife. The therapist was unable to calm him down and, in fact, felt an escalation of alarm and anxiety in herself. She called Keith's probation officer to both warn her and have her call Keith's wife. The probation officer and Keith's wife lived 6 hours away.

What ensued were 2 hours of calls involving the therapist, the client, the probation officer, and the estranged spouse. The client's rage produced rapid results. The therapist and the probation officer contacted the ex-wife and acted as intermediaries. The ex-wife made contacts with Keith, and a negotiation followed that concluded with positive results; Keith's anger dissolved. His wife was safe, and the problem was resolved, at least for the time.

It is interesting to observe the behavior of those involved in this particular situation and to hear about their reactions. First of all, everyone responded to the rage by moving in the direction that seemed most productive, but also in the direction pushed by the batterer: contact with his ex-wife. The threats produced immediate results, once again reinforcing the notion that *violence works*. The probation officer and the therapist talked about feeling manipulated, emotionally battered, and unable to slow down until the problem was resolved.

Keith sent the counselor a thank-you card and an apology. He talked about feeling appreciative of her efforts. The air was cleared; communication was open and honest. They had been through a crisis together and had come out of it with a positive resolution. A residue of misgiving and distrust remained, even though good feelings returned. The cycle of fear and hope had begun for the counselor.

CASE STUDY (continued)

If peripherally involved individuals react with fear to their minimal involvement with a batterer by changing their behaviors, why should one be surprised by the extreme behavior changes undergone by battered women and their children?

The vicariously traumatized helping professional can also experience an overidentification with the client or an emotional distancing; thus, self-care becomes extremely important. Support from family and friends, exercise, play, rest, nutrition, peer support, and networking with others working in the field are essential for creating a balanced emotional environment (Zorza, 1998). Experiencing and expressing the feelings that this work elicits becomes critical to preserving mental health. Much like having the stomach flu, catharsis promotes healing.

However, when a family member becomes privy to the pain and danger of an abusive relationship, the traumatic effect is magnified.

CASE STUDY

A FATHER'S CHOICE

Dick had watched the transformation take place. Nina had become a successful engineer, earned good money, bought her own home, had friends all over the world, and had landed a great position working for Euro-Disney. His daughter, his baby, the child who had followed him everywhere, had learned to ride the big Harley motorcycles that he loved, but had also become anxious, jumpy, and isolated. She had recently borrowed money from her parents to buy baby furniture.

Dick was worried. Nina's marriage to a rugged, handsome rugby player she met while in France seemed to change her. The most dramatic change in Dick's mind came after the birth of his first grandson, who was the apple of his eye.

At first, Nina seemed very happy, and her family was happy for her. Ned was charming and, by his own account, successful in business. Nina and Ned moved back to California after their marriage. It was after Tim's birth that Nina began to confide in her father. Nina told Dick that Ned was controlling and did not seem to care much about Tim, who had been born 2 months prematurely and had some physical problems.

Dick had noticed a few things about Ned that had disturbed him. Ned was cocky and a braggart, and he seemed to stretch the truth. He had talked about his love of motorcycles and his numerous experiences riding big bikes, but he really did not know much about them and was uncomfortable on the long ride he took with Dick and his friends. Dick also noticed that Nina was dressing differently and seemed to look to Ned for approval of her clothing. Ned did not take Nina to the hospital during her pregnancy when she was experiencing difficulty. He also refused to come to the hospital when infant Tim had to have surgery.

One day, Nina and Tim came to Dick's house. His daughter was asking for her parents' help and a place to stay. Nina took her father aside and told him that she was leaving Ned. Everything seemed to pour out of her as she told her father of the constant criticism, the violence (mostly directed at property), and the restrictions that Ned placed on her contact with her friends. She had gotten over the fact that Ned had spent her money and had demanded that she return to work when Tim was very small and very ill, but she could not handle his lack of involvement and concern for Tim.

Dick became a focus of Ned's campaign to "get his wife and son back where they belonged." The phone calls and taped messages were ongoing. Ned was intimidating and screamed, "I'll be your worst God-damned nightmare." He called the Department of Children and Family Services (DCFS) repeatedly, reporting his estranged wife and her family for child abuse and neglect. At one point, DCFS made a midnight visit with the intention of removing Dick's grandson from their home because of the frequency and severity of the reports. DCFS dismissed all of the allegations when they found no evidence of abuse or neglect.

Visitations were uncomfortable to horrific. Ned was surly to the family and made numerous trips to hospital emergency rooms when Tim had mosquito bites, a rash, or a cough, attempting to gather evidence that Nina and her parents were unfit caretakers. He subjected Tim to blood tests, X rays, and other procedures. Ned also became the perfect father at work, with neighbors, and even with his personalized license plates proclaiming he was "TIMSDAD." A social worker from DCFS told Nina that she was a battered woman and gave her a shelter hotline number. She began attending groups, and her father became her only confidant and protector. He took over the visitation transfers. Turning Tim over to Ned was painful. Watching his daughter become frightened and nervous was excruciating. In addition, taking his own wife to the doctor, hearing that her blood pressure was skyrocketing, and having the doctor tell him, "Dick, the stress is killing her, you have to do something," was unbearable.

And Ned had upped the ante. He was filing continuous court documents, screaming threats on the phone, and beating on Dick's front door to the point that neighbors got involved. Ned began to stalk Nina. He sat outside of their house in his car to observe her comings and goings. On another occasion, in the emergency room, Ned pushed Dick into the wall. Dick, a former Japanese prisoner of war and survivor of the death march on Corregidor, began sleeping curled up in the fetal position on the living room floor. He described himself as the "last wagon in the wagon train," the only defense for his wife, daughter, and grandson.

Dick secretly bought a gun to protect himself and his family. He carried it in the waistband of his pants when Ned came to pick up Tim. Ned's menacing behavior was escalating, and the family's trepidation was escalating as well. Ned had begun to act out in front of other people in the neighborhood, and his harassing legal maneuvers were becoming more frantic.

Then, on a Saturday morning, Ned arrived at Dick's home for another visitation. He was belligerent and derogatory. Nina and her mother were in another room when they heard the first shot. Ned, wounded and bleeding, fled down the street of the quiet middle-class neighborhood in which Dick had lived for more than 20 years. Neighbors reported that Dick walked down the street as if he were in a trance. He fired four more shots into Ned. Ned died on the street. Dick had believed that the nightmare would never end for his daughter, his grandson, his wife, and himself. In his fugue-like state, Dick had ended the nightmare.

SUMMARY

This chapter has pointed out that redefining partner violence is crucial to its understanding. Fear, both objective and subjective, is an integral aspect of the meaning of male-to-female abuse. Fear actually causes enduring change in brain functions. In addition to fear, anger is a near-universal reaction to assault. Wife beating accounts for a large number of injuries to women and the murder of men, women, and other family members. Assaults are costly to society in terms of medical, legal, and criminal justice services.

Learning experiments on animals have provided a number of human analogs that furnish a useful framework for understanding the behavior of battered women. Learning theory offers information about a number of learned reactions: (a) the generalization of fear to other cues in the environment, (b) the effects of punishment variables on the extent of suppression of behavior (e.g., intermittent punishment), (c) the effects of a gradual build-up or decline of assaults, and (d) the creation of an atmosphere typified by chronic anxiety. Over time, couples learn to accept the battering in their relationship.

Research also portrays women's aggression as primarily self-defensive, whereas men's is power oriented. Furthermore, men's aggression successfully intimidates women, whereas women's assaultive behavior does not usually frighten men. Men show little worry about criminal justice sanctions, one of the many factors alluding to the patriarchal nature of male-to-female violence. Some researchers and societal agents have implied gender equality in spousal violence, and have even gone so far as to suggest a Battered Husband Syndrome. Research has clearly contradicted this assumption. Given the broad nature of learning principles and their applicability to behavior in general, becoming a battered woman could happen to anyone.

5 Meltdown
The Impact of Stress and Learned Helplessness

She has lost her faith in the world's essential predictability, fairness and safety, and approaches even ordinary routines like driving with the hesitancy of an outsider, a foreigner in a hostile land.

—Jay (1991, p. 23)

CHAPTER OVERVIEW

Stress is part of everyday life and can result from either positive or negative events. Apparently, most individuals do not handle stress productively and pay a heavy price both physically and psychologically for chronic mismanagement. Posttraumatic stress disorder (PTSD) is a psychological manifestation of a trauma, such as exposure to war or chronic abuse. Learned helplessness is also a significant condition brought about by violence or, more specifically, by the inability to stop it. Effects of PTSD and learned helplessness may eventually culminate in a cluster of cognitions, feelings, and behavior that constitutes the battered woman syndrome. The core of fear and paralysis typifying this syndrome helps to explain the inexplicable: why battered women stay and why they sometimes kill.

VIOLENCE-INDUCED STRESS

In humans, a moderate amount of stress is essential to growth and development, but prolonged, intense stress debilitates the body and the soul. The concept of stress incorporates both psychological and physiological reactions to stress(ors). Loss of a job constitutes a negative stressor, whereas going on vacation constitutes a positive stressor. Psychological reactions to stress include cognitive impairment (e.g., confusion and poor test performance) and emotional responses (e.g., anxiety, anger, aggression, and depression). (Readers who enjoyed Willard and Ben will find an early experiment on stress in rats conducted by Selye, 1946, in Appendix C, Section 8.)

CASE STUDY

NICKIE AND TOM

To describe Nickie now is to describe her life with Tom, a successful businessman. Tom was obsessed with Nickie's life prior to their relationship. In particular, he wanted open disclosure of previous sexual experiences. His interrogation would sometimes last for hours. He read her private papers and journals and went through her picture album. He found pictures of her standing next to male friends and relatives. These pictures served as a basis for his distrust, even though he was aware that she had had no prior sexual experience. She had come to this relationship as a virgin.

When she married Tom, she had not anticipated how much he would mistrust and control her. She had nearly earned her doctorate, and she wanted to keep things at home on an even keel until her qualifying exams were completed. She recognized that she had given up some important things to keep her relationship together. She had given up her friends and family, but only for a time, to make it easier for her husband to feel secure.

Nickie had known that Tom was jealous, but she expected it to diminish over time. She understood his jealousy and fear so well, in fact, that his frenzied fantasies of her infidelities became real to her. She began to wonder if she had repressed the memories of affairs she had never had. His reality had become hers. Her ability to define herself apart from him became obscured.

Nickie did not understand why she cried a lot, or why she was unable to concentrate. She did not know why she shook when she talked or why she was afraid. She had not been physically abused. She had no idea how she had gotten from there to here, or when the change had begun, only that it seemed complete.

Researchers experimentally, and clinicians anecdotally, have documented the physiological toll of chronic apprehension. A longitudinal study found that mental health and physical health varied with abuse levels (Campbell & Soeken, 1999). Generally, the women in the Follingstad, Brennan, Hause, Polek, and Rutledge (1991) study reported that their physical and emotional health had been better both before and after the violent relationship. One study of Nicaraguan battered women showed a clear relationship between the abuse of either the wife or her child and the woman's level of emotional distress (Ellsberg et al., 1999). Similarly, a review and statistical analysis of a number of studies concerned with interpersonal violence identified a large number of violence-induced stress symptoms (Weaver & Clum, 1995).

CASE STUDY

MEI

I started having stomach pains the second year that we lived together, after the violence began. It was weird. I would be visiting a friend, and after I'd been there a few hours, I'd get a stabbing pain in my abdomen and feel sick. It was like the alarm ringing in the morning telling me that it was time to get up and go, and I would get up and go because I knew if I didn't, something bad would happen when I got home.

There is ample evidence that the impulsive and unpredictable behavior of abusers produces stress and feelings of helplessness in the people most affected by that behavior (Barnett & Hamberger, 1992; Campbell, 1990; Langford, 1996; O'Leary et al., 1994). Cole and Sapp (1988) found that the lower the level of internal control, the greater the level of stress (see Weaver & Clum, 1995, for a review).

Women in physically or emotionally destructive relationships can become hypersensitive to changes in specific situations and in their partners' eyes, speech, tone of voice, and facial expressions that may signal an onset of aggression. It seems that the battered women who can foresee a violent assault are so entrenched in this pattern that their greater exposure and familiarity have made them both more fearful and perhaps more accurate in predicting whether abuse will recur (Langford, 1996). No matter how practiced they may be, however, they can never predict when and how with exact precision.

Laboratory research can provide a scientific basis for these recent findings about battered women. Seligman (1968) and Seligman and Meyer (1970) were able to demonstrate that rats who were unpredictably shocked developed a chronic state of fear and ulcers. In another study, college students obliged to view photographs of graphic crime scenes without control over the timing of the presentations reported much more stress than did students who had control over the timing (Geer & Maisel, 1972; see also Abbot, Schoen, & Badia, 1984; Katz & Wykes, 1985). Knowing what to expect seems to provide an illusion of control.

POSTTRAUMATIC STRESS DISORDER

Traumatic events are the most obvious source of negative stress for anyone. Experiences such as earthquakes, nuclear accidents, plane crashes, and physical assaults produce severe stress reactions in almost everyone, sometimes called *disaster syndrome* (Atkinson, Atkinson, Smith, & Bem, 1990). A disaster syndrome encompasses three psychological stages: (a) shock, disorientation, and bewilderment; (b) passivity and lack of capacity to initiate tasks, accompanied by the inability to follow orders; and (c) anxiety and concentration difficulties. When a traumatic event has a prolonged reaction, it is called posttraumatic stress disorder (PTSD), a diagnosis first applied to Vietnam veterans (Kulka et al., 1990). Recent psychiatric studies undertaken by the Veterans Administration found evidence suggesting that soldiers physically or sexually abused as children had a greater sensitivity to developing PTSD than did soldiers who did not have a history of childhood abuse (Bower, 1992; King, King, Foy, Keane, & Fairbank, 1999).

PTSD received medical status in 1979 (American Psychiatric Association, 1980). Similar symptoms, however, have been associated with war for more than a century. These symptoms had been classified, depending on the war with which they were associated, as *nostalgia, shell shock,* and *battle fatigue.* Prior to the Vietnam War, medical professionals and others suspected that an individual who did not get over a traumatic experience in a reasonable amount of time was inherently disturbed or pathological. "Reasonable" was usually defined by the individuals who had a significant investment in the victim's emotional recovery.

Recognition of an external stressor as the precursor to PTSD produced a radical contrast to the *innate character defects* theory (see Adler, 1990). "In short, the diagnosis tacitly recognizes that the world can drive a normal person crazy" (Jay, 1991, p. 22). One significant consequence of the PTSD diagnosis in war veterans has been the provision of an appropriate status for trauma victims.

The definition of the disorder is comparatively recent and is evolving (Herman, 1992). PTSD is an anxiety disorder produced by an uncommon, extremely stressful event (e.g., assault, rape, military combat, death camp) and characterized by (a) reexperiencing the trauma in painful recollections or recurrent dreams; (b) diminished responsiveness (numbing), with disinterest in significant activities and with feelings of detachment and estrangement from others; and (c) such symptoms as exaggerated startle response, disturbed sleep, difficulty in concentrating or remembering, guilt about surviving when others did not, and avoidance of activities that call the traumatic event to mind (Goldenson, 1984).

A mass of scientific data documenting forgetting (i.e., repression of traumatic war experiences) has also emerged. A review of this literature indicates that recovery of these memories, sometmes through psychotherapy, leads to a remission of PTSD symptoms (Karon & Widener, 1997). Recent research has shown that the brain structure known as the amygdala is involved in a set of recurrent and long-lasting symptoms that occurs in response to PTSD (Rausch et al., 1996).

Living in a war zone caused PTSD in about 15% of the Vietnam veterans (American Psychiatric Association, 1980). Similarly, a survey of 4,008 adult women revealed that 69% of them had been exposed to some type of traumatic event over their lifetimes. Exposure to sexual assaults, aggravated assaults, or homicides involving a close relative occurred among 36% of the sample. Over a lifetime, the prevalence of PTSD was 12.3%. The rate of PTSD was significantly higher among crime victims (25.8%) than among noncrime victims (9.4%). Historical factors most closely related to PTSD included a direct threat to life or an actual injury (Resnick, Kilpatrick, Dansky, Saunders, & Best, 1993).

Other studies have estimated even higher percentages of PTSD symptoms: (a) 24 of 30 rape victims (80%) (Kramer & Green, 1991); (b) 24 of 25 adult incest victims (96%) (Donaldson & Gardner, 1985); and (c) 66% of 19 family survivors of homicide victims (Amick-McMullen, Kilpatrick, Veronen, & Smith, 1989). Some experts (Foa, Olasov, & Steketee, 1987) consider female victims of sexual assault and other assault victims to be the largest major group of PTSD victims. Riggs, Kilpatrick, and Resnick (1992) established that levels of PTSD symptomatology in women raped or assaulted by a husband were comparable to levels in women raped or assaulted by strangers. Astin, Lawrence, Pincus, and Foy (1990) demonstrated a significant relationship between childhood sexual victimization and PTSD. In the Amick-McMullen et al. (1989) study of homicide victims' relatives, the more dissatisfied family members were with the criminal justice system (e.g., charges against the perpetrator were reduced), the worse their PTSD symptoms.

Some have argued that marital rape is not a serious crime, not as serious a crime as a stranger-perpetrated rape, or both. The facts support a different conclusion. Sexually assaulted wives are just as traumatized as women assaulted by strangers (Monson et al., 1996; Riggs et al., 1992; Sullivan & Mosher, 1990). As one court held, "When you are raped by a stranger you have to live with a frightening memory. When you are raped by your husband, you have to live with your rapist" (*Warren v. State,* 1985).

In terms of physical and psychological injury, the effects of marital rape are extremely damaging and long-lasting (Campbell, 1989b; Riggs et al., 1992). Sexually abused women report more physical health symptoms, including pain, and seek more medical care than do nonsexually abused women (see Eby, Campbell, Sullivan, & Davidson, 1995; Koss, Koss, & Woodruff, 1991b). They also have poorer subjective health ratings (Golding, Cooper, & George, 1997).

One correlate of stress-related illness is having a network of close friends from whom the victim feels she or he must hide a shameful trauma. In other words, the traumatized individual actively inhibits disclosure (Pennebaker & Susman, 1988). According to Jay (1991), there is a "relentless external pressure on the victim to maintain the breach between the private, ravaged self and the public, acquiescent persona" (p. 22). Listening to trauma victims tell their stories creates stress, because the listener sees the pain and empathizes with the fear (Kessler, McLeod, & Wethington, 1985). Trauma, once- or twice-removed, still shakes the security of those peripherally involved in the world of the traumatized. For example, 8 weeks after the Loma Prieta earthquake in San Francisco, a study revealed that victims were still thinking about it, but they had stopped talking about it because others did not want to listen. In another study, parents bereaved by a child's death discovered that many of their friends and relatives avoided them, thus reducing opportunities for them to talk out their feelings and sending a strong message that implied that the time for being sad and the time for being heard were over (Pennebaker, 1991).

In an effort to create an analogy between the experiences of combat soldiers and those of battered women, we have inserted parallel wording in a quotation from Goodwin's (1987) description of PTSD victims.

> Due to circumstances of war [her married life], extended grieving was unproductive [and not allowed] and could become a liability [exacerbating her batterer's guilt, leading to increased outbursts]. Grief was handled as quickly as possible [to make way for the honeymoon stage]. Many soldiers [battered women] reported feeling numb. They felt depressed and unable to tell anyone. "How can I tell my wife [neighbor/friend/family member/pastor]? She'd never understand. How can anyone who has not been there understand?"
>
> Essentially, Vietnam-style [home-style] combat held no final resolution of conflict for anyone. Regardless of how one might respond, the overall outcome seemed to be an endless production of casualties with no perceivable positive results. They found little support from their friends and neighbors back home, the people in whose name so many people were drafted into military service [a battering relationship]. They felt helpless. They returned to the United States trying to put some positive resolution to this episode in their lives, but the atmosphere at home was hopeless. They were still helpless. (p. 8)

PTSD in battered women represents a configuration of factors: high arousal, high avoidance, intrusive memories, memory loss, and cognitive confusion. A number of researchers have diagnosed PTSD in battered women. Houskamp and

Foy (1991) indicated that 45% of their sample met full criteria on the *DSM-IV* for PTSD (also see Astin, Ogland-Hand, Coleman, & Foy, 1995; Kemp et al., 1991). In two samples of battered women seeking treatment, more than 60% experienced PTSD symptoms (Saunders, 1994). A more recent study revealed that 81% of a group of physically abused women and 63% of a verbally abused group met PTSD criteria (Kemp, Green, Hovanitz, & Rawlings, 1995). Prior to the research documenting PTSD, Painter and Dutton (1985) noted that some abused women behaved like disaster victims who continued to suffer extreme emotional reactions brought about by prolonged stress.

The extent and severity of exposure to violence, as judged by the revised Conflict Tactics Scale (CTS), is significantly correlated with severity of PTSD symptomatology in battered women. Sustained contact with the batterer through such events as court appearances, along with his continuing threats, "is likely to have significant influence on symptomology" (Houskamp & Foy, 1991, p. 374). Kemp et al. (1991) established that subjective abuse-related stress and actual assault level correlated positively with PTSD, anxiety, and depression. For the most part, the more severe and more chronic the trauma, the more extreme the symptoms (see Astin et al., 1990; Houskamp & Foy, 1991).

GINGER AND FERNANDO

CASE STUDY

Ginger went to counseling because her supervisor told her that "whatever it is that is bothering you is negatively affecting your work." Ginger's symptoms included emotional anesthesia (diminished responsiveness), inability to concentrate or complete projects she had started, difficulty in getting to sleep, and nightmares when she finally did sleep. She was a nurse and earned substantially more money than Fernando, who worked in a restaurant. They had been married for 5 years.

The beatings had been going on for the past 3 years, but the humiliation and emotional assaults had gone on longer than that. One night, while she was making dinner, she heard Fernando muttering in the living room. She knew that he was angry. Then, she heard something break. When she looked in the living room, her new coffee table had been flattened, and her crystal bowl was flying into the wall. Ginger tried to calm him, but he stormed out of the apartment. She cleaned up the mess one more time.

On one occasion, Fernando screamed at her in front of her sister because "she thinks she is too important to do my laundry and is too busy with her important job to cook and clean for me." He called her *gorda* (fat) and told her she was ugly

CASE STUDY (continued)

and disgusting, and no one would want her. Then, a week later, he beat her for coming on to a neighbor in the elevator.

The ultimate humiliation for Ginger was coming home from work and finding Fernando in bed with a prostitute. This time, she did the screaming, and this time, he beat her for embarrassing him. Later, he suggested that they both be tested for HIV.

Ginger closed herself off from friends and family. She lost interest in her life and avoided any situation that could put her in jeopardy. In fact, Ginger appeared more depressed and anxious than many of her clients in the psychiatric unit at the hospital.

Avoidance behavior is a central feature of PTSD and a basic coping strategy employed by Ginger and other battered women. In one study of battered women, physical arousal (i.e., hypersensitivity) was the most common symptom manifested; denial (i.e., avoidance) symptoms were second; reexperiencing symptoms (i.e., intrusive thoughts) was third (Kemp et al., 1995). An earlier study showed similar results, and that the levels of stress suffered by the women were actually higher than those found for a community sample of Vietnam veterans (Green, Lindy, Grace, & Glese, 1989).

Learning experiments with animals offer an explanation for some of the PTSD-associated behaviors of battered women. Rats in a Skinner box learn to press a bar to escape from or avoid a shock. In escape and avoidance learning, the animal must learn to make a response (press the bar) to escape or avoid pain. (See Appendix C, Sections 10 and 11, for a learning explanation of avoidance behavior.)

A battered woman might learn to avoid battering through self-protective actions (Langford, 1996). For example, if she is talking to a friend on the phone when the threats occur, she may hang up and start dinner, move to what she considers to be a safe area of the house, or leave the area entirely. She may avoid going home or move out for a period of time, avoid intimacy, or withdraw from her partner emotionally (Wuest & Merritt-Gray, 1999).

One of the most remarkable aspects of responses learned through avoidance conditioning techniques is their persistence (or failure to extinguish). In one experiment, dogs learned to avoid a traumatic shock by jumping over a barrier after a warning signal (tone). In a second phase, the experimenters turned off all the equipment so that the dogs were not shocked no matter what they did. When the investigators occasionally presented the tone during this period, the dogs continued jumping over the barrier. They continued jumping for more than 200 trials! They never learned that they did not need to jump to avoid a painful shock. They seemed unwilling to take the risk of not jumping (Solomon, Kamin, & Wynne, 1953).

An extrapolation of the persistence of avoidance learning to battering relationships may help explain the inflexible behavior of some battered women. Battered women who have escaped beatings through some behaviors, such as being sexually available, compliant, or nonconfrontive with their partners, may come to rely on these behaviors and may use them even when no beating is imminent. The problem of persistent nonadaptive responding will also become apparent to therapists working with individuals conditioned in this manner. Battered women may feel unable to make changes in their behavior. Moreover, the extreme fear brought about by the abuse may not diminish (extinguish) for many years.

An investigation of the effects of abuse on attachment styles uncovered two results (Justice & Hirt, 1992). Compared to nonabused women, abused women scored significantly higher on Emotional Detachment, specifically on the factors of Angry Withdrawal and Availability. Angry Withdrawal reflects an avoidance coping style. Availability refers to the expectation that responses to one's needs will not be positive. PTSD in battered women represents this combination of high arousal and high avoidance.

In an English study of male and female victims of violent assaults (including battered women), behavioral changes were apparent in 66% of the sample immediately after the assault. These changes remained for at least 6 months in 25% of the victims (Shepherd, 1990). The most common behavioral change was avoidance of the location where the attack had occurred. Other symptoms were physical problems and emotional distress.

Researchers have established that a number of subjective and objective factors mediate a victim's response to trauma. Some factors include the duration, frequency, and intensity of catastrophic events. A comprehensive review of studies on stress and interpersonal violence found that subjective factors, such as one's perception of the degree of threat and level of self-blame, contributed twice as much to the magnitude of psychological distress as did objective factors, such as physical injury or use of a weapon (Weaver & Clum, 1995).

Amick-McMullen et al. (1989) introduced a learning conceptualization (two-process avoidance theory) to explain the occurrence and maintenance of PTSD. In this theory, two processes occur: classical conditioning (fear) and operant conditioning (avoidance response, e.g., run to a safe location) (Mowrer, 1947; Rescorla & Solomon, 1967). In the first process, a person (or animal) becomes classically conditioned to fear a stimulus, such as the ringing of the phone paired with an aversive message (e.g., "Your brother has been killed"). In the second process, the person becomes operantly conditioned to respond by asking others to answer the phone to avoid the fear generated by the stimulus of the phone message.

Preventing the fear associated with such a message is reinforcing and therefore maintains the avoidance behavior. Unfortunately, one core feature of PTSD is the constant cognitive reexperiencing of the stressful event. This recurrence helps to maintain a high level of anxiety. To counteract the anxiety generated by the mental replays, an individual must repeatedly expend energy to monitor his or her actions. Even when someone is feeling less stressed, the occurrence of a very similar event can elicit the fear all over again. In learning terms, experiencing the fear again, after a respite, is called *spontaneous recovery* (i.e., of the fear; refer to Appendix C, Section 12).

CASE STUDY

WANDA AND PAUL

Wanda paid a high price for having fun. Paul went through her closet, removed her fancy dresses, and ripped them to shreds. He wanted to punish her for dancing with other men at her cousin's wedding. Actually, this was not the first time that she had been punished for "indiscretions." He had slapped her and had broken the phone because she had talked with her sister twice in one week.

Wanda spent a lot of time questioning her behavior. Activities that used to seem normal became distorted in her own mind: "Maybe I do spend too much time on the phone or with my family." "I shouldn't have danced with other men at my cousin's wedding."

A little at a time, Wanda withdrew and avoided contact with people who upset Paul. If she was on the phone, and Paul entered the room, she jumped. She forgot what life before Paul had been like, and that she used to be happy.

FRUSTRATION AND PROBLEM SOLVING

For a battered woman, her desire to be close to her partner and to have a happy home is countered by the reality of her husband's violence. Frustration generated by this approach-avoidance conflict may diminish her ability to solve problems effectively. For animals caught in an approach-avoidance situation, frustration develops when a problem leading to a reward becomes unsolvable, and attempts at solution are painful and presumably create fear. Some of the consequences for the laboratory animals were the development of inflexible, rigid behavior; refusal to behave; and unsuccessful attempts to escape. (Turn to Appendix C, Section 14 for an explanation of Maier's 1949 animal experiment on frustration.)

How is this animal research relevant to human behavior? Maguire and Corbett (1987) found that crime victims (robbery and assault) experienced severe symptoms, including an inability to perform ordinary tasks. Presumably, the fear generated by the need to focus on surviving is at the root of any special problem-solving difficulties noted in battered women (see Pelletier-Brown, 1998). Launius and Jensen (1987) studied problem solving in three different groups of women: (a) nonbattered women in therapy for anxiety and depression, (b) nonbattered women who were not in therapy, and (c) battered women. All three groups received everyday problems to solve, such as, "You are in a long line in the theater and two people cut in ahead of you. You don't appreciate this. What can you do?"

Battered women selected and generated fewer effective solutions to the situations presented than did the other groups. In a test involving a hypothetical abuse situation, however, they showed no deficit. In fact, data indicated that battered women solved a higher number of relationship problems than did nonbattered women (Campbell, 1989a). Nevertheless, in situations with their male partners, they were more passive and less assertive than the other women (also see Claerhout, Elder, & Janes, 1982; Launius & Lindquist, 1988).

Several investigations have established that battered women's coping strategies are deficient compared to samples of nonbattered women (e.g., Anson & Sagy, 1995; Kemp et al., 1995). Battered women were less apt to use active coping strategies (obtaining social support, reframing stressful events, and seeking spiritual support), but significantly more apt to use passive strategies (fantasizing) (Finn, 1985; Hodson, 1982; Nurius et al., 1992). The use of wishful thinking is especially prevalent in battered women. In a group of violent crime victims (not only battered women), one investigator found a positive link between the severity of symptoms and *both* avoidance and active coping styles (Kemp et al., 1995; Sutliff, 1995). Walker (1984) conjectured that active coping behaviors such as confrontation might escalate the abuse. One study found that as stress levels increased, effective coping strategies decreased (Gellen, Hoffman, Jones, & Stone, 1984).

Problem-solving deficits seem to be situation-specific and an outcome of the cognitive distortions associated with PTSD. Survival mandates a focus of attention on the person who controls the situation. From this perspective, the battered woman's attention and problem-solving abilities seem to be pointed in the practical direction (Campbell, 1989a). Trimpey (1989) speculates that a battered woman's inability to effectively generate solutions to some problems is caused by the anxiety brought on by pervasive physical and psychological violence. Russell et al. (1989) found that abused women were significantly more anxious, confused, and fatigued than were nonbattered women. In an important longitudinal study, battered women's self-care was similar to that of other adult women, but worsened over the 3½-year duration of the study for those still involved in abusive relationships (Campbell & Soeken, 1999).

Finn (1985) and Maertz (1990) demonstrated that problem-solving deficits were not solely a consequence of abuse, but also an outcome of the stress induced by unsuccessful problem-solving attempts. Negative effects of extreme stress are not limited to battered women. Depressed and anxious subjects in other populations also manifest problem-solving deficits (Gotlib & Asarnow, 1979; Nezu & Ronan, 1986).

Effects of frustration in animals vary, however, depending upon the design of the experiment. Amsel and Rousel (1972) rewarded rats twice, first after a short run and again after another run. After the animals adjusted to that pattern, the researchers removed the first reward. The animals began to run faster to get the second reward. In other words, the rats performed more but got less. Researchers interpreted this outcome as increased performance motivated by frustration. Analogously, battered women may be willing to do more to get less. In their frustration, they may be willing to try harder to please a partner who gives them less.

Increased performance, as a consequence of frustration, sharply contrasts with apathy and rigid responding as outcomes. It seems to us that the differences in the consequences (inflexibility vs. increased motivation) of the two types of frustration experiments arise from tangential differences generated by the dissimilarity in experimental procedures. That is, inflexibility (as in Maier, 1949) arises from the frustration accompanied by pain and fear, whereas increased motivation (as in Amsel & Rousel, 1972) emanates from frustration without fear and pain. Applying the findings of both these studies to abusive relationships, the more a battered woman is frustrated by her inability to improve her relationship and to end the violence, the more motivated she is to continue trying (Amsel & Rousel, 1972). Nevertheless, as fear increases, active problem-solving behavior diminishes (Maier, 1949). (Appendix C, Sections 14 and 15, review the animal research more fully.)

Clinical experience supports the notion that although battered women are creative and tenacious problem solvers, they may be trying to solve the wrong problem. Most battered women are striving to stop the violence by focusing on changing the abuser's behavior. One therapeutic goal should be to help them refocus their efforts instead on their own safety and the safety of their children. Designing safety or temporary escape plans can be useful in this regard.

LEARNED HELPLESSNESS

Additional theoretical rationales help complete the picture of why battered women stay. Gerow (1989) defines learned helplessness as "a condition in which a subject does not attempt to escape from a painful or noxious situation after learning in a previous, similar situation that escape is not possible" (p. 193). Hiroto (1974) empirically documented learned helplessness in humans using a sample of college students in an uncontrollable noise experiment. (See Appendix C, Section 15 for a more detailed description of the original animal experiment by Maier and Seligman, 1976.)

According to Martin Seligman (1975), there are three components to learned helplessness: (a) motivational impairment (passivity), (b) intellectual impairment (poor problem-solving ability), and (c) emotional trauma (increased feelings of helplessness, incompetence, frustration, and depression). Seligman particularly emphasized the similarity between learned helplessness and clinical depression (Peterson & Seligman, 1984). In the intervening years, as the learned helplessness model was applied to battered women, Peterson, Maier, and Seligman (1993) cautioned against misapplication. What appears to be passivity brought on by uncontrollable abuse may actually be passivity brought on by explicit and direct reinforcement. Many aspects of female socialization include rewards for being passive (e.g., Eagly & Johnson, 1990).

The constructs of internal and external locus of control reflect the degree to which an individual believes that the occurrence of rewards is dependent on his or her own behavior. This level of belief is a correlate of helplessness. External control is the perception that outcomes and reinforcements are dependent on forces outside of the individual (beyond one's control), such as God, luck, fate, chance, or powerful others. Internal control represents the perception that reinforcements depend on some quality or trait of the individual, such as his or her skill or interpersonal behaviors (Rotter, 1954).

Walker (1977) was the first researcher to extrapolate the original learned helplessness findings to battered women. Both Walker and Hendricks-Matthews (1982) suggested that learned helplessness causes battered women to make causal attributions that tend to keep them entrapped in the relationship, and one study detected higher levels of externality in victims than in nonvictims (Theodore, 1992). For example, a battered woman is likely to blame herself for the violence, as if she has done something to provoke the attacks. Unfortunately, society tends to reinforce this view. Making use of the reformulated learned helplessness model, Carlisle-Frank (1991) conjectured that battered women might have internal beliefs about controlling the violence in their homes, while having external beliefs about their ability to escape. In fact, battered women may have learned that they could not escape by actually having tried to do so, a type of *learned externality*.

There has been some disagreement over the appropriateness of applying the learned helplessness model to battered women (see Rhodes & McKenzie, 1998, for a review). In addition to depression, investigators testing the model have examined locus of control, coping styles, and help-seeking behavior. Walker (1984) used the Levenson Locus of Control Scale (Levenson, 1973) to measure three different types of control (internal, powerful others, and chance) in battered women. She tested the hypothesis that battered women would score high on the powerful others and chance dimensions. The women, however, scored high on all three scales. From these data, Walker suggested that battered women believe that they have a great amount of control over their lives, and that they will eventually be able to change their batterer's behavior—a sort of learned hopefulness as described previously (also see Arias, Lyons, & Street, 1997; Follingstad et al., 1992).

Wauchope (1988) attempted to use the relationship between help-seeking behavior and severity of violence as a test of learned helplessness theory. Her findings indicated that as the severity of violence increased, women were more likely, rather than less likely, to seek help (also see Gelles & Harrop, 1989). She interpreted her findings as failing to support learned helplessness theory.

A later study found that severity of abuse was not only related to increased help-seeking behavior, but also to increased levels of helplessness. The researchers concluded that help-seeking behavior and helplessness are not equivalent or mutually exclusive. In fact, they theorized that women who are severely abused become helpless, believing that the only avenue of escape is through the assistance of others; thus, they seek help (Wilson, Vercella, Brems, Benning, & Renfro, 1992). Furthermore, Marshall (1996) discovered that different types of abuse, such as psychological, physical, or sexual abuse, are related to different ways of seeking help.

Other researchers also have found that battered women rank high on help-seeking behaviors (Campbell, Miller, Cardwell, & Belknap, 1994; Goodman et al., in press; Hutchison & Hirschel, 1998; Sullivan, 1991a). A 1996 national random telephone survey of 6,766 women identified 2,811 female survivors of partner violence, 226 of whom had been assaulted within the past 5 years. Of the assaulted group, 38% contacted the police, 32% sought a restraining order, and 31% sought medical care. Many of these women (41%) failed to access any services. Factors associated with failure to obtain help were as follows: (a) higher income; (b) no children in the house; (c) employment, homemaker, or school activities; (d) higher educational attainment; (e) nonminority racial status; and (e) youthfulness (Hathaway et al., 1998). Finally, in one study of battered women with protection orders, 78% did seek help other than emergency protection orders, but almost half (46%) turned to neighbors and friends rather than to shelters (Keilitz et al., 1998).

Unfortunately, those seeking help may feel even more helpless because of society's response. Some criminal justice personnel, for instance, may disparage victims, blame them, side with the batterer, and trivialize their abuse. According to Erez and Belknap (1998), the one-size-fits-all approach to criminal justice processing leaves some women feeling powerless and depressed.

JANICE

Janice finally called the police, who arrested her violent boyfriend, Adam. The police officers were sensitive and supportive about her assault, and they gave her a shelter hotline number. The shelter advocate listened to Janice's story and made appropriate referrals to a battered woman's group, a victim advocate in the courts, and a therapist.

The court advocate and the city prosecutor got Janice ready for her day in court, which occurred 6 weeks after the incident. She was not prepared, however, for the complexity of the system or the outcomes. Her injuries were tangible and substantial. Six weeks after her boyfriend punched her in the face, her eyes were still bruised and swollen. The doctor had removed the stitches over her upper lip, but the scar was an angry red.

Janice was not emotionally ready to see Adam again. When he appeared in court, he was different. He seemed contrite, and the judge thought so, too. The final results of Janice's hours of help-seeking ended this way:

- Adam had to attend an abusers' group counseling program.
- He had to pay restitution to Janice, which was supposed to be $100 a month for 2 years but totaled only $50. She received the money before Adam's records were buried in a probation bank caseload of 5,000.
- Janice's therapist advised her to make contact with Adam's therapist, but the therapist never returned the call.
- Janice lost her job because of time lost while she sought medical attention and made court appearances.
- She then lost her apartment because of her lost income and because Adam did not pay the restitution that she needed for her rent.

Janice, a 35-year-old professional woman, lost her home, her job, and her boyfriend. Adam kept his home, his job, and found a new romantic interest while he was attending his recovery program.

Evidence from studies of help-seeking activity and other studies suggests that learned helplessness may be a contributing factor to battered women's behavior, but probably not the most important component in keeping them entrapped (see Rhodes & McKenzie, 1998, for a review). It seems probable that, like problem-solving deficits, learned helplessness may be situation-specific, a finding consistent with the animal studies (Maier & Seligman, 1976). A battered woman may have learned helplessness regarding certain areas of her life, but not all. Another possibility is that as the abuse occurs more frequently and the severity escalates, the learned helplessness generalizes. Consider the cases of battered women who believe that homicide or suicide are their only viable options.

Battered women are very focused on the abuse and the abuser. It becomes the predominant theme of family life and the pivotal feature around which everything else revolves. It would make sense that generalized problem solving and coping might be impaired as energy goes to problem solving and coping with the abuser. For the most part, the behavior of the battered woman has little long-term effect on what happens within the relationship. If she stops talking to friends on the phone because it upsets him, sooner or later, something else will trigger the controlling behavior or the violent episode. Even her effective problem solving may only delay the abuse; it will not stop it. Support for the lack of control that battered women have over an abuser's behavior comes from a study of abusive couples' arguments. *None* of a wife's behaviors successfully suppressed a husband's violence once it began (Jacobson et al., 1994).

According to the model of social support provided by Dunkel-Schetter, Folkman, and Lazarus (1987), people need to have social support systems in place, including a network of individuals who can function appropriately in times of stress. Seeking help is easier if there is someone tangible from whom to seek it. A number of battered women lack adequate and available social support systems. Unfortunately, having a support network in place may be a double-edged sword. For example, a friend might listen with concern to a neighbor's story of abuse, but then insist that the neighbor's only answer is an immediate divorce. This theory of social obstruction, set forth by Gurley (1989), proposes that helpfulness and harmfulness are independent dimensions that may coexist.

THE BATTERED WOMAN SYNDROME

> While the law specifically, and society in general, have offered little help to the battered wife, and indeed may be partially responsible for the actions of those who strike back violently, many of these women now face homicide charges brought by the same society and its legal system. (Anonymous, cited in Nerney, 1987, p. 21)

There has been confusion concerning the definition of the Battered Woman Syndrome (BWS). Some authors use the abusive acts committed against the woman as the defining aspects of BWS (e.g., severity, frequency of assaults) (see Campbell, 1990). Walker (1985a), in contrast, conceptualizes the syndrome as a severe stress reaction, a subcategory of PTSD. Basic personality components of BWS include fear, depression, guilt, passivity, and low self-esteem (Douglas, 1987).

In 1992, Dutton developed a model of PTSD that suggested that battered women experience great stress from being battered, and this alters their cognitions. The disturbance in the woman's intimate relationships (e.g., attachment) is a factor as well. Not all women react to battering the same way because they vary in the levels of social support they receive, the level of concurrent stress in their lives, the level of premarital (e.g., childhood) abuse they have experienced, and the severity of the current violence directed against them. Given the difficulties in defining BWS, Follingstad (1998) speculates that it might be best just to drop the BWS terminology and simply rely on the PTSD framework and the more specific definition by the American Psychiatric Society.

BWS may be conceptualized as a set of personality attributes brought on by abuse that render the victim more able to survive in the relationship and less able to escape it. The battered woman's belief that escape is impossible, and the depression that accompanies this belief, lead to her entrapment in the relationship. The three components of the syndrome are as follows: (a) behaviors brought on by victimization, (b) learned helplessness behavior, and (c) self-destructive coping behaviors.

The Violence Against Women Act (VAWA) of 1994 (Public Law 103-322, Title IV) called for a report on a number of factors involving BWS: (a) medical and psychological bases; (b) the use of BWS in trials; and (c) the perceptions of judges, prosecutors, and defense attorneys regarding the effects of BWS evidence in criminal trials (U.S. Department of Justice, 1996). The report found the following:

1. The name BWS does not satisfactorily reflect the scientific knowledge accumulated, and it carries the implication of a malady or a single pattern of responses to battering. Also *there is no "battered woman's defense" per se,* only expert testimony.

2. There is an extensive body of literature about the dynamics of battering and stress reactions to battering.

3. Expert testimony tends to increase knowledge about domestic violence and improves the ability of juries to reach decisions.

When accepted by the court, defense attorneys have used PTSD symptomatology to negotiate and diminish responsibility for a criminal act (Sparr, 1996). The PTSD defense presents several challenges to defense attorneys. Primarily, a diagnosis of PTSD stems from *subjective* self-reports. Obviously, people striving to avoid criminal punishments might try to distort their symptoms. Furthermore, defense attorneys must show a causal connection between PTSD symptoms and the alleged criminal act. That is, something about the symptoms (e.g., a flashback) *caused* the defendant to commit the criminal act. Attorneys also must show that the defendant's PTSD stemmed from a specifiable stressor (e.g., rape), rather than from past childhood traumas or other stressful events (Sparr, 1996).

Some legal scholars use BWS to expand the concept of legal self-defense. This defense holds that a battered woman is virtually held hostage in a violent household by a man who isolates and terrorizes her, convincing her that if she leaves, he will track her down and kill her. Violence and threats usually occur more frequently, and even when there is a period of alleged nonviolence, abused women do not feel safe. A mood of danger has been created that predisposes the victim to an ongoing state of chronic fear and arousal (hypervigilance). DePaul (1992) describes the syndrome as "the situation of a long-time victim of physical, sexual, and psychological abuse who loses self-confidence, feels trapped, and eventually strikes back, assaulting or killing the abuser" (p. 5) (also see Mones, 1992).

An account of 1988 data on 540 spouse murder cases from the nation's 75 largest counties detailed several outcomes. Husbands were defendants in 59% of the cases and wives in 41%. Juries or judges convicted 87% of male defendants and 70% of female defendants (Langan & Dawson, 1995; see Felson & Messner, 1998). In terms of provocation, prosecutors' files indicated that at or around the time of the murder, husbands had assaulted 44% of the female defendants, whereas wives had assaulted only 10% of male defendants (Langan & Dawson, 1995; also see Follingstad, Brondino, & Kleinfelter, 1996; O'Keefe, 1997).

Although it is possible that battered women's behavioral repertoires included the elements seen in BWS before the battering, it is more likely that the fear engendered by the violence produced the conditions. At the very least, violence by a loved one can create what civil law calls the "exacerbation of a pre-existing condition." Legal scholars and battered women's advocates argue that the experiences of battered women are unique and should be explained to a jury (Dodge & Greene, 1991). According to DePaul (1992),

> Without expert testimony to explain how women come to feel so dependent or fearful that they cannot leave an abusive relationship, juries often are left to won-

der why the woman did not walk out long before she felt compelled to retaliate. (p. 5)

One investigation of jurors' knowledge about the experiences of battered women found that jurors were relatively informed about the findings of empirical research on a number of issues: Violence escalates in a relationship; women are anxious and depressed, feel helpless, and suffer in many ways; battered women are afraid that their spouses might kill them; and leaving the batterer may lead to further harm. Individuals who serve on juries have much less information about other factors: battered women blame themselves, feel dependent on their husbands, accept their spouses' promises to change, can predict when the violence will occur, even occasionally provoke an assault to end the build-up of tension, and come to believe that they must use deadly force to stay alive (Greene, Raitz, & Lindblad, 1989).

Expert testimony should focus on the impact of violence and the woman's perception of threat. As an example, suppose a woman's husband indicates in obvious or subtle ways that he is going to give her "what for" when he gets up from his nap. Further suppose that he has beaten her previously under similar circumstances. She might believe the time has come to keep him from waking up. The threat, which has been paired with certain violence in the past, takes on a reality of its own. The nap itself can become a generalized cue that signals to a woman that danger lies ahead. The nap can become a blinking red light (see STEPS to End Family Violence, 1987).

Jurik and Winn (1990) wanted to determine whether homicide by females has been affected by women's liberation, and whether gender differences were still relevant. Their sample included 108 male-perpetrated homicides and 50 female-perpetrated homicides. Results indicated that when women kill, they generally kill in their own homes during domestic conflict. They are prone to kill male partners within a context of economic dependence, past attacks, and victim-initiated violence. In contrast, men are more likely to kill someone away from the home, and they usually initiate the violence when they kill (see also Goetting, 1991). Although more men kill women than the reverse, women almost always kill in an intimate setting. An estimated 37% of women inmates reported that the victim of their violence had been a relative or intimate. Among these offenders, two thirds had killed either their spouse or a family member (sibling, child) (Greenfeld & Minor-Harper, 1991).

In one study of more than 1,600 homicides, self-defense characterized almost all killings by females, but almost none by males. A number of other actions and motives typified male killers, but not females: (a) Men often hunt down and kill spouses who have left them; (b) men kill as part of a planned murder-suicide;

(c) men kill in response to revelations of wifely infidelity, although men are generally more adulterous than women; (d) men kill after subjecting their wives to lengthy periods of coercive abuse and assaults; and (e) men perpetrate family massacres (Wilson & Daly, 1992).

The Report of the Governor's Committee to Study Sentencing and Correctional Alternatives for Women Convicted of Crime, State of Maryland, 1988 (cited in "Violence and Women Offenders," 1990) established that 43% of the women in prisons and jails in Maryland had been physically abused, and 33% had been sexually abused. According to California State Assembly member Sheila Kuehl (personal communication, April 16, 1992), who worked on the California Clemency Project for battered women who kill, 93% of the women imprisoned for homicide in California claim to have killed their batterers.

In a study of men and women in Florida prisons for spousal homicide, 73% of the women reported being physically abused by their husbands (Barnard, Vera, Vera, & Newman, 1982). For men, the precipitating event was usually some form of perceived rejection. Barnard and his colleagues called these murders of wives by husbands *sex-role threat homicides.* In contrast, the women killed in response to what they saw as an attack or threat by their partner. In reality, most battered women who kill are no threat to society. Nevertheless, few women are acquitted at trials; most (72%-80%) are convicted or accept a plea, and many receive very long sentences (Osthoff, 1992). A battered woman may perceive homicide to be her only viable option. Defense attorney Leslie Abramson (cited in Gibbs, 1993) has argued: "Morally and legally, she should not be expected to wait until his hands are around her neck" (p. 43). She believes that whereas men may kill out of wounded pride, women most often kill out of fear (Abramson, 1994).

The BWS defense, however, is controversial. A number of observers worry that husband killings will go unpunished. "What message are we giving women when they can kill their husbands and get away with it?" Across the years, the authors have not seen or heard of any hesitation in using the "heat of passion" defense. This defense is notoriously one-sided, a gendered defense for men who killed their wives or their wives' lovers when they found them in flagrante delicto (in the act of sexual intercourse). Its use has gradually expanded to include other female infractions (e.g., when a woman leaves her spouse).

The standard for assessing the nature of self-defense has been euphemistically called the reasonable man's defense. In other words, what would a reasonable man do in this situation? Reasonable women and children may have different perceptions about what is life-threatening and react in different and distinct ways (Osthoff, 1992).

PATRICIA

Patricia was the top student in her nursing program and a grandmother when she killed her husband. Her abuse had been primarily sexual (rape and sodomy with injury) and emotional (threats to kill her or her children). He had pushed her around for years, but she did not even count that behavior as violent.

Her case was given to an overworked public defender, and the battered woman's expert received preparation for her testimony one hour before she appeared on the stand. Even though there were several people who could have corroborated the deceased's "weird behavior," the only witness her attorney called in her defense was a teacher who had a love affair with Patricia and remained her friend.

Patricia was planning to leave her abusive husband when he threatened to sexually abuse her 3-year-old grandson. She paid a neighbor $300 to kill her abuser. The prosecutor charged Patricia with murder for financial gain, because she was the beneficiary on her husband's $1,500 life insurance policy. She confessed to everything on the stand except wanting the money or wanting him dead. She wanted the jury, the judge, the attorneys, and everyone in the courtroom to understand that she just wanted to protect her grandson.

Patricia did not have the benefit of a fully developed battered woman's defense. The judge, using the reasonable man defense as a yardstick, found her guilty of murder with special circumstances. Patricia is serving a life sentence without the possibility of parole.

According to Schneider (1986), the reasonable man standard needs extension to a reasonable woman standard. Increasingly, this viewpoint is being heard. Many states now allow expert testimony on BWS, which was previously seen as more prejudicial than informative. Virtually all states are reexamining cases in which females claimed they killed a spouse or lover who abused them. The governors of California, Florida, Illinois, Maryland, and Ohio have already commuted some sentences or granted clemency (Ammons, 1994).

The 1987 Committee on Domestic Violence and Incarcerated Women recognized that the criminal justice system does not act effectively to protect women from being beaten ("Panel Says," 1987). A battered woman may not be able to obtain a restraining order or keep it in effect. She may be unable to obtain even temporary financial support for a 30-day period. The court will most likely allow her abuser visitation with the children. In the end, no one can guarantee her safety ("Domestic Violence in the Courts," 1989). The 1987 Committee concluded that the criminal justice system's response was "inconsistent and inadequate" ("Panel Says," 1987). A New York Committee on Domestic Violence (STEPS to End Family Violence, 1987) has concluded that killing an assaultive male should not be the only option left to battered women. When leaving is more dangerous than staying, but staying amounts to living in daily terror, the battered woman's dilemma can reach its final, catastrophic climax. It remains an ongoing societal struggle to find a balance between expressing compassionate concern for victims of marital violence and condoning violence as the justifiable response.

SUMMARY

A woman's acceptance of responsibility for the violence in her home, coupled with her inability to stop it, create confusion and frustration, and obstruct certain forms of effective problem solving. If she is unable to see any relationship between what she does and what happens to her, it is likely that she will feel helpless and depressed.

Results from learning experiments have explained and simplified the mechanisms underlying a battered woman's avoidance-motivated behaviors as well as the development of PTSD symptoms. Whereas the concept of learned helplessness helps explain some aspects of her behavior, such as her problem-solving deficits and ineffective coping styles, PTSD provides a broader psychological and physiological framework. PTSD documents more fully the experiences of individuals exposed to chronic or severe trauma, such as battering. If society will not help the battered woman and she cannot stop the violence and perceives that she has no other options, a day may come when she makes a lethal choice: to kill her abuser.

Catalysts for Change 6

CHAPTER OVERVIEW

This chapter is dedicated to the community change agents of the 1970s who uncovered a problem that had been buried and unnamed. That problem is the violence directed against women in their homes—the places that have been synonymous with women's safety. Without the feminist movement, battered wives would still be deadbolted into their houses and manacled to their abusers. These grassroots pioneers began organizing to create solutions. This chapter is about those solutions and the solutions for the future.

IMPORTANCE OF PREVENTION

"The progressive nature of domestic violence, along with such consequences as substance abuse, depression, and attempted suicide, underscores the importance of early recognition and intervention" ("The Battered Woman," 1989, p. 104). In addition to the life-altering consequences for women, exposure of children to family violence has profoundly negative effects. Given the serious consequences to women, children, and society, steps to prevent battering are essential.

For change to happen, basic ideological transformations must occur, and "men have a particular role to play in educating other men about the nature of abuse and how men can change" (Adams & McCormick, 1982, p. 171). Glen Good, President of the Society for the Psychological Study of Men and Masculinity (SPSMM), a division of the American Psychological Association, has brought attention to the problems of masculine socialization (see also Pollack, 1999). According to Good (1998),

> Problems like violence, substance abuse, relationship issues, parenting problems, and poor health habits need attention. We also need to develop intervention for more recently identified masculinity-related problems, such as lack of emotional

> competence, defensive self-sufficiency, poor sexual integrity, and uninvolved fathers. (p. 3)

Males are both killers and victims. Homicide is the second leading cause of death for young men ages 15-24 and the leading cause of death among young Black men (see DuRant, Cadenhead, Pendergrast, Slavens, & Linder, 1994, for a review). Today's adolescents are in grave conflict about the masculine role, as is society. It is time for society to change its model of masculinity. People need to let real boys be diverse, loving, caring, and emotionally expressive (Good, 1998).

Society needs to change not only its model of masculinity, but also its treatment of women everywhere. Organizations that have traditionally championed human rights should recognize the inhumane treatment of women around the globe as a *human rights* issue (Rosen, 1991). Murphy and Meyer (1991) proposed that "treatment in the area of spousal violence should be part of a larger movement designed to alter the social factors that contribute to violence against women and that keep women trapped in abusive relationships" (p. 99).

Children exposed to family violence suffer from increased anxiety, low self-esteem, truancy, low school achievement, and other behavioral problems (Jaffe, Hastings, & Reitzel, 1992). Toddlers as young as three are affected (Main & George, 1985). Early and appropriate intervention with children can counteract the insidious consequences of exposure to parental violence, but interventions must be designed according to the emotional, behavioral, cognitive, social, and physiological functioning of the child.

Lynn Loar, a children's advocate, and Carol Rathmann, Director of the Sonoma County Humane Society, have pioneered a program to teach abused and neglected children gentleness with living things. The program facilitators introduce the children to gardening, instilling in them a sense that they can nurture and cause beautiful or edible things to grow. They start the children with plants, because they know that children who live with abuse might also perpetrate it when they became frustrated. Loar and Rathmann did not want the children in their program to hurt an animal or carry the guilt of having harmed a pet. Once the fledgling farmers have mastered the gentle caretaking of plants and flowers, they are promoted to playing with large, sturdy animals.

The volunteers and staff at the Sonoma County Humane Society want to teach children that touch does not need to be frightening; it can be healing, gentle, and loving. They want to promote trusting relationships between the children and adults. The children learn both empathy and compassion through human interaction and by tending the animals. They learn to be patient, because the plants and animals have different schedules from those of the people who care for them. These traumatized children learn that they can be superheroes who nurture and protect other living creatures, and that they themselves are worthy of care and attention. They learn values that are incompatible with violence (Loar & Rathmann, 1994).

Children living in abusive families need to label and deal with their emotional reactions to the violence. They need to develop safety skills and learn how to develop social support networks. They also need to understand that they are not responsible for the violence in their families (Gruzinski, Brink, & Edleson, 1988). An exciting new treatment developed by Alicia Liberman and her associates (cited in Zorza, 1999b) considers the mother and the child as dual victims of domestic violence and treats them both through a series of weekly home visits. The treatment led to a dramatic reduction in PTSD symptomatology in both mother and child, a decrease in the number of mothers who returned to their abusers, and an amazing increase in children's tested IQs (10-25 points).

Education is an essential piece of primary prevention programs and has the potential to reach across generational and cultural differences. There is a great need for education that conveys the message that family violence will not be tolerated (Kaci, 1990; Straus, 1983). Evidence suggests that public service announcements and documentaries have been successful in that regard (Kaci, 1990). In New Jersey, advocates have initiated a program to offer information to battered women. The underlying philosophy is that knowledge about domestic violence and the belief that they are not alone will crack through denial and isolation and reinforce action. Some doctors allow educational films to be shown in their waiting rooms and in hospital lobbies. These films enlighten the public about the causes and effects of spouse abuse; the legal consequences; and remedies, including emergency protective orders and local resources.[1]

Prevention programs are also available in some schools. Barrie Levy and The Southern California Coalition on Battered Women developed a curriculum for junior and senior high schools called "Prevention Skills for Violence-Free Relationships" (Levy, 1984). One outgrowth of the program was the development at Jordan High School in Long Beach, California, of a family support group for students who lived in violent households or who had experienced dating violence. More recently, the Los Angeles Commission on Assaults Against Women (LACAAW) developed their "In Touch With Teens" curriculum. This innovative program uses teens and adults as facilitators (Aldrige, Friedman, & Occhiuzzo Giggans, 1995). Jaffe, Suderman, Reitzel, and Killip (1992) documented favorable changes in attitudes, behavior, and intentions following a large-scale, secondary school prevention program. Gender differences indicated that females had a greater sensitivity to domestic violence and women's equality than did males. Evidence is accumulating that education can change attitudes toward wife abuse (Wolfe et al., 1996). Even a 20-minute oral presentation to university students about domestic violence produced some changes (O'Neal & Dorn, 1998).

One area of concern is that teenagers do not define or recognize dating violence as a problem (Levy, 1993; Parrot & Bechhofer, 1991). Schools can become more involved in education and prevention (Krajewski, 1996). For example, one program prepared teens to provide resources and referrals for abused peers (Creighton & Kivel, 1993). There is also a clear need to design programs that attempt to reduce attitudes supportive of male violence (Avery-Leaf, Cascardi, O'Leary, & Cano, 1997; O'Keefe & Treister, 1998; Thorne-Finch, 1992). It is also crucial to educate parents about how to help their teens avoid dating violence (Levy & Occhiuzzo Giggans, 1995).

Jaffe, Hastings, and Reitzel (1992) make several recommendations for schools: (a) train personnel to recognize the behavior of children exposed to domestic abuse, (b) teach children conflict resolution skills, (c) establish a board to enlist agency services for referrals, and (d) develop a school protocol for handling disclosures. Because of mandatory child abuse reporting laws in every state, the school may intervene in spouse abuse because of the possibility of child endangerment. Along similar lines, screening for violence can be expanded to schools and pediatricians' offices, and parenting education can be provided (Sleutel, 1998).

One societal change that is necessary to prevent the transmission of violence across generations is to attack the problem of children's exposure to violence more effectively. By 1998, the legal system had made some headway but still failed to safeguard children's physical and mental health needs in a number of critical situations (Johnson, 1998). Utah has led the way to correcting some of these needs by including a child "witnessing parental abuse two or more times" as a form of child maltreatment chargeable as a misdemeanor (cited in Edleson, 1999).

Responding to research indicating that children chronically exposed to violence at home or in their communities are at much higher risk of becoming juvenile delinquents and adult criminals, President Clinton said that "children's exposure to violence has tremendous negative consequences . . . for them and for all the rest of us" ("President Announces Crackdown," 1998, p. 6). Clinton further stated: "It's time to send a message through the court that when a man assaults or kills someone in the presence of a child, he has committed not one horrendous act, but two" (p. 7) (also see Osofsky, 1998). The old saying, "an ounce of prevention is worth a pound of cure," has particular relevance when considering the consequences to future generations.

EMPOWERMENT OF BATTERED WOMEN

Empowerment strategies are an essential component of recovery for women already victimized by intimate violence. Empowerment involves two major aspects: (a) gaining power and (b) taking action along specific dimensions (e.g., personal/interpersonal or social/collective levels). *Individual empowerment* incorporates the notion of intrapsychic change. *Social or environmental empowerment* refers to deficiencies in the structure of forces in society (see The Center on Crime, Communities & Culture of the Open Society Institute, 1999, for national resources).

Women often pass through several different empowerment stages before they are able to change their feelings and cognitions about being battered. During the first stage, women feel fearful, angry, and powerless. During the second stage, victims become more aware of the danger of being victimized, and they start to place the blame for battering on the abuser. In the last stage, the woman is able to be more assertive and self-determined. She is likely to escape through getting a job or going back to school (see Paquet, Damant, Beaudoin, & Proulx, 1998, for a review).

Conditions central to the maintenance of abusive home environments are the self-perpetuating nature of family violence and the isolation in which it thrives. Battered women's programs can effect change by intervening in these processes. A number of studies have provided empirical evidence of favorable changes fostered by shelter programs. In one short-term outreach treatment, women reported a decrease in abuse and an increase in life satisfaction and perceived coping ability (McNamara, Ertl, Marsh, & Walker, 1997). A small study of 20 sheltered women showed that after 3 weeks in the shelter, the women were significantly less depressed, more hopeful, and had higher internal locus of control scores (Dziegielewski, Resnick, & Krause, 1996; also see Sedlak, 1988b, for a review).

Shelters also help women to seek appropriate support services in the community (Gondolf, 1988a). An emerging trend is to provide transitional housing and other postshelter services (Orava, McLeod, & Sharpe, 1996; Tutty, 1996). Battered women generally have favorable opinions of staff and the shelter experience. When funding problems force staff into multiple roles and increase their workloads, however, some residents have voiced concerns about the lack of staff's availability for one-on-one counseling (Tutty, Weaver, & Rothery, 1999).

In our opinion, battered women in a shelter can begin a restoration process by virtue of being separated from their abusers, feeling safe, having people with whom to talk about their problems, and working at a practical level to solve some of these problems. Battered women who have formed close relationships with other shelter residents or shelter staff are more likely to leave their abusive relationships (Dalto, 1983).

Hotline counselors and shelter staff are generally very creative and aware of community resources. Shelter workers explore options with a battered woman to help her devise a safety and housing plan. Referrals may include a funded, after-hours hotel; other emergency shelter (mission or church); a 24-hour coffee shop; or a friend or relative's home. Usually, within a week, space will become available in a battered women's program. For safe space outside of the area, a battered woman sometimes can obtain a small financial grant through such agencies as Traveler's Aid, Catholic Charities, Lutheran Social Services, or the YWCA.

The role of shelters has expanded as the special needs of underserved populations has come to the forefront (see Huisman, 1996, about Asian women; Valencia & Van Hoorn, 1999, about Latinas). For instance, shelters have begun training staff and upgrading facilities to accommodate disabled women (Reyna, 1995). Many shelters are now wheelchair accessible (ramps, wider doors) and have connections with specialized agencies in the community to meet the needs of disabled women. One point of progress has been the inclusion of special telecommunication devices for hearing-impaired callers (Danis et al., 1998).

Shelter programs are also becoming better prepared to meet the needs of older battered women (Vinton, 1998; also see Boudreau, 1993; Pillemer & Finkelhor, 1989). Wisconsin, one of the first states to implement special programs for abused elder women, has assisted other states in the development of protocols and programming. In a 1992 Florida survey of 6,026 women who were sheltered during the previous year, approximately 2% were over 60 years of age. In a 5-year follow-up study of these shelters, special programming had increased, as had the percentage of older staff members, volunteers, and board members (Vinton, Altholz, & Lobell, 1997). About one third offered outreach services, and 19% offered individual interventions for elder victims.

At the national level, the Women's Initiative of the American Association of Retired Persons (AARP) convened a forum bringing together service providers working with the elderly, battered women's advocates, and researchers. The Administration on Aging, an agency of the federal government, funded six demonstration projects in 1994-1995 that focused on the protection of older women against partner abuse (AARP, 1993, 1994; McKibben, 1988).

An AARP study recommended the use of safe houses, a type of sister-to-sister program for sheltering abused older women. Another innovative approach is the formation of multidisciplinary community teams (Hwalek, Williamson, & Stahl, 1991; Nachman, 1991; Nerenberg et al., 1990). Using a team approach not only improves victim identification, but also allows for joint decision making about which agency and type of intervention is best suited to the task (Matlaw & Spence, 1994).

Whether battered women choose to leave or stay in the relationship, either temporarily or permanently, appropriate counseling needs to be part of the package for real change to occur. Many professionals see the woman's choice as one between staying or leaving. A battered woman often experiences the conflict as, "Don't help me end the relationship, help me end the abuse" (Landenburger, 1989).

Although abused women who have counseling are significantly more likely to leave than women who do not (Frisch & MacKenzie, 1991), *leaving* as the measure of success of counseling is an inaccurate and invalid criterion (Brown, 1998). Leaving is a process for most battered women. Counselors need to acknowledge a battered woman's psychological upheaval during the process of leaving and help her regain an emotional balance. Women need to feel safe and eliminate the chaos in their lives. They especially need to salvage some sense of self-confidence and reclaim their selves (Brown, 1997; Kirkwood, 1993; Moss et al., 1997; Wuest & Merritt-Gray, 1999).

Battered women not only grieve their loss of self, but also the loss of their abusive partner. There are those who ask, "Where's the loss?" Most battered women, however, feel great deprivation and loss when their relationships end (Walker, 1984). Whereas some argue that battered women are grieving the loss of a relationship, others suggest that they are grieving the loss of their dreams and hopes (see Hoff, 1990; Landenburger, 1989; Wuest & Merritt-Gray, 1999). Negating that loss does not help the women. Assessing battered women's losses and dealing with them in a support group enables women to develop a new sense of self-determination and avoid the immobilizing effects of grief (Varvaro, 1991).

Some of the most important work with battered women is the remaking of their belief systems (see Malloy, 1986). To make this change, shelters, therapists, and battered women's support groups should help women to stop believing that they caused or can stop the abuse (Wetzel & Ross, 1983). One effective approach to changing beliefs is cognitive reappraisal. She must make some cognitive readjustments along the lines of defining the meaning of the violence, what caused it, and what role it plays in her life now (D'Zurilla, 1986).

There are several other ways to accomplish an attitudinal shift: (a) breaking the silence and isolation by confiding in someone else (Vaughn, 1987); (b) getting education regarding sex roles and their relationship to domestic violence and power inequality; (c) building resources outside of the relationship (Wilson et al., 1989); (d) developing empathy for other battered women and compassion for herself; and (e) grieving the loss of the relationship and her idealistic beliefs (Ferraro, 1979; Russell & Uhlemann, 1994).

Appropriate counseling should address the very real restrictions that women face in the world, in their relationships, and in stereotypic roles. At a practical level, counselors can role-play job interviewing techniques, assertion skills, parenting skills, and even basic apartment or house-hunting approaches. Gestalt techniques and other cognitive problem-solving strategies used in a group setting can be effective in helping abused women restore independent decision-making skills. Holiman and Schilit (1991) found that role playing, expressing feelings, and problem sharing assisted the women in altering their feelings of powerlessness. Some believe that self-defense training for women is critical. Self-defense training can tap into a woman's physical power. It offers her a constructive physical outlet for her emotions (Cummings, 1990).

Douglas and Colantuono (1987) have pinpointed the importance of social support in recovery from chronic abuse (also see Kemp et al., 1995). In one review, 63% of battered women who had little or no support returned to their abusers. In contrast, of those who had strong support systems, only 19% returned (Johnson, 1988). One of the great assets of 12-step and other self-help programs is the abundance and continuity of support that they provide. Chang (1989) has theorized that supportive involvement with others is critical in the transformation of a battered woman into a self-saver.

Sullivan and her associates proposed an experimental longitudinal study to ascertain specific community resources that women perceived as empowering (Sullivan, Basta et al., 1992; Sullivan, Rumptz, Campbell, Eby, & Davidson, 1996; Tan, Basta, Sullivan, & Davidson, 1995). Investigators assumed that the most effective interventions would be defined by the women themselves. This strategy also allowed the battered women to direct the intervention process.

An initial step was conducting a needs assessment survey of 141 sheltered women. The results indicated that more than 60% of the women needed legal assistance, and more than half needed jobs, further education, transportation, material goods, health care, social support, financial assistance, child care, and resources for their children. Almost 40% of the women needed housing (Sullivan, Tan, Basta, Rumptz, & Davidson, 1992).

The findings laid the groundwork for the development of a postshelter program that used female students as advocates. The advocates received training in the dynamics of woman battering, empathy, and active listening skills, as well as in strategies for generating and accessing community resources. Once an advocate was assigned to a woman, she began working with her one-on-one for 4 to

6 hours per week for a period of 10 weeks. Interventions were varied, practical, and specific to the woman's situation.

One advocate accompanied her client to a divorce workshop to learn about her legal rights. Another met with the formerly battered woman and a police officer for coffee to discuss a safety plan. Some advocates helped women register for school, look for work, meet neighbors, and locate child care. In other words, the advocates offered more than referrals. They helped the women make the system work for them.

The researchers assessed the effectiveness of the individually tailored interventions by asking the battered women to respond to six interviews: the first one immediately upon leaving the shelter, and successively at 10 weeks, 6 months, 12 months, 18 months, and 24 months. Some additional contacts also occurred between interviews. The results substantiated a strong relationship between social support and the psychological well-being of battered women. The participants who worked with advocates were significantly more effective in obtaining resources than were those without advocates. Furthermore, these battered women reported less depression and more satisfaction with their quality of life. Most notably, they experienced less physical violence by the end of the 2-year period (Sullivan & Bybee, 1999).

Throughout the world, women are slowly making progress in ending domestic violence. One program in Iztacalco, Mexico, rechanneled their efforts from changing legislation to raising public awareness. They used small-scale media, such as buttons and posters, to change attitudes about the legitimacy of wife abuse (Fawcett, Heise, Isita-Espejel, & Pick, 1999). Some Ecuadorian villages assign a compadre to newlywed couples. The compadre's job is to intervene at the first sign of discord. The Marshall Islanders of Oceania use community chastisement provided by the village elders to confront and curtail the problem of spousal abuse (Counts et al., 1992). Other countries, such as Chile, Nicaragua, and Japan, also report renewed efforts and some progress in reducing wife abuse and other forms of family violence (e.g., Ellsberg et al., 1999; Kozu, 1999; McWhirter, 1999).

When women choose to stay with their abusers, eliminating the abuse is critical. Counseling, as one method of changing batterers' behavior, has not produced universally satisfactory results according to program evaluation studies of court-sponsored programs. Depending on variables, such as the number of counseling sessions, the length of the follow-up period, the measure of recidivism, and the type of counseling provided, effectiveness has varied. For those studies considered methodologically sound, the majority found modest but statistically significant reductions in recidivism (Healey et al., 1998). Over the years, methodological problems, such as small samples, no comparison groups, and high attrition rates, have rendered these studies' judgments of effectiveness uncertain (see Healey et al., 1998, for a review; see also Davis & Taylor, 1997; Gondolf, 1998b; Palmer, Brown, & Barrera, 1992). Using the most current and applicable statistical procedures, the reassault rate—as reported by women and supplemented by arrest records and batterers' reports over a 15-month follow-up period—is 39% (Gondolf, Chang, & Laporte, 1999). These results suggest that battered women cannot and should not depend on enrollment in a counseling program to ensure their future safety.

It is important to acknowledge, however, that counselors attempting to change chronic behaviors (e.g., substance abuse) and attitudes anticipate some form of recidivism. Many batterers' programs tend to take a resocialization stance, highlighting attitudinal and belief change, as well as behavioral change. These programs do not refer to cure, but something more like recovery (Billings-Beck, Fromm, & Harris, personal communication, 1998). Increasingly, it has become clear that criminal justice agencies must become aware of the key components of an integrated criminal justice response. The system needs to develop a coordinated, systemwide response to battering, including law enforcement, prosecutors, judges, probation offices, and victim advocates (Healey et al., 1998).

INSTITUTIONAL INTERVENTIONS

Society plays a critical role in empowering (or failing to empower) battered women. In fact, there may be no totally effective *individual* solutions to battering. It is society's (not a woman's) responsibility to change practices and policies that encourage battering. Much of the intervention that occurs must happen at the most basic level. Society must change its view of women as subordinate to men and change the structure that imposes that subordination (see Paquet et al., 1998).

A number of experts suggest that those interested in helping battered women should focus their efforts on a holistic community response that networks with all of the systems that affect families. The actions of certain individuals, such as police officers, judges, emergency room personnel, employers, counselors, and clergy, all influence women's actions and ability to leave or stay away from their abusers (Sullivan, 1991a; Wuest & Merritt-Gray, 1999).

Because the church is the first place to which many women turn in a crisis, the religious community has an opportunity to make important contributions in assisting couples caught up in the cycle of violence. Thompson (1989) claims that clergy should help victims determine the best theological choices, yet realistically offer them a number of possible options. She goes so far as to advise victims "to shop around and get second or third opinions from religious helpers in the community" (p. 38).

Some religious organizations have taken very active roles in aiding spouse abuse victims by starting shelters or by designing and conducting training programs for shelter staff and the religious community (Martin, 1989). The clergy can take several helpful actions when a woman discloses her victimization: (a) consider her safety first, (b) believe her account, (c) talk about the violence directly, (d) encourage her to seek additional resources, (e) respect her need for self-determination, (f) be sensitive to cultural differences, and (g) give her spiritual support. It is likewise important to avoid common pitfalls: (a) believing that the problem has disappeared or will do so, (b) believing the denials or minimizations, (c) believing that an upstanding church member could not be assaultive, (d) suggesting forgiveness prematurely before real changes are made, (e) using a couple's counseling approach, (f) conceptualizing marital violence as noncriminal, and (g) actively trying to "rescue" the woman (Cooper-White, 1996).

Garanzini (1988), a Jesuit priest with a doctorate in counseling and education psychology, addressed the appropriate role of pastors from a different perspective. First, he highlighted the legal obligations that ministers have to report child abuse and neglect and how best to meet this requirement. Second, he summarized research-derived warning signs that pastors might use in identifying and helping at-risk families, and he called attention to several general problem areas that families are likely to face. Finally, he suggested a group of strategies that pastors might adopt to combat family violence: (a) establish regular supportive relationships with trained professionals in counseling, services for families, and family medicine; (b) recognize family violence by founding peer support groups for families and by including family violence as a topic for sermons; and (c) establish pastoral teams or mobilize special ministries to assist at-risk families.

Fundamentalist clergy may be particularly unsupportive of battered women because of their ultraconservative attitudes about marriage and sex roles. It is appropriate to address all of these beliefs by questioning them or reinterpreting them, reframing certain Biblical writings, and placing them within a broader context. Reframing can include highlighting the responsibilities of husbands and emphasizing the second account of creation, which gives both males and females dominion over the earth. This approach places many of the issues faced by a fundamentalist battered woman within her own framework (Whipple, 1987; also see McDonald, 1990; Ruether, 1983).

Helping battered women achieve economic independence also plays a pivotal role in avoiding victimization (Browne et al., 1999). Working away from home appears to be a crucial survival strategy, possibly because it lessens the battered woman's economic, social, and emotional dependence on her husband (Wilson et al., 1989; also see Browne et al., 1999). Programs geared to assist battered women in finding employment should be sensitive to their possible lack of self-confidence and job skills, and the effects of battering on work performance. Employers can play a key role in helping women escape from abusive relationships by boosting victims' self-confidence (Wuest & Merritt-Gray, 1999). Positive employer feedback makes battered women feel successful at work, which, in turn, implies to them that they are worth something. An employer who cuts a woman some slack or allows her to have time off is profoundly influential in her ability to take control of her life.

Taking a broader, long-term view, economic equality for battered women may be an approach to interrupting the intergenerational transmission of abuse. When women leave their violent homes, they usually take their children with them. From Hackler's (1991) view, leaving is a prevention strategy for reducing future crime, because it removes the children from a violent environment.

One growing solution to a combination of problems is the development of transitional housing programs. These programs provide continued assistance in helping women find and participate in essential activities (e.g., vocational training, education, job-searching skills, counseling) over a period of 3 to 18 months beyond the customary shelter stay (Loren, 1994; Tsesis, 1996). In addition, transitional housing is low-cost housing.

The history of widespread medical proaction is short. In 1989, McLeer and Anwar (1989) reported that identification of battered women in the emergency room rose from 5.6% to 30% when protocols were in place that simply asked how injuries occurred. According to Campbell and Alford (1989), sexual abuse of battered women has been routinely ignored. In 1992, hospital accrediting bodies decreed that emergency room personnel *must* try to identify battered women and provide appropriate referrals (Joint Commission on Accreditation of Healthcare Organizations [JCAHO], 1992; Shepherd, 1990; Zorza & Schoenberg, 1995). Doctors specializing in obstetrics and gynecology are in a particularly valuable position to identify sexual abuse, especially during pregnancy.

The American Medical Association (AMA) issued a booklet to be used in detecting and treating victims of family abuse (Children's Safety Network, 1992; Schornstein, 1997). Because of these efforts, hospital employees became increasingly willing to screen patients and to attend training seminars (e.g., Hambleton, Clark, Sumaya, Weissman, & Horner, 1997; Smith, Danis, & Helmick, 1998). Moreover, medical schools began including domestic violence in their curricula (Alpert & Cohen, 1997; Smith et al., 1998).

Although the AMA supports screening patients for domestic violence, educating medical staff, and appropriate intervention, it does not support mandatory reporting. The AMA's objections rest on well-established policies about confidentiality. Little research, if any, has systematically studied the effects of mandatory reporting laws (Lund, 1999). Reactions to the laws have been mixed.

Although some evidence suggests that the laws are protecting victims and dealing more effectively with offenders, some medical personnel and some victims have voiced complaints. Generally, battered women's advocates fear that mandatory reporting will discourage victims from seeking help; they feel that it is too controlling, too intrusive, and even dangerous (Currens, 1998; see Zorza & Schoenberg, 1995).

VIOLENCE AGAINST WOMEN ACT

Because of the $1.62 billion Violence Against Women Act (VAWA) (Biden, 1994), the criminal justice response to domestic violence and sexual assault has improved dramatically. A key provision of the bill was the $800 million funding of research grants. To identify areas where VAWA's impact was problematic, representatives of The Urban Institute visited a number of sites where they interviewed battered women, shelter directors, and others (The Urban Institute, 1998; see Klein, 1995). Based on the Institute's 1997 recommendations, the National Institute of Justice (NIJ) began soliciting grant proposals covering several areas, including the following: (a) judicial training, (b) interventions for domestic violence offenders, (c) mandatory reporting, and (d) mediation in domestic violence cases (NIJ, 1999a). Another set of grants focused on interpersonal violence in the Native American community (NIJ, 1999b).

An example of grant money well spent involves the use of Internet-based preparation of court-acceptable protective orders and custody documents. When this computer program is made available in a safe and supportive location, such as a shelter, it allows victims and advocates to prepare complete petitions. Currently, advocates are modifying the program for non-English-speaking users and for application across state lines (Zorza & Klemperer, 1999).

Because antistalking legislation had received the least amount of attention, the Bureau of Justice Assistance (BJA) convened a seminar of leading experts to develop a model antistalking law. The participants also made recommendations concerning sentencing of stalkers, pretrial release provisions, strategies for implementing stalking statutes, and a national research agenda on stalking (BJA, 1996).

Additional areas of focus for helping battered women were as follows: (a) waivers of fees for such documents as restraining orders; (b) interstate enforcement of protective orders; (c) reforming court procedures (e.g., plea bargaining); and (d) training law enforcement personnel, particularly judges. Concerns regarding privacy and confidentiality have been scrutinized (Zorza, 1995). For example, mothers may face a double bind in trying to obtain medical attention for their children because abusers can get legal access to their children's medical records. If a battered woman obtains medical care, the abuser may be able to locate her through the addresses provided to medical personnel. Another necessity for battered women is the acknowledgment of privileged communication, the type honored between doctor and patient or between attorney and client. Many states have upheld victim-counselor privileges, but others have not.

In recent years, there have been positive changes in restricting public access to postal, motor vehicle, and voting records, particularly in regard to victims of domestic violence. In many states, addresses and telephone numbers that were previously easily obtained are now more difficult to access. In November 1998, Vice President Al Gore announced that the federal government would make it easier for victims to change their social security numbers with written evidence of domestic violence from a shelter, physician, or law enforcement agent ("Abuse Victims," 1998; see "Two New York Lower Court Welfare-Related Confidentiality Decisions," 1999, for continuing problems).

Fortunately, the plight of crime victims, in general, has garnered increasing public support. Although federal funding of crime victim compensation has increased, funding of victim service organizations is insufficient to assist victims over any extended period of time. Without community support, many women must return to their batterers because housing and child care are not available (Klein, 1995). All but one of the states has passed a Victims' Bill of Rights, and 22 states have passed constitutional amendments requiring certain crime victim services (Tomz & McGillis, 1997).

Senator Jon Kyl introduced a federal constitutional amendment on April 1, 1998, to guarantee legal rights to crime victims. Of particular importance to the safety of battered women is the provision that victims would have the right to be notified of a batterer's escape or release from custody ("Sponsors Introduce New Draft," 1998).

One outgrowth of VAWA's $1 million funding has been the establishment in Texas of the National Domestic Violence Hotline (NDVH) (1-800-799-SAFE), available 24 hours per day. The hotline received calls from all 50 states, averaging about 300 calls per day during the first 7 months of operation. Most callers had seen messages about the hotline in the media. About 50% of the calls originated from currently or formerly abused women; 14% came from family and friends of battered victims; almost 5% were from self-identified batterers; and the rest were from individuals, such as service providers, professionals, and elected officials.

NDVH workers provided 24,441 referrals, primarily to shelters. They surmised that the greatest gap in services was inadequate shelter capacity, followed by legal resources, criminal justice response, and housing. An analysis of calls to the hotline revealed some very important information. It became clear that a number of populations were underserved: foreign language speakers needing

AT&T's translators, and women who were hearing disabled or had other disabilities. Another group with difficulty obtaining services was women in rural areas. Overall, the hotline has the potential to provide a vast amount of information relevant to understanding and intervening in domestic violence (Danis et al., 1998).

BATTERED WOMEN AND CHILD PROTECTIVE SERVICES

The problem of conflicting interests of children and battered women spurred CPS agencies to consider ways to integrate both concerns into child welfare practice. Social workers are receiving training that directs them to see both the woman and her children as clients who need protection. As urged by nearly every expert in the field, innovative approaches have increasingly included cross-agency collaborations (e.g., police, shelters, courts, CPS) (Aron & Olson, 1997; Brookoff, 1997; Davidson, 1995; Magen et al., 1995).

Several recommendations affecting child custody emanated from these collaborations:

1. Attend to safety issues. See the nonabusing parent and child as one-unit interventions that should focus on the safety of both the child and the adult victim of abuse (e.g., restraining orders, types of counseling recommended).
2. Hold the abuser, not the victim, accountable for his or her violence.
3. Set a context of domestic violence in the report to the court. Specify, for example, that the situation has occurred in a long-standing case of spousal violence.
4. Keep the domestic violence victim and the child together and in their home, unless there is a strong, compelling rationale not to do so.
5. Confront one's own stereotypes about mothers and fathers. One attorney reported that in 16 years of working in the courts, she had never seen a father charged with failure to protect when the child abuser was the mother.

According to Minnesota law, a defense of the nonabusive parent is to determine whether, at the time of neglect (or abuse), there was reasonable apprehension in the mind of the battered victim that acting to stop or prevent neglect would result in substantial bodily harm to her or her child. The American Bar Association's Center on Children created standards for evaluating *failure to protect* in the context of child sexual abuse, which also could be used in cases of spousal violence: (a) whether parents knew or had reasonable cause to believe their child had been abused and failed to take reasonable steps to prevent it; (b) the nature of the actions parents took to protect the child following disclosure of the abuse or neglect; and (c) whether parents voluntarily agreed to participate in specialized counseling programs and to accept other protective services.

CHANGING LEGAL INTERVENTIONS IN CHILD CUSTODY

Some of the more recent developments in the legal system have included family court interventions when child custody and domestic violence issues collide. Prior to the increase in awareness of domestic violence and its effects on children and adult victims, mandatory mediation of custody and visitation disputes was the "law of the land." As evidence has accumulated about domestic violence, credence in the superiority of joint custody over sole custody has slowly eroded (National Council of Juvenile and Family Court Judges, 1994). Data from the California Family Law Court Snapshot Study, conducted in June 1991, revealed that of parents who use mediation services, 48% report high levels of interparental conflict (Depner, Canatta, & Ricci, 1995). In response to these problems and a request from the court, Margaret Little, Director of Family Court Services for the Los Angeles Superior Court, obtained funds in 1998 for the development of a parenting curriculum specifically for spouse abusers (and their victims). Some studies have found that courts are very apt to consider alcohol or drug abuse as relevant to custody issues, but they are not inclined to perceive spouse abuse as an issue (National Center on Women and Family Law, 1994; cf. Sorensen et al., 1995). Recently, an appeals court in California reversed this trend by overturning the custody decision of Judge Nancy Wieben-Stock in the case of O.J. Simpson's two minor children. Judge Wieben-Stock had granted custody to O.J. Simpson, rather than the children's grandparents, despite evidence indicating that he beat and possibly murdered his ex-wife, Nicole Brown Simpson. The appeals court was adamant in its decision that domestic violence and homicide (even alleged) of a parent are critical elements in determining whether the surviving parent should be awarded custody of their children (see Fields-Meyer, Benet, Bernstein, & Dodd, 1998, and Zorza, 1999a, for reviews).

Experts in the field have increasingly called for proactive court approaches to mediation of custody. Guidelines for court intervention in domestic violence cases are available and should be followed, and sensitivity to cultural differences is imperative (Duryee, 1995; Landau, 1995; Wong, 1995). Screening of client suitability for mediation is crucial. In one survey, 80% of mediation programs claimed to use screening procedures, but further analysis revealed that only half of them actually interviewed husbands and wives separately (Pearson, 1997; see also Bryan, 1992; Davies, Ralph, Hawton, & Craig, 1995). Helpful approaches include options to avoid face-to-face contact, and options to bring a support person or legal counsel to the meetings. Finally, all court-connected services should have access to referral information for parents, such as how shelters or abuser counseling programs can be contacted (Newmark, Harrell, & Salem, 1995).

Overall, legal protections for domestic violence victims during divorce mediation have slowly been advancing ("Mediation Regulated," 1997). Battered women often find themselves in a catch-22 situation if they are trying to discontinue contact with an abusive partner (e.g., leave the city), as the court almost always mandates paternal visitation rights. Many battered women and children are terrified because batterers often use visitation as an opportunity to continue their abuse (Geffner & Pagelow, 1990; Hilton, 1992; O'Sullivan & Carper, 1998). It is important that guidelines for court-supervised visitation be developed and that funding of these services be made available (Straus, 1995). A 1997 survey of members of the National Coalition Against Domestic Violence (NCADV) found that their first legislative priority concerned child visitation and safety (NCADV, 1997).

The emphasis on maintaining marriages regardless of the cost to individual family members appears to be a tenet of many conservative religious and political groups espousing their version of "family values." One recent legislative approach developed in Louisiana has been to make some marriages (covenant) harder to dissolve than standard marriages. Although most experts agree that stable families have many benefits and provide the best climate for raising children, they reject the notion that making divorce harder to obtain is productive. Turning attention away from individual predilections and toward devising practical social policy changes should help attain more stable marriages (Marano, 1997).

POLICE TRAINING

Because police can play a pivotal role in interrupting the intergenerational cycle of violence, improving their training is a first step (Buchanan & Perry, 1985). In Hamberger's (1991) opinion, training of police should include their sensitization to the research on domestic violence, in particular, that violent women are rarely husband-beaters or mutual combatants. At least 85% of the victims of spouse assaults and admissions to emergency rooms are women (Greenfeld et al., 1998; Rand, 1997). Officers can be trained to improve their investigatory work and their comprehension of the psychosocial context of abuse. Stubbing (1990), a police trainer and advocate for battered women, has promoted training that includes hearing battered women speak of their terror and inability to get out, and listening to batterers describe their out-of-control behavior and how an arrest started to turn their lives around. Police trainees also heard the voices of children. According to one of the authors (A.L.), inclusion of battered women and children in police and probation training creates empathy—an effective tool for reaching the hearts of those who listen (Wuest & Merritt-Gray, 1999).

In 1996, the U.S. Department of Justice awarded a $385,000 grant to the city of Los Angeles to implement a program aimed at reducing domestic violence. The grant money enabled the Los Angeles Police Department (LAPD) to train officers to identify and arrest suspects in domestic abuse cases and to respond more effectively to victims ("City Receives Grant," 1996).

CASE STUDY

LONG BEACH, CALIFORNIA— A CREATIVE APPROACH

Many cities and municipalities are developing creative, collaborative, and holistic approaches to the problems associated with spousal violence. Long Beach, California, a multiethnic seaport city of 450,000 people, has a unique perspective and an effective collaboration of shelter advocates, police officers, city prosecutors, a domestic-violence dedicated court and follow-up team, probation officers, batterers' programs, child abuse agencies, and substance abuse programs.

Robbie Hill has been a member of the domestic violence unit of the Long Beach Police Department since 1993, and Nancy Rivera joined the team in 1994. Ruth Burton has been a battered women's advocate at WomenShelter of Long Beach since 1993. These three women are integral members of the Domestic Abuse Response Team (DART). Patrol units call DART to the scene of a domestic violence incident if any of the following criteria are met: (a) department personnel are implicated; (b) there is serious injury, the victim refuses medical attention, or both; (c) there have been two or more prior incidents involving this family; (d) spousal rape has occurred; and/or (e) the case falls under the rubric of intimate relationships, past or present.

Robbie and Nancy handle the investigation, and they call Ruth only after the victim signs a consent form. On-call DART counselors will come out if the victim needs help, whether or not the victim meets DART criteria. According to Robbie, "Sometimes, we know just by reading the report that the victim needs to speak to a counselor." All three team members agree that most of the women feel more comfortable with a counselor present during the interview.

Robbie says, "The victim feels our true concern. It's not just a job to us. We're there for more than a criminal investigation. We're there for them. We give them information and provide options (e.g., shelter referrals, legal possibilities). We offer vertical prosecution all the way up the line. That is, victims and perpetrators see the same people. We follow through." Ruth and Nancy believe that it is this team approach that is so successful. "DART is 10% Rambette [Rambo's sisters], 10% maintaining perspective, 40% police work, and 40% social work. We are there for each other and have a common goal."

That statement could not have been made a decade ago. The relationship between the grassroots shelter movement and the traditionally hierarchical criminal justice system has been historically thorny. This recent marriage, however arranged, seems to be working.

A case moves from investigation to prosecution. Steve Shaw and Sharon Panian have been the consistent team representing victims in the City Prosecutor's Domestic Violence Unit. The unit handles each case from filing through arraignment, pretrial hearing, trial, and postsentencing hearings.

Steve and Sharon both agree that working domestic violence misdemeanors does not appeal to many prosecutors because of the unusual difficulties associated with these cases. Steve says, "Misdemeanors are more difficult to prove because there is less evidence, and juries take felonies more seriously. About 90% of the victims either recant or seriously minimize the incident. The victim who is bleeding and pleading for police protection on Friday night comes to court on Monday to tell the prosecutor that it was all just a misunderstanding. Victims and witnesses are often uncooperative and hostile. Most of the women say that their abuser is a good husband and father most of the time."

Both city prosecutors understand why this happens. From Sharon's point of view, "The prosecutor who keeps the defendant in jail may be revictimizing the victim. Many of the cases involve battered women who are financially dependent on their batterers. For these victims, a black eye once or twice a year may be a small price to pay for food and shelter for the victim and her children."

Sharon and Steve are willing to take a chance on which cases to file. They are committed to protecting the victim by making the best legal decision possible, even if they believe they will lose the case. Both are creative and see every situation, every victim, every perpetrator, every family as different. Both agree that prosecuting partner abuse is not a job for everyone; it is 20% law and 80% social work.

When a domestic violence case is successfully prosecuted, the defendant often completes a year-long counseling program. According to Steve, "These perpetrators frequently return to court saying they were glad they were forced to attend the group sessions. Sometimes, the victims are grateful and things are better for them and for their families. Those are the moments that make the job worthwhile and keep us going."

The city prosecutors are able to work innovatively because they are working with a court that is also responsive to partner assault on a case-by-case basis. Deborah Andrews is one of the few judges who presides over a courtroom that handles domestic violence cases exclusively. The judge reflects, "The focus of my court is to treat each defendant individually, to provide logical consequences, and to give feedback that is often positive. I spend a lot of time explaining court orders. As a judge, I don't have to go into such detail, but it pays off. The defendants understand what is expected of them and what it means if they fail to comply. I see people over and over again during the process, and I know their stories."

Judge Andrews works closely with the abusers' programs in the area and holds an annual meeting with the providers. She knows many of the facilitators personally and understands the relevance of these programs. When defendants return to court with their progress reports, she may ask them, "What's going on in group?" "What have you learned so far?" "What's a time-out?" "Why do you think you received a positive progress report?" She addresses issues directly and speaks directly to the perpetrators (not through their attorneys).

Judge Andrews will not issue a fee waiver for batterer treatment. She believes that defendants should pay something for their counseling programs. She and her bailiff, Deputy Arnie Gonzales, believe that treating defendants disrespectfully gives them the wrong message. "You can be respectful and still hold a defendant accountable for his behavior," she concludes.

Long Beach employs another arm of accountability in regard to the batterer and as a program of the court. It is the only court in the state that uses domestic violence case monitoring. Elena Villacres and Joe Quick are part of the Court Referral Information Services Program (CRISP), which has been offering services since 1994. CRISP staff members are the administrative experts and liaisons between the court and the batterers' programs.

Defendants leave the courtroom and report to the CRISP office. Elena and Joe speak to the perpetrators, reinforcing Judge Andrews's orders. In brief, defendants are able to choose a program from the approved probation list. Batterers have 21 days to enroll in the selected group. After that time period, CRISP staff calls the offenders' programs to check on their enrollment status. If they have failed to comply, the court issues a bench warrant for their arrest.

CRISP handles violations of court orders and notifies the court clerk. If there is a red item (serious infraction), the judge receives immediate notification. Elena states, "CRISP is like Switzerland. We're neutral, but our rules are not meant to be broken. The defendants have to respect the law, other individuals, and be responsible for their actions." Joe Quick describes CRISP as a work in progress.

In addition to the unified response of shelter staff, batterers' programs, and the criminal justice system, Paula Cohen, Staff Attorney for Long Beach Legal Aid's Domestic Violence Project, has coordinated the work of child and spouse abuse advocates. These efforts culminated in the development of the Long Beach Area Child Abuse and Domestic Violence Prevention Council. This coalition brings together formerly hesitant (at best) allies with ostensibly differing agendas, until they sit down together (see Witwer & Crawford, 1995, for a review of the literature and for recommendations on community coordination).

Communication and respect among all of the cogs in the wheel have been critical to the success of the Long Beach model. There are several themes that are consistent throughout these programs: (a) Each of the members of this criminal justice team perceives him- or herself as part enforcer and part social worker, and they consider each function necessary; (b) they do not believe that one size fits all, but look upon each victim and perpetrator as a distinctive individual; (c) this work is not for everyone; and (d) supportive interaction at every level in the system is crucial, because as much for the victims as the perpetrators, isolation is an enemy.

CASE STUDY (continued)

To really help battered women, the entire community needs to be involved. Shelters, medical personnel, employers, police, and members of society at large need to become involved. Although counseling and advocacy should work toward empowering survivors of abuse on an individual level, more emphasis should be placed on empowering women by changing the community (Barkley, 1997; Morton, 1997). Many small communities use creative interventions to confront violence between adult intimates. When the systems work together, safety and support are the possible outcomes. Margaret's case demonstrates a successful coupling of social services and the criminal justice system (also see Boles & Patterson, 1997).

MARGARET AND JOE

CASE STUDY

Margaret was a teacher, mother of four children, and wife of an abusive husband. Joe was the stepfather of the three older children. The youngest child was a product of Joe and Margaret's 7-year marriage. Margaret and the children became increasingly wary and fearful of Joe. His vicious verbal tirades had worsened over the years, and he had added hitting, choking, and throwing things to his repertoire.

Her impetus to take action came from her oldest daughter's school counselor. Margaret's daughter had been an outstanding student, member of the Pep Squad, and popular. The counselor was concerned because the girl was withdrawing from her friends, seemed depressed, and was failing in two classes. Did Margaret know of any reason for this? Was anything unusual happening at home?

CASE STUDY (continued)

Margaret could truthfully answer, "No." What was happening at home was not unusual.

Margaret made contact with a local battered women's hotline. She decided that she did not need shelter, and she obtained a temporary restraining order with an order for Joe to leave the house. He left, but not for long. He would park his car across the street and leave it there. Margaret and the kids were terrified. One night, she came home from work to find the kids sitting in the living room very quietly. The lights were out. Joe came from out of the shadows and pinned Margaret against the wall, saying, "Where's your protection now? Who's going to help you now?" Finally, he left.

Joe had intimidated Margaret and the kids before, and it had worked. He was always able to return. This time, Margaret stood her ground. She again made contact with the local shelter. A shelter worker advised her over the phone and agreed to advocate for her when she returned to court.

The shelter worker suggested that Margaret get written statements from her neighbors about seeing Joe, because he was wise enough to leave before the police could arrive. She also suggested that Margaret take a close-up picture of the car (when he parked it across the street) with a dated newspaper on it, and then take a picture of the car and newspaper in relation to her house. These photographs and written statements would substantiate Margaret's allegations that Joe was violating the restraining order.

Armed with her evidence and her advocates, Margaret appeared in court. The judge issued a bench warrant for Joe's arrest, and he was picked up. Joe has stopped harassing Margaret and the kids. She made the system work.

NOTE

1. For more information about these films, correspond with the New Jersey Coalition Against Domestic Violence, local coalitions, or the Corporate Alliance to End Partner Violence in Chicago.

7 Voices of Hope
Survivors Speak

Heroism is not inherent in human nature. It is not their initial helplessness that must astonish us, but the way they finally overcame it.
—Simone de Beauvoir (cited in Steiner, 1966, p. xxii)

CASE STUDY

GLORIA AND MILES

Gloria is 44, has her bachelor's degree, is a mother of three children, and works as an registered nurse. Her son will be graduating from U.C. Berkeley this year, and her daughters are in high school. Gloria is a devout Catholic; a dedicated mother; and an open-minded, free-thinking, and compassionate human being. She is also a formerly battered woman who has spent the past decade pulling her life back together.

Gloria married her high school sweetheart, who was an athlete, popular, jealous, and abusive. She was pregnant before they got married, and she had to deal with the shame that that engendered in her, but she thought that getting married would end the jealousy, violence, and shame. Besides, she was in love.

They both attended college. He graduated, but did not work regularly. She took early childhood education classes and worked in day care centers from the time she was 22 until she was 29 years old. She supported the family much of the time, but turned the money over to Miles. Miles had an economic principle upon which he operated: His money was his, and so was hers.

The first time she left Miles was 4 months after they married. Miles hit her and threw her around. He accused her of "coming on" to his friends, dressing like a slut, not looking sexy enough, and on and on. The yelling, swearing, threats, name-calling, and beatings happened in front of her children. Gloria says that she never enjoyed being hit or thought it was sexually exciting. What she did feel was shame and hope. She thought that if she could just change a little, things would get better. "If I could have cooked better, looked better, or did what he wanted more often, things would improve. I even tried smoking marijuana with him. Hope kept me going."

"It is also important to know that I was coming from knowing nothing about battered women." The first article that she read on battered women was about Francine Hughes (*The Burning Bed*). She learned that Francine was appearing on television, and she asked a neighbor to watch the kids because she knew she would be upset.

One night, Miles came home angry and drunk. There was an argument, and he beat her with a pop bottle. "I don't know what I saw when I looked in the mirror afterward, but it scared me. I looked at the kids, looked in the mirror, and said to myself, "I'm going to die if I don't do something."

She started writing letters about what was happening to her. She wrote to the YWCA, NOW, Catholic Social Services, and the Salvation Army. While she was waiting for answers to the letters, Gloria went to Parents Anonymous (she did not know what it was, and she was not abusing the kids) and to a group called Recovery (for self-esteem). The only response that she received was from the YWCA, and they asked her to come in for a "talk." Later, Gloria found out that they wanted to know if she was crazy.

The Y took action. They set up three seminars on domestic violence to see who would show up. Of course, Gloria was there. From the meetings, a women's group evolved, and she was part of that program. The group was empowering, and Gloria also felt proud about having been an impetus for the YWCA involvement. Gloria began making plans to leave months before she actually left. She made a wheel with "things to take care of a day at a time." One of the tasks was to write letters to everyone who had helped her. She put them in the mailbox on her way out of town.

Gloria and her children trekked (by car) across the country to a shelter for battered women. It was 1977. She started college again in 1978. She put herself through school on welfare and side jobs (Avon, college work-study). She also went into therapy to get over Miles and the fantasies that she still had about building a life with him. She says that it has taken her 14 years to feel that she could be interested in another man, and she is still wary.

Gloria's son went away to college and wrote his first sociology paper on domestic violence. It gave Gloria and James a real opportunity to talk. Her children are doing well, and they are proud of their mother. Gloria's daughter heard a lecture in school on spouse abuse. That evening, she told her mother that she had lots of courage, and that she was brave to leave. Gloria's eyes were full of emotion when she related that story.

CASE STUDY: PEGGY

Peggy was married for 12½ years to the "All-American Boy." He was the man whom other women wanted, and he was the man who was going to protect her from her abusive stepfather. He was the father of their four children, and he was also the man who blackened her eye on their honeymoon. Peggy's husband was an alcoholic who continued to abuse her throughout their marriage. When Peggy left him, her children ranged in age from 5 to 9. After he and Peggy separated, he neither supported the children financially nor visited them. Peggy's first husband had an alcoholic father who beat his mother.

Peggy's second husband was charming, romantic, and more brutal than the first. She lived with him for 4 months and left after a beating. He followed her, promising that things would change and that life would be wonderful once again. He was extremely romantic and affectionate. But very quickly, he began drinking and using drugs again, and Peggy left him in December 1975.

Peggy was terrified of her second husband, and although she left him, it took her 5 years to gather the courage to divorce him. Peggy had undergone corrective ear surgery, because her husband had battered her to the point of deafness. Peggy had been asked if she went to therapy. She replied, "No, I went to school, and that saved my life."

Peggy supported herself and her four daughters by tending bar until the gradual loss of hearing became a total loss of hearing. The only sounds she heard were the phantom noises in her head, which are typical for people who experience hearing loss. She used state vocational aid, which paid for tuition, classes on deafness, sign language, and an interpreter. She also received Aid to Families with Dependent Children. She completed her first semester with a 4.0 grade point average.

Peggy had a temporary restraining order, but her husband continued to harass her from the court-ordered distance. She changed her phone number and moved several times, but he always found her and drove around the neighborhood on his motorcycle. Peggy was often terrified, but she continued courageously to complete her schooling and maintain a positive attitude.

Dr. Bud Martin of American River College in Sacramento was a major influence and source of support in Peggy's life during those difficult times. His class, Personal and Social Adjustment, was the beginning of her journey to healing. She wrote her first term paper in that class. It was an inspired autobiography called, "A Case for the Battered Woman." She took every course Dr. Martin taught, and he encouraged her to finish school.

In February 1979, Peggy and her family suffered a great personal tragedy. Her 17-year-old daughter passed away as a result of a brain tumor. Her determined voice still breaks as she recalls her daughter's last day. Peggy's resolve to

CASE STUDY (continued)

graduate and to change her life probably gave her the focus and resolve to complete her last semester.

Peggy became an expert in sign language and received her Bachelor of Arts in special education and deafness in January 1980. She graduated with an overall grade point average of 3.5. Peggy volunteered for the Long Beach Police Department's emergency translation team. In 1986, she began working for Su Casa, a battered women's shelter in southern California.

In 1988, Peggy was recruited by the daytime drama, *Days of Our Lives*, as a consultant and, later, as a cast member. She has become a national spokesperson for the problems of battered women and the double jeopardy experienced by battered women who are hearing-impaired. Peggy was invited to sit on a panel at a conference at Gallaudet College (the only liberal arts college in the world for the deaf). Peggy spoke on deafness and domestic violence.

CASE STUDY

CHRISTY AND DICK

Christy is a vivacious woman in her late 40s. Her sons are grown, and her marriage is 32 years old. She finds it hard to believe that she is still married and does not recommend her path to other women. She is happy now and feels in control of her life. That journey started a decade ago.

Christy met Dick when she was 18, and she married him when she was 20. They met in junior college. He was from a wealthy family and had attended a private high school. Christy's financial roots were much less auspicious. Her mother was a single parent. Both Christy and Dick came from abusive families. Christy calls herself a "classic case of the Fifties." She had her children in rapid succession and became emotionally and financially dependent on her husband. Although she worked as a kindergarten teacher and supported her family for a year and a half, she stayed home as soon as Dick's career was established, and she gave everybody her best and took the leftovers.

Christy maintained friendships, but she says that all her friends were like her: upper middle class, at-home moms, and abused. According to Christy, "What I have seen from other women is that they thought they were never good enough, because they were always told they weren't. We all believed it had to be perfect because it would make our husbands happy, but they're never happy, and it's never perfect. I used to plan a really fancy dinner and have it ready right when he got home, so he didn't have to wait and we could have a nice evening."

It took about 6 years for his rage to control her life, and it was about 15 years before she had a word, other than "uncomfortable," to describe what was happening to her. Dick was very jealous. She had saved letters from a high school boyfriend and had them locked in a little box. On one occasion, he took the hinges off the box to read the letters. Dick was a drinker, and as he drank more, he became more verbally abusive and neglectful. He did not hit Christy. He broke things that she liked, threw the coffee table, hit the walls, and told her what to do. She did not always take it from him. She got angry, but did not push him too far.

It was not until she started attending small seminars on mental health issues that she began to change. She started and stopped going to Al-Anon two or three times. At that time, nobody had heard of a battered women's group. And at 40, she began working as a fitness instructor, and she was very successful. Dick felt threatened, but she refused to stop moving forward. She was always searching to make her life better.

Christy told me that "recognition is an inside job." She found a wonderful support group through Al-Anon and has been a regular for more than 2 years. She said that there were several things that really made a difference to her, and she wanted to pass on that information to other women:

Networking: "I had to meet other women to get through my own denial and know that I wasn't alone."

Assertiveness Programs: "I needed to know I had a choice. I didn't have to take whatever was in front of me."

Anger: "When I found out that I had a choice, I got angry and nasty because Dick had made me think I didn't have one. When I got angrier than I was fearful, he backed off. I have eventually found a middle road. Billy Joel's record, "My Life," became my song. Remember that men who abuse women have a tremendous case of Alzheimer's Disease. They don't want to remember how they've hurt you. Sometimes, I remind him, but I actually like him now, and he respects and likes me. I know this couldn't happen in every case."

DO WOMEN REMAIN IN ABUSIVE RELATIONSHIPS?

Lehnen and Skogan (1981), in analyzing data from the National Crime Survey, found that most victims were divorced or separated at the time of their interview. These data imply that "many or even most women leave abusive relationships" (p. 239) (also see Rogge & Bradbury, 1999). Generally, studies find that about one third of battered women fleeing to shelters return to their partners. Gondolf

(1988b) discovered that 24% of shelter women planned to return, with an additional 7% undecided. Strube and Barbour (1984) found that 62% of their sample were separated or divorced at a follow-up period, 1 to 18 months postshelter. Herbert, Silver, and Ellard (1991) found that 66% of a group of 132 battered community women had left. Of those remaining, 50% had left at least once.

These findings indicate that leaving is often an ongoing process culminating in change, rather than a single event. In a study of 512 abused women living in a shelter, 74.2% had separated from their mates at least once, and some had separated more than 10 times (LaBell, 1979). According to Browne (1983), the average battering relationship lasts about 6 years—the same length of time as the average marriage. A number of experts have conceptualized leaving an abusive relationship as a process, perhaps with several stages (Landenburger, 1989; Merritt-Gray & Wuest, 1995; Moss et al., 1997). Basically, battered women must traverse several changes in beliefs: (a) acknowledging their relationship as dangerous, (b) realizing it will not get better, (c) experiencing some catalyst (e.g., abuse of a child), (d) giving up the dream of an idealized committed relationship, and (e) accepting that it will never be over (e.g., having to share child custody) (Moss et al., 1997).

LEAVING AN ABUSER

What does it take for women to make a decision to take action? For the women interviewed here (by A.L.), breaking the isolation was a critical step. A second essential factor seemed to be the introduction of a person into the battered woman's life who was supportive and encouraging, and who somehow convinced her that she was important. Once she has taken little steps, she has tangible evidence that she can take bigger ones. A battered woman needs a new mirror on reality, and other human beings can hold the looking glass.

KAREN'S CATALYSTS FOR CHANGE

We started our book with Karen Connell, and it seems appropriate to end with an update. What were Karen Connell's catalysts for change? During the later 1970s and early 1980's, the system was basically unresponsive to battered women, so Karen's catalysts did not come from the system. Karen's leaving was influenced by several factors. She saw her son, Ward, changing from a decent, fairly happy little boy into a person who screamed and swore at her—a person like her husband. A friend gave Karen a shelter hotline number. Finally, on the day she made up her mind to leave, her husband, Michael, raped her.

For the last 3 years of her marriage, Michael had not worked. He stayed home and virtually held her hostage. Her time and actions were monitored, and Michael placed a tap on the phone. Her "free" day was the morning she worked at Ward's co-op nursery. Karen planned her escape with a shelter advocate. On the day she worked at the co-op, she took Ward and went to the shelter. For the first time in years, she and Ward were safe. They never lived with Michael again.

KAREN REVISITED

Karen's surgery saved her life and her voice. Although her vocal cords were cut, she has been miraculously able to tell her story. Karen's whispering voice has screamed the plight of battered women to millions of people through radio and television interviews and speaking engagements. She served on the staff of the Sojourn shelter for battered women in Santa Monica, California, and worked as a victim advocate for the Los Angeles City Attorneys' Domestic Violence unit. Karen is currently self-employed as an accountant and financial planner. Ward continues to struggle with the abuse that he witnessed and directly experienced. In 1986, Karen received the Governor's Award for her work with survivors of spouse abuse.

Appendix A

A Compilation of Statistics on Abuse of Intimates

APPENDIX A A Compilation of Statistics on Abuse of Intimates

Researchers	*Organization*	*Reported By*	*Sample Type*	*Sample Size*	*Assessment*	*Period of Time*	*Outcome (Rate)*		
PHYSICAL ASSAULTS									
Straus and Gelles (1986)	Family Violence Laboratory	University	Married/ divorced; males/ females	3,500	Conflict Tactics Scales (CTS)[a]	Lifetime	*Percentage of perpetrators of abuse*		
								Males	*Females*
							Nonsevere abuse	1.3	12.1
							Severe abuse	3.0	4.4
Tjaden and Thoennes (1998)	Center for Policy Research	National Institute of Justice and Centers for Disease Control and Prevention	Married/ divorced/ cohabiting/ dating; males/ females	16,000 (8,000 males, 8,000 females)	Modified CTS	Lifetime	*Percentage of victims of abuse* (n = *79)*		
								Males	*Females*
								7.4	22.1
Craven (1997)	Census Bureau	Bureau of Justice Statistics (BJS)	Male/female assault victims over 12 years old	11,068,600	National Crime Victimization Survey questionnaire (NCVS)[b]	1 year	*Number of victims of abuse, by gender*		
								Males	*Females*
							Total incidents	6,228,500	4,840,100
							Percentage of victims of abuse, by relationship		
								Males	*Females*
							Stranger	63.4	38.4
							Known to victim	36.6	61.6
							Current/ex-spouse or boy/girlfriend	2.8	20.7
							Other relative	3.6	6.6
							Friend/acquaintance	30.2	34.3

Bachman and Saltzman (1995)	Census Bureau	BJS	Current/ former spouse or boyfriend/ girlfriend	960,000	NCVS questionnaire	1 year (1992-1993)	*Percentage of intimate victims of abuse, by gender* *Males* 15; *Females* 85

NOTES: Victims reported about 50% of these incidents to the police. The rate of victimization for separated women was three times higher than the rate for divorced women and 25 times higher than the rate for married women.

RACIAL DIFFERENCES

Greenfeld et al. (1998)	Census Bureau	BJS	Females	Not provided	NCVS questionnaire	1 year	*Percentage of female victims of abuse, by race* Whites 0.8 Hispanics 0.9 Blacks 1.2 Others (e.g.Asians) 0.6

NOTE: About half (49%) of White victims, about two-thirds (68%) of Black victims, and close to half (44%) of Others reported the crime to the police.

INJURIES CAUSED BY INTIMATES

Rand (1997)	Consumer Product Safety Commission	BJS	Emergency room patients	1,417,600	National Electronic Injury Surveillance System (NEISS)	1 year	*Number of persons injured, by gender* *Males* 862,000; *Females* 554,700; *Not Specified* 900 *Number and percentage of injuries, by relationship* Current/ex-spouse: *Males* 15,400 (1.80%); *Females* 88,400 (15.90%) Current/ex-boy-/girlfriend: *Males* 23,000 (2.75%); *Females* 116,000 (20.90%)

(continued)

APPENDIX A Continued

Researchers	*Organization*	*Reported By*	*Sample Type*	*Sample Size*	*Assessment*	*Period of Time*	*Outcome (Rate)*
Zlotnick et al. (1998)	Center for Population Research of the National Institute of Child Health and Human Development Demography and Ecology	University	Male/female cohabitants	7,506	Injury questions by telephone survey	1 year	*Percentage of sample injured, by gender (n = 826)* *Males* 27 *Females* 73
SEXUAL ASSAULTS							
Bachman and Saltzman (1995)	Census Bureau	BJS	Women	500,000	NCVS questionnaire	1 year (1992-1993)	*Percentage of sexual assaults by lone offenders* Stranger 23 Acquaintance/friend 40 Other relative 9 Total intimates 29 Husband 9 Ex-husband 4 Boyfriend/ex-boyfriend 16

HOMICIDES									
Greenfeld et al. (1998)	Federal Bureau of Investigation (FBI)	Police departments	Murdered males/ females over 12 years old	446,370	Written reports	1976-1996	*Average percentage of people killed, by relationship to victim*		
								Males	*Females*
							Total unknown	34.4	27.8
							Total known to police	65.6	72.2
							Spouse	3.7	18.9
							Ex-spouse	0.2	1.4
							Nonmarital partner	2.0	9.4
							Others	59.6	42.5
STALKING									
Tjaden and Thoennes (1998)	Center for Policy Research	National Institute of Justice and Centers for Disease Control and Prevention	Married/ divorced/ cohabiting/ dating; males/ females	16,000 (8,000 males, 8,000 females)	Modified CTS	Lifetime	*Percentage of sample stalked*		
								Males	*Females*
								2	8

NOTE: Male intimates physically assaulted (81%) and sexually assaulted (31%) of the victims they stalked.

(continued)

APPENDIX A Continued

Researchers	Organization	Reported By	Sample Type	Sample Size	Assessment	Period of Time	Outcome (Rate)
DATING POPULATIONS							
Bachman and Saltzman (1995)	Census Bureau	BJS	Dating males and females	Not provided	NCVS questionnaire (for assaults); *Uniform Crime Reports* (FBI) (for murders)	1 year (1992-1993)	*Victimization by current/former dating partner* *Males* / *Females* Simple assault: 2.0% / 16.0% Murder: 1.4% / 10.3%
LESBIAN POPULATIONS							
Tjaden, Thoennes, and Allison (1999)	Center for Policy Research	National Institute of Justice and Centers for Disease Control and Prevention	Cohabiting females	Seventy-nine female co-habitants, from a sample of 8,000 females	Modified CTS		*Percentage of female victims* 11.4
ELDER ABUSE							
Bachman and Saltzman (1995)	Census Bureau	BJS	Females over 65 years old	Not provided	NCVS questionnaire	1 year (1992-1993)	*Percentage of females victimized by male intimates* 1.2

Pillemer and Finkelhor (1988)	University	University	Males/ females 65 years and older residing in Boston	2,020 (65% were females)	CTS	Lifetime	*Percentage of victims of abuse (n = 65)* *Males* / *Females* By spouse: 5.1 / 2.5
Tatara and Kuzmeskus (1997)	National Center on Elder Abuse		Males/ females 60 years and older	293,000	Official written records of state agencies	FY95 and FY96	*Percentage of victims of abuse, by gender* *Males* / *Females* 32.4 / 67.3 *Percentage of perpetrators, by gender* *Males* / *Females* 47.4 / 48.9 *Percentage of victims of abuse, by relationship* Adult child 36.7 Spouse 12.6 Other family 10.8 Grandchild 7.7 Sibling 2.7 Service provider/ volunteer 3.5 Other categories 13.4 Unknown 5.1

a. The Conflict Tactics Scale (CTS) contains 18 self-report questions about abuse (perpetration and victimization).
b. The National Crime Victimization Survey uses approximately 10 or more items about crime victimization. Researchers conduct both surveys by telephone.

Appendix B
General Learning Information

UNDERSTANDING DIVERGENCE IN RESEARCH FINDINGS

In reading research results, one needs to bear in mind that a number of variables influence the findings. For example, the nature of the sample, the size of the sample, and the specific questions asked all determine the final outcome. Because investigators are prone to using different questionnaires and focusing on particular problems, their results are likely to differ. Sometimes, apparently divergent results may not vary as much as a superficial reading leads one to believe.

LEARNING RESEARCH

A few basic assumptions govern learning research: (a) A similarity exists between human behavior and animal behavior; (b) the results of laboratory experiments with animals using reinforcement and punishment can be extrapolated to describe human behavior; and (c) it is necessary to postulate the effects of some nonobservable factors in humans, such as religious attitudes or beliefs in the traditional family, just as one postulates the existence of hunger as a motivation in food-deprived animals. Even when it is impossible to scientifically observe internal factors (e.g., sexist attitudes), it may be possible to verify them through empirically based research, such as questionnaires. Furthermore, Follingstad et al. (1992) asserted that "literature from the laboratory study of human aggression is particularly relevant for considering what happens in battering relationships" (p. 110).

This book incorporates several important experiments conducted on dogs and rats that have provided outcomes that seem to have significant applications for understanding why battered women may learn to stay with abusive husbands. (Early researchers conducted a number of animal studies before enactment of newer guidelines governing animal research.)

I. Classical Conditioning: Pavlov and His Dog

It is possible to condition emotional reactions. Laboratory experiments have demonstrated that human beings can learn to fear what they previously felt neutral about, liked, or even loved. The procedure used is called *classical conditioning.* Classical conditioning is simply pairing two stimuli to produce a response, such as in the famous case of Pavlov and his dog. Pavlov and his dog are the Jeff and Lassie of psychology. Pavlov sounded a tone, placed meat powder on the tongue of his hungry pet, and the dog salivated. After several pairings of the tone and the meat powder, the animal salivated after hearing the tone, but before the meat powder arrived; that is, the dog salivated to the presentation of the tone by itself.

With classical conditioning, a reward (e.g., food) or aversive event (e.g., shock) occurs regardless of the subject's response. For example, Pavlov put the food in the dog's mouth whether or not the dog salivated. Pavlov, not the dog, controlled the presentation of the food.

II. Extinction and Spontaneous Recovery

Extinction refers to the decrease in responses when no reinforcement follows the designated response. Research has shown that when learning takes place under intermittent reinforcement schedules (occasional rewards), it takes animals longer to stop responding (resistance to extinction).

Pavlov also noted an interesting side effect of his learning experiments. If he continued to sound the tone, but failed to present the food, the salivation diminished slowly; it was extinguished. If he waited a few days to present the tone (without the food) to the dog again, the dog once again salivated (spontaneous recovery). This pattern went on for days and did not seem to extinguish completely. The dog had to learn that the tone was no longer significant and did not mean that food was on the way.

III. Operant Conditioning: Skinner and His Rat

Operant conditioning refers to a basic form of learning primarily covering voluntary behaviors, such as driving a car or swimming. In contrast to classical, or Pavlovian, conditioning, operant conditioning requires the individual to earn a reward, or to work to eliminate a painful circumstance. B. F. Skinner, the famous behaviorist, developed the operant paradigm. In Skinner's (1938) experiments, behavior is shaped by rewarding (reinforcing) responses in a step-by-step manner as the animal approximates (successive approximation) the desired behavior. Skinner's classic work involved putting a rat in a box containing a bar. Skinner has retained his immortality with psychology students, not just for his research, but because the box was given his name, the Skinner box.

In a Skinner box, the animal receives rewards (food pellets) as he slowly learns the desired behavior, the bar press. As the rat stands on its hind legs near the bar, a food pellet arrives in the food dish. When the rat touches the bar, another food pellet arrives, and so on until the rat presses the bar and receives food regularly. This process is called *shaping.* The animal learns that the reward is dependent on its own behavior; that is, it has control over the outcome of its behavior. The consequences of behavior (getting food or avoiding pain) control the animal's rate of lever pressing.

1A. Reinforcement Definitions

Reinforcers: Reinforcers are events that increase responding.[1]

Positive reinforcer: A positive reinforcer is any event that, when added to a situation, increases the probability that an organism will make a behavioral response.

Animal Examples

Primary (unlearned) reinforcers: food and water

Secondary (learned) reinforcers: sound of a bell signifying food is coming (Secondary reinforcers have previously been paired with primary reinforcers.)

Human Examples

Primary (unlearned) reinforcers: food and water

Secondary (learned) reinforcers: smile, money, praise, approval, sexual contact, and affection

Negative Reinforcer: A negative reinforcer is any event that, when taken away, increases a behavioral response.

Animal Examples

Primary (unlearned) negative reinforcer: shock

Secondary (learned) negative reinforcer: sound of a bell signifying that a shock is coming

Human Examples

Primary (unlearned) negative reinforcer: shock

Secondary (learned) negative reinforcer: frown, criticism, name-calling

1B. Additional Facts About Reinforcement

1. Reinforcers greatly enhance learning, but learning can take place without reinforcement.
2. In general, the larger the reinforcer, the greater (or faster) the learning.
3. When reinforcement is not given after a response, the number of responses declines (extinction occurs).
4. Contingent (earned, dependent, or related) reinforcement produces much better learning than does noncontingent reinforcement. A rat that must press a lever to earn food will learn to do so far better than a rat who is given the food without having to press a lever.
5. Delaying the presentation of the reinforcer retards learning.
6. Presenting the reinforcement on every trial in classical conditioning speeds up learning, whereas intermittent reinforcement (IR schedule) retards learning.
7. Presenting the reinforcement intermittently in operant conditioning will still induce learning, but the schedule of reinforcers (IR) will help maintain the behavior longer than if every trial is rewarded.
8. If motivation (e.g., hunger) is increased, learning occurs more rapidly.
9. Enjoyable activities (e.g., watching TV) can act as reinforcers as much as can stimuli such as food and water.
10. After a behavior is learned, it is harder to extinguish it if intermittent reinforcement had been used.

1C. Punishment Definitions

Punishers: Punishers are events that decrease responding.

Positive punisher: A positive punisher is any event that, when added to a situation, decreases a behavioral response.

Animal Examples

Primary (unlearned) positive punisher: bar slap—shock for pressing a bar to obtain food

Secondary (learned) positive punisher: a tone signifying bar slap will occur

Human Examples

Primary (unlearned) positive punisher: spanking beating

Secondary (learned) positive punisher: pouting, disapproval, swearing

Negative punisher: A negative punisher is any event that, when taken away, decreases a behavioral response.

Animal Examples

Primary (unlearned) negative punisher: Water is removed when the animal eats.

Secondary (learned) negative punisher: A bell signaling food is turned off when the animal presses the bar for food.

Human Examples

Primary (unlearned) negative punisher: dessert taken away after a meal

Secondary (learned) negative punisher: deprivation of TV privilege; time-out (removal from others)

1D. Additional Facts About Punishment

1. Punishment is not the opposite of reinforcement. A noxious event like a shock does not always decrease responding (Skinner, 1938). "Punishment typically produces a change in behavior much more rapidly than other forms of instrumental conditioning, such as positive reinforcement or avoidance" (Domjan & Burkhard, 1989, p. 259).
2. The less intense and briefer the duration of the punishment, the less the suppression (Karsh, 1962). Mildly punished behaviors will recover (Appel, 1963).
3. Severity of punishment = duration × intensity.
4. If the first punishment is severe, but successive punishments are milder, the punished behavior will be inhibited (Sandler et al., 1966).
5. If the first punishment is mild, and successive punishments become more severe, behavioral suppression will usually not occur (Sandler et al., 1966). An animal continues to adjust and respond for the reward that is also present in the situation.
6. If punishment is discontinued, recovery may occur (Catania, 1984).
7. If the punishment is contingent upon the animal's behavior, the animal will learn to eliminate the responses (Camp, Raymond, & Church, 1967).
8. If the punishment is not contingent upon the organism's response, the organism will probably not learn to inhibit the undesirable responses (Hunt & Brady, 1955).

9. Punishment is more effective if given immediately after the undesirable behavior. If the punishment is delayed, the animal probably will not learn to suppress the undesirable behavior (Kamin, 1959).
10. The more consistent the punishment, the greater the decrement in the number of responses. Intermittent punishment does not maintain suppression of the punished behavior (Azrin et al., 1963). (Note that, in contrast, intermittent reinforcement schedules are very effective.)
11. If alternative, rewarded responses are available, the animal will inhibit the punished behavior more readily (Herman & Azrin, 1964).
12. A behavior that is both reinforced and punished is likely to recur (Azrin & Holz, 1966). If an animal both receives a mild shock and a pellet of food for a response, it will continue responding.
13. If a cue such as a light is used to signal forthcoming punishment, future presentations of the light will reduce behavior (Dinsmoor, 1952).
14. When punishment of a certain response is used as a discriminative stimulus (a signal) that a reinforcer will follow, the punished behavior will not be inhibited, but probably will be increased (Azrin & Holz, 1961).
15. Higher levels of shock generally lead to more aggression by the punished organism toward objects or other people (Azrin, 1970; Ulrich et al., 1964) or toward oneself (Logan & Wallace, 1981).
16. Inescapable shock leads to a general inhibition of responding, which implies that the organism has developed a conditioned emotional response of fear (Estes & Skinner, 1941).
17. Inescapable punishment works proactively to prevent responding (Klee, 1944) and to reduce future problem solving. Dogs exposed to inescapable shock suffered from "learned helplessness" (Maier, Seligman, & Solomon, 1969).
18. Exposure to prior shock enhances the effects of mild punishment, but decreases the effects of intense punishment (Church, 1969).

NOTE

1. These terms, examples, and definitions appear in Willet and Barnett (1987).

Appendix C
Specific Learning Experiments

1. The Use of Both Punishment and Reinforcement in Humans

Ayllon and Azrin (1966) conditioned schizophrenics to respond to a punishment (noxious noise) coupled with reinforcement (token), and not to respond to a no-punishment, no-reinforcement condition. When the time between reinforcements lengthened, schizophrenics continued to select a punished response even without the accompanying reinforcement.

2. Conflict in Animals

Brown (1948) and Miller (1959) used rats to demonstrate several different types of conflict (approach-approach, approach-avoidance, avoidance-avoidance, and double approach-avoidance). For example, one goal consists of water and shock, whereas the other consists of food and shock. An animal faced with such a dilemma often runs halfway toward one of the goals and then retreats. Momentarily, it runs halfway toward the other goal, and then returns. Presumably, its approach behavior represents the desire for the positive goal (food or water), whereas its avoidance behavior reflects fear of the shock. The animal's degree of vacillation assesses its level of conflict or ambivalence.

3. Punishment as a Discriminative Cue for Reinforcement

When a cue (e.g., a tone) serves as a signal for forthcoming punishment, that same cue will reduce future behavior (Dinsmoor, 1952). Experiments by Holz and Azrin (1961) using pigeons indicated that if punishment were necessary to obtain a reward, the animal will accept the punishment. Pigeons learned to respond on a (variable interval) to punishment (shock) coupled with reinforcement (food), and not to respond to punishment alone (extinction). Because getting food depended on getting shocked, the pigeons increased their pecking even though they had to endure shocks. Punishment became a discriminative stimulus (cue) for a reward (signaled forthcoming food reinforcement).

4. Punishment-Facilitated Attachment

Rosenblum and Harlow (1963) detected significant variations between baby monkeys in attachment behavior with a monkey surrogate mother who differed in terms of her aversiveness. The babies who were given an opportunity to cling to a terry cloth "mother" in a situation involving the delivery of air blasts (punishment) spent more time with her than did a comparison group of monkey given access to a "mother" without the punishment. These findings suggest that punishment enhances the baby's responsiveness to the mother.

5. Extinction Failure: Responses Fixated Through Punishment

When rats receive punishment that is not sufficient to suppress their behavior, their behavior may become almost impossible to extinguish (Azrin et al., 1963). In a human example, a child who is inconsistently punished for throwing tantrums may continue throwing the tantrums for a very long time, even when the parents walk away (remove the reinforcement of attention). In other words, if a parent reacts to a child's tantrum by giving him or her attention, such as, "Don't cry. We are going to the park later. Come on, now, this is not worth crying about," the attention serves as a reward for throwing the tantrum.

6. The Gradual Build-up of Punishment

Using an increasing level of shock to punish a rat for pressing a lever does not lead to suppression of lever-pressing. Instead, the rat learns to adjust to the ever-increasing level of shock; it continues to press the lever (Sandler et al., 1966).

7. Matching Behavior

The Matching Law states that the relative frequency of responding on an alternative (e.g., Choice A—highly rewarded—or Choice B—less rewarded) matches the relative frequency of reinforcement for responses on that alternative. Interpreted, this statement implies that an animal will work harder on one alternative if it receives a higher reward (e.g., A) than it will for another alternative of lesser reward (e.g., B). That is, the organism matches its responses to the frequency (amount, value) of a reward.

It may be possible to apply the matching behavior seen in animal experiments on making choices to the escalation of abuse in marital violence (Herrnstein, 1970). (In learning theory, noxious events such as electrical shocks for animals or physical violence for humans can be used as either punishers—to decrease behavior—or as negative reinforcers—to increase behavior through avoidance.) It may be possible to apply the idea of matching to the escalation of abuse in battering. First, assume that various forms of abuse, such as threats or swearing, function as negative reinforcers. Because negative reinforcers increase the probability of future responses, one abusive behavior (e.g., swearing) might lead to responsive threats by the partner (a matching response), leading to shoving by the first partner (matching), and so forth. Each abuse (negative reinforcer) serves to increase the other partner's abusive response (which serves as a negative reinforcer), so that, overall, the abuse escalates.

8. Stress

Hans Selye (1946) was the first to offer a relatively complete picture of the devastating effects of response-based stress on rats. Different stressors, such as infection and heat, caused a nonspecific response of the body that went through three stages: (a) alarm (the body mobilizes its defenses), pushing energy use to the limit; (b) resistance (the body returns to normal and copes with the stressor); and (c) exhaustion (the body can no longer adapt to the stressor; symptoms occur; death may follow).

Human bodies may well go through similar stages when the stressor is emotional. If so, the experiments explain psychosomatic illnesses—real physical illnesses whose origins lie in emotional stress.

9. Predictable and Unpredictable Shock

Abbot et al. (1984) gave rats a choice between a signaled and unsignaled shock. The animals could not avoid the shock; they could only control their own ability to predict it. If the rat pressed the bar at the beginning of a sequence of trials, it earned a warning tone before every shock. If it did not press the bar at the beginning, it received no warning signal. All of the rats showed a marked preference for the signaled shock as reflected in their rapid learning of the bar press. The construct of control might be implied here.

10. Signaled Avoidance: Use of a Warning Signal

Bolles, Stokes, and Younger (1966) performed an experiment designed to examine escape and avoidance. In avoidance, rats learned to perform a task, such as running to the other ("safe") side of a box, at the sound of a tone (a learned signal) that signified that a shock was imminent. In escape, the animals could get away only after receiving the shock. They could not prevent it by performing a learned task (e.g., moving to the other side of a shuttle box).

11. Nonsignaled Avoidance: Use of Temporal Cues to Know When to Make an Avoidance Response

Work with laboratory animals in nonsignaled avoidance experiments also appears to be pertinent to issues of control raised in battering relationships. In a series of studies, Sidman (1953) placed rats in precarious situations that required them to respond (almost continuously at certain points during the experiment) to avoid the pain of being shocked. In these experiments, there was no handy signal, such as a tone, to warn the animal of the forthcoming shock. To a certain extent, the rat had to estimate when a response was necessary by paying attention to time (temporal cues).

A clock was set to deliver shocks to an animal provided it made no response. If the animal made an appropriate response (such as pressing a bar), the clock was reset, allowing the animal to rest before the clock was reactivated to deliver another shock. In other words, the rat could adjust his behavior to avoid or minimize the shock.

Actually, Sidman used two clocks in his experiment. The Shock-Shock (S-S) clock's timer was set to control the interval between shocks (e.g., 2 seconds) if the animal made no response (e.g., pressing a lever). In other words, an animal that did nothing or made the wrong response would receive a shock every 2 seconds ad infinitum until a power failure brought temporary relief.

The other clock was called the Response-Shock (R-S) clock. This clock controlled the elapsed time between a response and the delivery of a shock. To activate this clock, the animal had to make the appropriate response. If the R-S clock was set for 4-second intervals, the rat could relax for 4 seconds before responding again (pressing the lever). This behavior prevented the shock and reset the clock for another 4-second, safe period. If the animal did not respond appropriately, the 2-second S-S clock took over again, and the animal was shocked every 2 seconds.

Although there was no tangible cue that a shock was coming—no loud noise, light, or other event (conditioned stimulus) to warn the rats that a shock was imminent—they apparently learned to avoid shocks by attending to temporal cues, that is, to anticipate and to respond at specific time intervals.

This procedure, controlled by two clocks, is one of the most demanding schedules ever devised by research psychologists. It required constant vigilance and rapid response. It also took a long time to learn. The animals virtually lived "on the edge." For animals tested over several days, fatigue made it impossible for them to avoid all shocks and, in fact, to attend to the time interval cues. The rats could learn to avoid shock, even most shocks, but the rats were never able to avoid *all* shocks.

12. A Warning Signal Generates Fear

Brown and Jacobs (1949) exposed rats to different fear experiences. The first group of rats received a warning signal that ended with a shock. The second group received the same warning signal, but no shock. Later, both groups experienced the opportunity to turn off the warning signal by crossing from one side of a shuttle box to the other. The light remained on until the rats crossed over. The results indicated that the first group, the group that received the warning signal followed by the shock, learned to make the shuttle response significantly faster than the second group. The researchers interpreted these findings as signifying that the first group learned the shuttle response to reduce the fear generated by the warning signal. The termination of fear is reinforcing.

13. Motivation Following Frustration by Nonreward

Amsel and Rousel (1972) allowed rats to run in a straight runway to the first goal box for food, and then onward in the alley to a second goal box for additional food. After learning this procedure, the researchers frustrated the animals by not providing them with any food in the first goal box. When this occurred, the frustrated rats ran even faster than they had originally to the second goal box. They also ran faster than a control group of rats, which continued to receive the food reward in the first goal box. Apparently, frustration produced by the absence of anticipated reward in the first goal box intensified the rats' motivation to reach the second goal box.

14. Frustration and Its Consequences

Animals caught in an approach-avoidance situation develop frustration (Maier, 1949). One outcome of their frustration is stereotyped responses. For example, Maier, Glazer, and Klee (1940) trained rats to jump from a jumping stand into a slightly closed door. Food was behind the door as a reinforcer for jumping to the correct color (e.g., white, rather than black). Later, after the jumping was well-established, the problem was made unsolvable. For a number of trials, the animals received reinforcement on half of their jumps to the formerly correct color (i.e., white) and on half of their jumps to the formerly incorrect color (i.e., black). After this frustration training, the animals exhibited a number of unusual behaviors: (a) rigid responses, for example, only jumping to the "right"; (b) apathy, or refusal to jump at all; (c) peculiar postures that seemed catatonic; and (d) attempts to get out of the test situation altogether by jumping over the test apparatus into the laboratory area.

One of the most fascinating occurrences was that the animals walked to the correct door if the experimenter placed a little bridge between the jumping stand and the door. If the bridge was removed and the door opened so that the animal could actually see the food, he still would not jump to obtain it. His behavior was inflexible and self-defeating. The rat did not perform the correct response even when he knew what it was. This compulsive behavior is labeled "fixated."

15. Learned Helplessness in Dogs

Researchers who were using dogs for testing subjected one of three groups of dogs to inescapable shock trials (Maier & Seligman, 1976). A second group could escape, and a third comparison group received no shocks at all. Later, the experimenters tried to teach the dogs a new task—how to jump over a barrier to avoid a shock. The dogs given inescapable shocks were almost unable to learn the new task. The other two groups of dogs learned to avoid shocks in the new task quickly. The shocked dogs had apparently learned that nothing they did made a difference (learned helplessness).

References

Abbot, B. B., Schoen, L. S., & Badia, P. (1984). Predictable and unpredictable shock: Behavioral measures of aversion and physiological measures of stress. *Psychological Bulletin, 96,* 45-71.

Abbott, J., Johnson, R., Koziol-McLain, J., & Lowenstein, S. (1995). Domestic violence against women: Incidence and prevalence in an emergency department population. *Journal of the American Medical Association, 273,* 1763-1766.

Abram, K. M. (1990). The problem of co-occurring disorders among jail detainees. *Law and Human Behavior, 14,* 333-345.

Abramson, L. (1994, July 25). Unequal justice. *Newsweek, 124*(4), 25.

Abuse victims get new federal cards. (1998, November 5). *Los Angeles Daily News,* p. 12.

Abusive relationships and Stockholm Syndrome. (1991, September 23). *Behavior Today, 22*(39), 6-7.

Ackerman, M. J., & Ackerman, M. C. (1996). Child custody evaluation practices: A 1996 survey of psychologists. *Family Law Quarterly, 30,* 565-586.

Adams, D. C. (1984, August). *Stages of anti-sexist awareness and change for men who batter.* Paper presented at the annual meeting of the American Psychological Association, Toronto.

Adams, D. C. (1986, August). *Counseling men who batter: A profeminist analysis of five treatment models.* Paper presented at the annual meeting of the American Psychological Association, Washington, DC.

Adams, D. C. (1988). Treatment models of men who batter: A profeminist analysis. In K. A. Yllö & M. Bograd (Eds.), *Feminist perspectives on wife abuse* (pp. 176-199). Newbury Park, CA: Sage.

Adams, D. C., & McCormick, A. J. (1982). Men unlearning violence: A group approach based on the collective model. In M. Roy (Ed.), *The abusive partner: An analysis of domestic battering* (pp. 170-197). New York: Van Nostrand Reinhold.

Adler, A. (1927). *Practice and theory of individual psychology.* New York: Harcourt, Brace & World.

Adler, T. (1990, May). PTSD linked to stress rather than character. *APA Monitor, 21*(5), 12.

Aguilar, R. J., & Nightingale, N. N. (1994). The impact of specific battering experiences on the self-esteem of abused women. *Journal of Family Violence, 9,* 35-45.

Aguirre, B. E. (1985). Why do they return? Abused wives in shelters. *Social Work, 30,* 350-354.

Aldarondo, E. (1996). Cessation and persistence of wife assault: A longitudinal analysis. *American Journal of Orthopsychiatry, 66,* 141-151.

Aldrige, L., Friedman, C., & Occhiuzzo Giggans, P. (1995). *In touch with teens: A relationship violence prevention curriculum for youth ages 12 to 19.* Los Angeles: Los Angeles Commission on Assaults Against Women.

Alexander, P. (1997, June). *The measurement of role reversal as a mediator of intergenerational transmission of violence.* Paper presented at Program Evaluation and Family Violence Research Conference, Durham, NH.

Allen, D. M. (1988). *Unifying individual and family therapies.* San Francisco: Jossey-Bass.

Alpert, E. J., & Cohen, S. (1997). Educating the nation's physicians about family violence and abuse. *Academic Medicine, 71*(Suppl. 1), S3-S110.

Alsdurf, J. M. (1985). Wife abuse and the church: The response of pastors. *Response, 8*(1), 9-11.

American Association of Retired Persons. (1993). *Abused elders or older battered women? Report on the AARP forum.* Washington, DC: Author.

American Association of Retired Persons. (1994, January 12). *Survey of services for older battered women.* Unpublished final report. Washington, DC: Author.

American Psychiatric Association. (1980). *Diagnostic and statistical manual of mental disorders* (3rd ed.). Washington, DC: Author.

Amick-McMullen, A., Kilpatrick, D. G., Veronen, L. J., & Smith, S. (1989). Family survivors of homicide victims: Theoretical perspective and an exploratory study. *Journal of Traumatic Stress, 2,* 21-35.

Ammons, L. L. (1994). Discretionary justice: A legal and policy analysis of a governor's use of the clemency power in the cases of incarcerated women. *Journal of Law and Policy, 3,* 1-79.

Amsel, A., & Rousel, J. (1972). Behavior habituation, counterconditioning, and a general theory of persistence. In A. H. Black & W. F. Prokasy (Eds.), *Classical conditioning II: Current research and theory* (pp. 409-426). New York: Appleton-Century-Crofts.

Andelin, H. B. (1963). *Fascinating womanhood.* New York: Bantam. (Pacific Press edition)

Anderson, K. L. (1997). Gender, status and domestic violence: An integration of feminist and family violence approaches. *Journal of Marriage and the Family, 59,* 655-669.

Andrews, B., & Brewin, C. R. (1990). Attributions of blame for marital violence: A study of antecedents and consequences. *Journal of Marriage and the Family, 52,* 757-767.

Anetzberger, G. J. (1987). *The etiology of elder abuse by adult offspring.* Springfield, IL: Charles C Thomas.

Anson, O., & Sagy, S. (1995). Marital violence: Comparing women in violent and nonviolent unions. *Human Relations, 48,* 285-305.

Appel, J. B. (1963). Punishment and shock intensity. *Science, 141,* 528-529.

Arias, I., Lyons, C. M., & Street, A. E. (1997). Individual and marital consequences of victimization: Moderating effects of relationship efficacy and spouse support. *Journal of Family Violence, 12,* 193-210.

Arias, I., & Pape, K. T. (1999). Psychological abuse: Implications for adjustment and commitment to leave violent partners. *Violence and Victims, 14,* 55-67.

Aron, L. Y., & Olson, K. K. (1997, March). *Efforts of child welfare agencies to address domestic violence: The experiences of five communities.* Washington, DC: Urban Institute.

Asher, S. J. (1990, August). *Primary, secondary, and tertiary prevention of violence against women.* Paper presented at the annual meeting of the American Psychological Association, Boston.

Astin, M. C., Lawrence, K. J., & Foy, D. W. (1993). Posttraumatic stress disorder among battered women: Risk and resiliency factors. *Violence and Victims, 8,* 17-28.

Astin, M. C., Lawrence, K. J., Pincus, G., & Foy, D. W. (1990, October). *Moderator variables of post-traumatic stress disorder among battered women.* Paper presented at the annual meeting of the Society for Traumatic Stress Studies, New Orleans.

Astin, M. C., Ogland-Hand, S. M., Coleman, E. M., & Foy, D. W. (1991, August). *PTSD in battered women: Comparisons with maritally distressed controls.* Paper presented at the annual meeting of the American Psychological Association, San Francisco.

Astin, M. C., Ogland-Hand, S. M., Coleman, E. M., & Foy, D. W. (1995). Posttraumatic stress disorder and childhood abuse in battered women: Comparisons with maritally distressed women. *Journal of Consulting and Clinical Psychology, 63,* 308-312.

Atkinson, R. L., Atkinson, R. C., Smith, E. E., & Bem, D. J. (1990). *Introduction to psychology* (10th ed.). New York: Harcourt Brace Jovanovich.

Avery-Leaf, S., Cascardi, M., O'Leary, K. D., & Cano, A. (1997). Efficacy of a dating violence prevention program on attitudes justifying aggression. *Journal of Adolescent Health, 21,* 11-17.

Avni, N. (1991a). Battered wives: Characteristics of their courtship days. *Journal of Interpersonal Violence, 6,* 232-239.

Avni, N. (1991b). Battered wives: The home as a total institution. *Violence and Victims, 6,* 137-149.

Ayllon, T., & Azrin, N. H. (1966). Punishment as a discriminative stimulus and conditioned reinforcer with humans. *Journal of the Experimental Analysis of Behavior, 9,* 411-419.

Azrin, N. H. (1970). Punishment of elicited aggression. *Journal of the Experimental Analysis of Behavior, 14,* 7-10.

Azrin, N. H., & Holz, W. C. (1961). Punishment during fixed-interval reinforcement. *Journal of the Experimental Analysis of Behavior, 4,* 343-347.

Azrin, N. H., & Holz, W. C. (1966). Punishment. In W. R. Honig (Ed.), *Operant behavior: Areas of research and application* (pp. 380-447). New York: Appleton-Century-Crofts.

Azrin, N. H., Holz, W. C., & Hake, D. F. (1963). Fixed-ratio punishment. *Journal of the Experimental Analysis of Behavior, 6,* 141-148.

Bachman, R. (1994, January). *Violence against women* (NCVS Report; NCJ No. 145325). Rockville, MD: U.S. Department of Justice, Bureau of Justice Statistics.

Bachman, R., & Coker, A. L. (1995). Police involvement in domestic violence: The interactive effects of victim injury, offender's history of violence, and race. *Violence and Victims, 10,* 91-106.

Bachman, R., & Saltzman, L. E. (1995). *Violence against women: Estimates from the redesigned survey* (Bureau of Justice Statistics Special Report; NCJ No. 154348). Rockville, MD: U.S. Department of Justice.

Bachman, R., & Taylor, B. M. (1994). The measurement of family violence and rape by the redesigned National Crime Victimization Survey. *Justice Quarterly, 11,* 499-512.

Baker, N. V., Gregware, P. R., & Cassidy, M. A. (1999). Family killing fields: Honor rationales in the murder of women. *Violence Against Women, 5,* 164-184.

Bandura, A. (1971). *Social learning theory.* Morristown, NJ: General Learning.

Barkley, K. M. (1997). *Social change and social service: A case study of a feminist battered women's shelter* [CD-ROM]. Abstract from: ProQuest File: Dissertation Abstracts Item: 9638071

Barling, J., & Rosenbaum, A. (1986). Work stressors and wife abuse. *Journal of Applied Psychology, 71,* 346-348.

Barnard, G. W., Vera, H., Vera, M., & Newman, G. (1982). Till death do us part: A study of spouse murder. *Bulletin of the American Academy of Psychiatry and Law, 10,* 271-280.

Barnett, O. W. (1990). *Forms and frequencies of abuse.* Unpublished manuscript, Pepperdine University, Malibu, CA.

Barnett, O. W., & Fagan, R. W. (1993). Alcohol use in male spouse abusers and their female partners. *Journal of Family Violence, 8,* 1-25.

Barnett, O. W., & Hamberger, L. K. (1992). The assessment of maritally violent men on the California Psychological Inventory. *Violence and Victims, 7,* 15-28.

Barnett, O. W., Haney-Martindale, D. J., Modzelewski, C. A., & Sheltra, E. M. (1991, April). *Reasons why battered women feel self-blame.* Paper presented at the annual meeting of the Western Psychological Association, San Francisco.

Barnett, O. W., Keyson, M., & Thelen, R. E. (1992, August). *Battered women's responsive violence.* Paper presented at the annual meeting of the American Psychological Association, Washington, DC.

Barnett, O. W., Lee, C. Y., & Thelen, R. E. (1997). Differences in forms, outcomes, and attributions of self-defense and control in interpartner aggression. *Violence Against Women, 3,* 462-481.

Barnett, O. W., & Lopez-Real, D. I. (1985, November). *Women's reactions to battering and why they stay.* Paper presented at the annual meeting of the American Society of Criminology, San Diego, CA.

Barnett, O. W., Martinez, T. E., & Keyson, M. (1996). The relationship between violence, social support, and self-blame in battered women. *Journal of Interpersonal Violence, 11,* 221-233.

Barnett, O. W., Miller-Perrin, C. L., & Perrin, R. D. (1997). *Family violence across the lifespan.* Thousand Oaks, CA: Sage.

Barshis, V. R. G. (1983). The question of marital rape. *Women's Studies International Forum, 6,* 383-393.

Bassuk, E. L., Weinreb, L. F., Buckner, J. C., Browne, A., Salomon, A., & Bassuk, S. S. (1996). The characteristics and needs of sheltered homeless and low-income housed mothers. *Journal of the American Medical Association, 276,* 640-646.

Baumeister, R. F., Stillwell, A., & Wotman, S. R. (1990). Victim and perpetrator accounts of interpersonal conflict: Autobiographical narratives about anger. *Journal of Personality and Social Psychology, 59,* 994-1005.

Bauserman, S. K., & Arias, I. (1990, November). *Application of an investment model of commitment to spouse abuse.* Paper presented at the meeting of the Association for Advancement of Behavior Therapy, San Francisco.

Beck, M., Springer, K., & Foote, D. (1992, April). Sex and psychotherapy. *Newsweek, 119*(4), 53-57.

Belle, D. (1990). Poverty and women's mental health. *American Psychologist, 45,* 385-389.

Belmore, M. F., & Quinsey, V. P. (1994). Correlates of psychopathy in a noninstitutional sample. *Journal of Interpersonal Violence, 9,* 339-349.

Bennett, L. W. (1998, Fall/Winter). Substance abuse and women abuse by male partners. *Family Violence and Sexual Abuse Bulletin, 14*(3-4), 38.

Bennett, L., & Fineran, S. (1997, July). *Sexual and severe physical violence of high school students: Power beliefs, gender, and relationship.* Paper presented at the Fifth International Conference on Family Violence Research, Durham, NH.

Bennett, L., Goodman, L., & Dutton, M. A. (1999). Systemic obstacles to the criminal prosecution of a battering partner. *Journal of Interpersonal Violence, 14,* 761-772.

Bennett, L. W., Tolman, R. M., Rogalski, C. A., & Srinivasaraghavan, J. (1994). Domestic abuse by male alcohol and drug addicts. *Violence and Victims, 9,* 359-368.

Bergen, R. K. (1995). *Wife rape: Understanding the response of service providers.* Thousand Oaks, CA: Sage.

Berger, P. J., & Berger, B. (1979). Becoming a member of society. In P. I. Rose (Ed.), *Socialization and the life cycle* (pp. 4-20). New York: St. Martin's.

Bergman, B., Larsson, G., Brismar, B., & Klang, M. (1988). Aetiological and precipitating factors in wife battering. *Acta Psychiatric Scandinavia, 77,* 338-345.

Berkowitz, L., & LePage, A. (1967). Weapons as aggression-eliciting stimuli. *Journal of Personality and Social Psychology, 7,* 202-207.

Berliner, L. (1998). Battered women and abused children: The question of responsibility. *Journal of Interpersonal Violence, 13,* 287-289.

Bernard, C., & Schlaffer, E. (1992). Domestic violence in Austria: The institutional response. In E. C. Viano (Ed.), *Intimate violence: An interdisciplinary perspective* (pp. 243-254). Bristol, PA: Taylor & Francis.

Bethke, T., & De Joy, D. (1993). An experimental study of factors influencing the acceptability of dating violence. *Journal of Interpersonal Violence, 8,* 36-51.

Beyer, L. (1999, January 18). The price of honor. *Time, 153*(2), 55.

Biden, J. R., Jr. (1994). *Turning the act into action: The violence against women law* [Committee on the Judiciary]. Washington, DC: U.S. Senate.

Blackman, J. (1988, August). *Exploring the impacts of poverty on battered women who kill their abusers.* Paper presented at the annual meeting of the American Psychological Association, Atlanta, GA.

Bograd, M. (1992). Values in conflict: Challenges to family therapists' thinking. *Journal of Marital and Family Therapy, 18,* 245-256.

Boles, A. B., & Patterson, J. C. (1997). *Improving community response to crime victims: An eight-step model for developing protocol.* Thousand Oaks, CA: Sage.

Bolles, R. C., Stokes, L. W., & Younger, M. S. (1966). Does CS termination reinforce avoidance behavior? *Journal of Comparative and Physiological Psychology, 62,* 201-207.

Bookwala, J., Frieze, I. H., Smith, C., & Ryan, K. (1992). Predictors of dating violence: A multivariate analysis. *Violence and Victims, 7,* 297-311.

Boudreau, F. A. (1993). Elder abuse. In R. L. Hampton, T. P. Gullotta, G. R. Adams, E. H. Potter, III, & R. P. Weissberg (Eds.), *Family violence: Prevention and treatment* (pp. 142-158). Newbury Park, CA: Sage.

Bourg, S., & Stock, H. V. (1994). A review of domestic violence arrest statistics in a police department using a pro-arrest policy: Are pro-arrest policies enough? *Journal of Family Violence, 9,* 177-192.

Bower, B. (1992). Prior abuse stokes combat reactions. *Science News, 141,* 332.

Bower, B. (1999, March 27). Friendly peril for disaster workers. *Science News, 155,* 203.

Bowker, L. H. (1984). Battered wives and the police: A national study of usage and effectiveness. *Police Studies, 7,* 84-93.

Boxer, A. M., Cook, J. A., & Herdt, G. (1991). Double jeopardy: Identity transitions and parent-child relations among gay and lesbian youth. In K. A. Pillemer & K. McCartney (Eds.), *Parent-child relations throughout life* (pp. 59-92). Hillsdale, NJ: Lawrence Erlbaum.

Braidbill, K. (1997, October). A deadly force. *Los Angeles Magazine,* pp. 68-69, 71, 130-132.

Brandwein, R. A. (1997, June). *The use of public welfare by family violence victims: Implications of new federal welfare "reform."* Paper presented at the Fifth International Family Violence Research Conference, University of New Hampshire, Durham.

Brenner, J. (1991). Feminization of poverty. In J. Lorber & S. A. Farrell (Eds.), *The social construction of gender* (pp. 193-209). Newbury Park, CA: Sage.

Briere, J., Woo, R., McRae, B., Foltz, J., & Sitzman, R. (1997). Lifetime victimization history, demographics, and clinical status in female psychiatric emergency room patients. *Journal of Nervous and Mental Disease, 185,* 95-101.

Brines, J. (1994). Economic dependency, gender, and the division of labor at home. *American Journal of Sociology, 100,* 652-688.

Brinkerhoff, M. B., & Lupri, E. (1988). Interpersonal violence. *Canadian Journal of Sociology, 13,* 407-434.

Brookoff, D. (1997, October). *Drugs, alcohol, and domestic violence in Memphis.* Washington, DC: National Institute of Justice.

Broverman, I. K., Vogel, S. R., Broverman, D. M., Clarkson, F. E., & Rosenkrantz, P. S. (1972). Sex-role stereotypes: A current appraisal. *Journal of Social Issues, 28,* 59-78.

Brown, G., Bhrolchain, M., & Harris, T. (1975). Social class and psychiatric disturbance among women in an urban population. *Sociology, 9,* 225-254.

Brown, J. (1997). Working toward freedom from violence: The process of change in battered women. *Violence Against Women, 3,* 5-26.

Brown, J. (1998, July). *The Process of Change in Abused Women Scale (PROCAWS): Stage of change, pros & cons, and self-efficacy as measurable outcomes.* Paper presented at Program Evaluation and Family Violence Research: An International Conference, Durham, NH.

Brown, J. K. (1992). Introduction: Definitions, assumptions, themes, and issues. In D. A. Counts, J. K. Brown, & J. C. Campbell (Eds.), *Sanctions and sanctuary: Cultural perspectives on the beating of wives* (pp. 1-18). Boulder, CO: Westview.

Brown, J. S. (1948). Gradients of approach and avoidance responses and their relation to motivation. *Journal of Comparative and Physiological Psychology, 41,* 450-465.

Brown, J. S., & Jacobs, A. (1949). The role of fear in the motivation and acquisition of responses. *Journal of Experimental Psychology, 39,* 747-759.

Browne, A. (1983). *Self-defensive homicides by battered women: Relationships at risk.* Paper presented at the meeting of the American Psychology-Law Society, Chicago.

Browne, A. (1987). *When battered women kill.* New York: Free Press.

Browne, A. (1990, December 11). *Assaults between intimate partners in the United States: Incidence, prevalence, and proportional risk for women and men.* Testimony before the U.S. Senate, Committee on the Judiciary, Washington, DC.

Browne, A., & Bassuk, B. A. (1997). Intimate violence in the lives of homeless and poor housed women: Prevalence and patterns in an ethnically diverse sample. *American Journal of Orthopsychiatry, 67,* 261-278.

Browne, A., Salomon, A., & Bassuk, S. S. (1999). The impact of recent partner violence on poor women's capacity to maintain work. *Violence Against Women, 5,* 393-426.

Browning, J., & Dutton, D. (1986). Assessment of wife assault with the Conflict Tactics Scale: Using couple data to quantify the differential reporting effect. *Journal of Marriage and the Family, 48,* 375-379.

Brush, L. D. (1990). Violent acts and injurious outcomes in married couples: Methodological issues in the National Survey of Families and Households. *Gender & Society, 4,* 56-67.

Brustin, S. L. (1995). Legal responses to teen dating violence. *Family Law Quarterly, 29,* 331-356.

Bryan, P. (1992). Killing us softly: Divorce mediation and the politics of power. *Buffalo Law Review, 40,* 441-523.

Bryant, V., Eliach, J., & Green, S. L. (1991). Adapting the traditional EAP model to effectively serve battered women in the workplace. *Employee Assistance Quarterly, 6*(2), 1-10.

Buchanan, D. C., & Perry, P. A. (1985). Attitudes of police recruits towards domestic disturbances: An evaluation of family crisis intervention training. *Journal of Criminal Justice, 13,* 561-572.

Bureau of Justice Assistance. (1996, June). *Regional seminar series on developing and implementing antistalking codes* [Monograph, NCJ No. 156836]. Washington, DC: Author.

Bureau of Justice Statistics. (1992). *Criminal victimization in the United States, 1991* (NCJ No. 139563). Washington, DC: U.S. Department of Justice.

Bureau of Labor Statistics. (1999). *Usual weekly earnings of wage and salary workers: Fourth quarter 1998* (USDL No. 99-15). Washington, DC: Author.

Burgess, A. W., Baker, T., Greening, D., Hartman, C. R., Burgess, A. G., Douglas, J. E., & Halloran, R. (1997). Stalking behaviors within domestic violence. *Journal of Family Violence, 12,* 389-403.

Burke, A. (1995, July 31). Valley needs more shelter beds. *Los Angeles Daily News,* p. 6.

Burkhauser, R. V., & Duncan, G. J. (1989). Economic risks of gender roles: Income loss and life events over the life course. *Social Science Quarterly, 70,* 3-23.

Burt, M. R., Newmark, L. C., Olson, K. K., Aron, L. Y., & Harrell, A. V. (1997, March). *1997 report: Evaluation of the STOP formula grants under the Violence Against Women Act of 1994.* Washington, DC: Urban Institute.

Burton, J., Foy, D., Bwanausi, C., & Johnson, J. (1994). The relationship between the traumatic exposure, family dysfunction, and post-traumatic stress symptoms in male juvenile offenders. *Journal of Traumatic Stress, 7,* 83-93.

Bushman, B. J., & Cooper, H. M. (1990). Effects of alcohol on human aggression: An integrative research review. *Psychological Bulletin, 107,* 341-354.

Butehorn, L. (1985). Social networks and battered woman's decision to stay or leave. *Dissertation Abstracts International, 46,* 1741B. (UMI No. 8513594)

Buttell, F. (1997). Domestic violence as a contributing factor in the decision to divorce: Perspectives of divorcing parents. *Family Violence and Sexual Assault Bulleltin, 13*(3-4), 25-29.

Buzawa, E. S., Austin, T. L., & Buzawa, C. G. (1995). Responding to crimes of violence against women: Gender differences versus organizational imperatives. *Crime & Delinquency, 41,* 443-466.

Byrne, C. A., Resnick, H. S., Kilpatrick, D. G., Best, C. L., & Saunders, B. E. (1999). The socioeconomic impact of interpersonal violence on women. *Journal of Consulting and Clinical Psychology, 67,* 362-366.

Cadoret, R. J., Leve, L. D., & Devor, E. (1997). Genetics of aggressive and violent behavior. *Anger, Aggression, and Violence, 20,* 301-322.

California panel urges reforms to curb gender bias in courts. (1990, May 1). *Criminal Justice Newsletter, 21*(9), 4-5.

Camp, D. S., Raymond, G. A., & Church, R. M. (1967). Temporal relationship between response and punishment. *Journal of Experimental Psychology, 74,* 114-123.

Campbell, D. (1993). Nursing care of African-American women: Afrocentric perspectives. *Association of Women's Health, Obstetric, and Neonatal Nurses' Clinical Issues, 4,* 407-415.

Campbell, J. C. (1989a). A test of two explanatory models of women's responses to battering. *Nursing Research, 38*(1), 18-24.

Campbell, J. C. (1989b). Women's responses to sexual abuse in intimate relationships. *Health Care for Women International, 8,* 335-347.

Campbell, J. C. (1990, December). Battered woman syndrome: A critical review. *Violence UpDate, 1*(4), 1, 4, 10-11.

Campbell, J. C. (1992). "If I can't have you, no one can": Power and control in homicide of female partners. In J. Radford & D. E. Russell (Eds.), *Femicide: The politics of women killing* (pp. 88-113). New York: Twayne.

Campbell, J. C., & Alford, P. (1989). The dark consequences of marital rape. *American Journal of Nursing, 87,* 946-949.

Campbell, J. C., & Humphreys, J. H. (1984). *Nursing care of victims of family violence.* Norwalk, CT: Appleton-Lange.

Campbell, J. C., Kub, J., Belknap, R. A., & Templin, T. N. (1997). Predictors of depression in battered women. *Violence Against Women, 3,* 271-293.

Campbell, J. C., & Lewandowski, L. A. (1997). Mental and physical health effects of intimate partner violence on women and children. *Psychiatric Clinics of North America, 20,* 353-374.

Campbell, J. C., Miller, P., Cardwell, M. M., & Belknap, R. A. (1994). Relationship status of battered women over time. *Journal of Family Violence, 9,* 99-111.

Campbell, J. C., & Sheridan, D. J. (1989). Emergency nursing interventions with battered women. *Journal of Emergency Nursing, 15,* 12-17.

Campbell, J. C., & Soeken, K. L. (1999). Women's responses to battering over time. *Journal of Interpersonal Violence, 14,* 21-40.

Cantos, A. L., Neidig, P. H., & O'Leary, K. D. (1994). Injuries of women and men in a treatment program for domestic violence. *Journal of Family Violence, 9,* 113-124.

Caplan, P. J. (1984). The myth of women's masochism. *American Psychologist, 39,* 130-139.

Carlisle-Frank, P. (1991, July). Do battered women's beliefs about control affect their decisions to remain in abusive environments? *Violence UpDate, 1*(11), 1, 8, 10-11.

Carlson, B. E. (1997). Mental retardation and domestic violence: An ecological approach to intervention. *Social Work, 42,* 79-89.

Carlson, C., & Nidey, F. J. (1995). Mandatory penalties, victim cooperation, and the judicial processing of domestic abuse assault cases. *Crime & Delinquency, 41,* 132-149.

Carlson, M. J., Harris, S. D., & Holden, G. W. (1999). Protective orders and domestic violence: Risk factors for re-abuse. *Journal of Family Violence, 14,* 205-226.

Carmen, E. H., Ricker, P. P., & Mills, T. (1984). Victims of violence and psychiatric illness. *American Journal of Psychiatry, 141,* 379-383.

Carmody, D. C., & Williams, K. R. (1987). Wife assault and perceptions of sanctions. *Violence and Victims, 2,* 25-38.

Cascardi, M., & O'Leary, K. D. (1992). Depressive symptomatology, self-esteem, and self-blame in battered women. *Journal of Family Violence, 7,* 249-259.

Cascardi, M., Vivian, D., & Meyer, S. L. (1991, November). *Context and attributions for marital violence in discordant couples.* Paper presented at the annual meeting of the Association for Advancement of Behavior Therapy, New York.

Catania, C. (1984). *Learning.* Englewood Cliffs, NJ: Prentice Hall.

Caulfield, M. B., Riggs, D. S., & Street, A. (1999, July). *The role of commitment in the perpetration of dating violence.* Paper presented at the 6th International Family Violence Research Conference, Durham, NH.

The Center on Crime, Communities & Culture of the Open Society Institute. (1999). *Domestic violence: National directory of professional services.* New York: Author.

Chalk, R., & King, P. A. (Eds.). (1998). *Violence in families: Assessing prevention and treatment programs.* Washington, DC: National Academy Press.

Chang, D. B. K. (1989). An abused spouse's self-saving process: A theory of identity transformation. *Sociological Perspectives, 32,* 535-550.

Chester, B., Robin, R. W., Koss, M. P., Lopez, M. P., & Goldman, D. (1994). Grandmother dishonored: Violence against women by male partners in American Indian communities. *Violence and Victims, 9,* 249-258.

Children's Safety Network. (1992). *Domestic violence: A directory of protocols for health care providers.* Newton, MA: Education Development Center.

Chin, K. (1994). Out-of-town brides: International marriage and wife abuse among Chinese immigrants. *Journal of Comparative Family Studies, 25,* 53-69.

Choice, P., Lamke, L. K., & Pittman, J. F. (1995). Conflict resolution strategies and marital distress as mediating factors in the link between witnessing interparental violence and wife beating. *Violence and Victims, 10,* 107-119.

Christian, J. L., O'Leary, K. D., & Vivian, D. (1994). Depressive symptomatology in maritally discordant women and men: The role of individual and relationship variables. *Journal of Family Psychology, 8,* 32-42.

Church, R. M. (1969). Response suppression. In B. A. Campbell & R. M. Church (Eds.), *Punishment and aversive behavior* (pp. 111-156). New York: Appleton-Century-Crofts.

City receives grant to combat abuse. (1996, December 21). *Los Angeles Daily News,* p. 8.

Claerhout, S., Elder, J., & Janes, C. (1982). Problem-solving skills of rural battered women. *American Journal of Community Psychology, 10,* 605-612.

Clarke, P. N., Pendry, N. C., & Kim, Y. S. (1997). Patterns of violence in homeless women. *Western Journal of Nursing Research, 19,* 490-500.

Clarke, R. L. (1986). *Pastoral care of battered women.* Philadelphia: Westminster.

Coan, J., Gottman, J. M., Babcock, J., & Jacobson, N. (1997). Battering and the male rejection of influence from women. *Aggressive Behavior, 23,* 375-388.

Cohen, J. H., Forjuoh, S. N., & Gondolf, E. W. (1999). Injuries and health care use in women with partners in batterer intervention programs. *Journal of Family Violence, 14,* 83-94.

Cohn, I. D. (1991). Sex differences in the course of personality development: A meta-analysis. *Psychological Bulletin, 109,* 252-266.

Cole, C. (1988). Routine comprehensive inquiry for abuse: A justifiable clinical assessment procedure. *Clinical Social Work Journal, 16,* 33-42.

Cole, T., & Sapp, G. (1988). Stress, locus of control, and achievement of high school seniors. *Psychological Reports, 63,* 355-359.

Coleman, D. H., & Straus, M. A. (1986). Marital power, conflict, and violence in a nationally representative sample of American couples. *Violence and Victims, 1,* 141-157.

Coleman, V. E. (1992, August). *Breaking the silence about lesbian battering: New directions in domestic violence theory.* Paper presented at the annual meeting of the American Psychological Association, Washington, DC.

Cook, P. W. (1997). *Abused men: The hidden side of domestic violence.* Westport, CT: Praeger.

Cook-Daniels, L. (1998, September/October). Abuse of lesbian and gay male elders. *Victimization of the Elderly and Disabled, 1*(3), 37, 47.

Cooper-White, P. (1996). An emperor without clothes: The church's views about treatment of domestic violence. *Pastoral Psychology, 45,* 3-20.

Counts, D. A., Brown, J. K., & Campbell, J. C. (Eds.). (1992). *Sanctions and sanctuary: Cultural perspectives on the beating of wives.* Boulder, CO: Westview.

Court allows suit questioning 911 domestic violence response. (1999, February 2). *Criminal Justice Newsletter, 30*(3), 3.

Court of appeals to rehear Lautenberg firearm case. (1999, February/March). *Domestic Violence Report, 4,* 37.

Craven, D. (1997). *Sex differences in violent victimization, 1994* (NCJ No. 164508). Washington, DC: U.S. Department of Justice.

Crawford, M., & Gartner, R. (1992). *Women killing, intimate femicide in Ontario 1974-1990.* Oshawa, Ontario, Canada: Women We Honour Action Committee.

Crawford, M., & Masterson, F. (1978). Components of the flight response can reinforce bar-press avoidance. *Journal of Experimental Psychology: Animal Behavior Processes, 4,* 144-151.

Creighton, A., & Kivel, P. (1993). *Helping teens stop violence: A practical guide to counselors.* Alameda, CA: Hunter House.

Cucio, W. (1997). *The Passaic county study of AFDC recipients in a welfare-to-work program: A preliminary analysis.* Patterson, NJ: Passaic County Board of Social Services.

Cummings, E. M. (1998). Children exposed to marital conflict and violence: Conceptual and theoretical directions. In G. W. Holden, R. Geffner, & E. N. Jouriles (Eds.), *Children exposed to marital violence* (pp. 55-93). Washington, DC: American Psychological Association.

Cummings, N. (1990). Issues of the 1990s. *Response, 13*(1), 4.

Currens, S. (1998, April/May). Kentucky coalition's concerns about mandatory reporting. *Domestic Violence Report, 3,* 49-50.

Dalto, C. A. (1983). Battered women: Factors influencing whether or not former shelter residents return to the abusive situation. *Dissertation Abstracts International, 44,* 1277B. (UMI No. 8317463)

Danis, F. S., Lewis, C. M., Trapp, J., Reid, K., & Fisher, E. R. (1998, July). *Lessons from the first year: An evaluation of the National Domestic Violence Hotline.* Paper presented at the meeting of Program Evaluation and Family Violence Research: An International Conference, Durham, NH.

D'Augelli, A. R. (1991). Gay men in college: Identity processes and adaptations. *Journal of College Student Development, 32,* 140-146.

D'Augelli, A. R. (1992). Lesbian and gay male undergraduates' experiences of harassment and fear on campus. *Journal of Interpersonal Violence, 7,* 383-395.

Davidson, H. A. (1995). Child abuse and domestic violence: Legal connections and controversies. *Family Law Quarterly, 29,* 357-373.

Davies, B., Ralph, S., Hawton, M., & Craig, L. (1995). A study of client satisfaction with family court counselling in cases involving domestic violence. *Family and Conciliation Courts Review, 33,* 324-341.

Davis, M. H., & Morris, M. M. (1998). Relationship-specific and global perceptions of social support: Associations with well-being and attachment. *Journal of Personality and Social Psychology, 74,* 468-481.

Davis, R. C., & Taylor, B. G. (1997). A proactive response to family violence: The results of a randomized experiment. *Criminology, 35,* 307-333.

Davis, R. L. (1998). *Domestic violence: Facts and fallacies.* Westport, CT: Praeger.

DeFronzo, J. (1997). Welfare and homicide. *Journal of Research in Crime and Delinquency, 34,* 395-406.

DeKeseredy, W. S. (1990). Male peer support and woman abuse: The current state of knowledge. *Sociological Focus, 23,* 129-139.

DeKeseredy, W. S., & Kelly, K. D. (1993). The incidence and prevalence of woman abuse in Canadian university and college dating relationships. *Canadian Journal of Sociology, 18,* 137-159.

DeLozier, P. (1992). Attachment theory and child abuse. In C. M. Parks & J. Stevenson-Hinde (Eds.), *The place of attachment in human behavior* (pp. 95-117). New York: Basic Books.

DePaul, A. (1992, January 16). New laws in California aid women victimized by violence. *Criminal Justice Newsletter, 23*(2), 5-6.

Depner, C. E., Canatta, K., & Ricci, I. (1995). Report 4: Mediated agreements on child custody and visitation: 1991 California family court services snapshot study. *Family and Conciliation Courts Review, 33,* 87-109.

De Stafano, A. M. (1988, October 7). New York teen antigay poll finds. *Newsday,* pp. 7, 21.

Dinsmoor, J. A. (1952). A discrimination based on punishment. *Quarterly Journal of Experimental Psychology, 4,* 27-45.

Dobash, R. E. (1976-1977). *The relationship between violence directed at women and violence directed at children within the family setting.* Appendix 38, Parliamentary Select Committee on Violence in the Family. London: HMSO.

Dobash, R. E., & Dobash, R. P. (1979). *Violence against wives: A case against patriarchy.* New York: Free Press.

Dobash, R. P., & Dobash, R. E. (1991). *Gender, methodology, and methods in criminological research: The case of spousal violence.* Paper presented at the British Criminology Conference, York, UK.

Dobash, R. P., Dobash, R. E., Cavanagh, K., & Lewis, R. (1998). Separate and intersecting realities: A comparison of men's and women's accounts of violence against women. *Violence Against Women, 4,* 382-414.

Dobash, R. P., Dobash, R. E., Wilson, M., & Daly, M. (1992). The myth of sexual symmetry in marital violence. *Social Problems, 39,* 71-91.

Dodge, M., & Greene, E. (1991). Juror and expert conceptions of battered women. *Violence and Victims, 6,* 271-282.

Domestic violence in the courts [Excerpted from Gender Bias in the Courts, Report of the Maryland Special Joint Committee on Gender Bias in the Courts, Annapolis, MD]. (1989). *Response, 12*(4), 3-6.

Domestic violence conviction bars gun possession by officers. (1997, January 2). *Criminal Justice Newsletter,* pp. 2-3.

Domjan, M., & Burkhard, B. (1989). *The principles of learning and behavior.* Monterey, CA: Brooks/Cole.

Donaldson, M., & Gardner, R. (1985). Diagnosis and treatment of traumatic stress among women after childhood incest. In C. R. Figley (Ed.), *Trauma and its wake* (Vol. 1, pp. 356-377). New York: Brunner/Mazel.

Douglas, H. (1991). Assessing violent couples. *Families in Society: The Journal of Contemporary Human Services, 72,* 525-534.

Douglas, M. A. (1987). The battered woman syndrome. In D. J. Sonkin (Ed.), *Domestic violence on trial: Psychological and legal dimensions of family violence* (pp. 39-54). New York: Springer.

Douglas, M. A., & Colantuono, A. (1987, July). *Cluster analysis of MMPI scores among battered women.* Paper presented at the Third National Family Violence Research Conference, Durham, NH.

Doumas, D., Margolin, G., & John, R. S. (1994). The intergenerational transmission of aggression across three generations. *Journal of Family Violence, 9,* 157-175.

Downs, W. R., & Miller, B. A. (1998). Relationship between experiences of parental violence during childhood and women's self-esteem. *Violence and Victims, 13,* 63-77.

Draper, T. W., & Gordon, T. (1986). Men's perceptions of nurturing behavior in other men. *Psychological Reports, 59,* 11-18.

Duncan, G. J. (1987). *Economic status of women.* Ann Arbor: University of Michigan, Institute for Social Research.

Dunford, F. W., Huizinga, D., & Elliott, D. S. (1990). The role of arrest in domestic assault: The Omaha police experiment. *Criminology, 28,* 183-206.

Dunkel-Schetter, C., Folkman, S., & Lazarus, R. S. (1987). Correlates of social support receipt. *Journal of Personality and Social Psychology, 53,* 71-80.

DuRant, R. H., Cadenhead, C., Pendergrast, R. A., Slavens, G., & Linder, C. W. (1994). Factors associated with the use of violence among urban black adolescents. *American Journal of Public Health, 84,* 612-617.

Duryee, M. A. (1995). Guidelines for family court services intervention when there are allegations of domestic violence. *Family and Conciliation Courts Review, 33,* 79-86.

Dutton, D. G. (1994). Patriarchy and wife assault: An ecological fallacy. *Violence and Victims, 9,* 167-182.

Dutton, D. G. (1998). *The abusive personality.* New York: Guilford.

Dutton, D. G., Fehr, B., & McEwen, H. (1982). Severe wife battering as deindividuation violence. *Victimology: An International Journal, 7*(1-4), 13-23.

Dutton, D. G., & Haring, M. (1999). Perpetrator personality effects on post-separation victim reactions in abusive relationships. *Journal of Family Violence, 14,* 193-204.

Dutton, D. G., & Painter, S. L. (1981). Traumatic bonding: The development of emotional attachments in battered women and other relationships of intermittent abuse. *Victimology: An International Journal, 6*(1-4), 139-155.

Dutton, D. G., & Painter, S. L. (1993a). The battered woman syndrome: Effects of severity and intermittency of abuse. *American Journal of Orthopsychiatry, 63,* 614-622.

Dutton, D. G., & Painter, S. L. (1993b). Emotional attachments in abusive relationships: A test of traumatic bonding theory. *Violence and Victims, 8,* 105-120.

Dutton, D. G., Saunders, K., Starzomski, A., & Bartholomew, K. (1994). Intimacy-anger and insecure attachment as precursors of abuse in intimate relationships. *Journal of Applied Social Psychology, 24,* 1367-1386.

Dutton, D. G., & Strachan, C. E. (1987). Motivational needs for power and spouse-specific assertiveness in assaultive and nonassaultive men. *Violence and Victims, 2,* 145-156.

Dutton, M. A. (1992). *Empowering and healing the battered woman: A model of assessment and intervention.* New York: Springer.

Dutton, M. A., Burghardt, K. J., Perrin, S. G., Chrestman, K. R., & Halle, P. M. (1994). Battered women's cognitive schemata. *Journal of Traumatic Stress, 7,* 237-255.

Dziegielewski, S. F., Resnick, C., & Krause, N. B. (1996). Shelter-based crisis intervention with battered women. In A. R. Roberts (Ed.), *Helping battered women* (pp. 159-171). New York: Oxford University Press.

D'Zurilla, T. J. (1986). *Problem-solving therapy: A social competence approach to clinical intervention.* New York: Springer.

Eagly, A. H., & Johnson, B. T. (1990). Gender and leadership style: A meta-analysis. *Psychological Bullletin, 108,* 233-256.

Eby, K. K., Campbell, J. C., Sullivan, C. M., & Davidson, W. S. (1995). Health effects of experiences of sexual violence for women with abusive partners. *Health Care for Women International, 16,* 563-576.

Edleson, J. L. (1999). The overlap between child maltreatment and woman battering. *Violence Against Women, 5,* 134-154.

Edleson, J. L., & Brygger, M. P. (1986). Gender differences in reporting of battering incidents. *Family Relations, 35,* 377-382.

Edwards, J. N., Fuller, T. D., Vorakitphokatom, S., & Sermsi, S. (1994). *Household crowding and its consequences.* Boulder, CO: Westview.

Eigenberg, H., & Moriarty, L. (1991). Domestic violence and local law enforcement in Texas. *Journal of Interpersonal Violence, 6,* 102-109.

Eisikovits, Z., & Buchbinder, E. (1996). Pathways to disenchantment: Battered women's views of their social workers. *Journal of Interpersonal Violence, 11,* 425-440.

Eisler, R. M., Skidmore, J. R., & Ward, C. H. (1988). Masculine gender-role stress: Predictor of anger, anxiety, and health-risk behavior. *Journal of Personality Assessment, 52,* 133-141.

Ellard, J. H., Herbert, T. B., & Thompson, L. J. (1991). Coping with an abusive relationship: How and why do people stay? *Journal of Marriage and the Family, 53,* 311-325.

Ellis, D. (1989). Male abuse of a married or cohabiting female partner: The application of sociological theory to research findings. *Violence and Victims, 4,* 235-255.

Ellis, D. (1992). Woman abuse among separated and divorced women: The relevance of social support. In E. C. Viano (Ed.), *Intimate violence: Interdisciplinary perspectives* (pp. 177-189). Bristol, PA: Taylor & Francis.

Ellis, L. (1998). Neodarwinian theories of violent criminality and antisocial behavior: Photographic evidence from nonhuman animals and a review of the literature. *Aggression and Violent Behavior, 3,* 61-110.

Ellsberg, M., Caldera, T., Herrera, A., Winkvist, A., & Kullgren, G. (1999). Domestic violence and emotional distress among Nicaraguan women. *American Psychologist, 54,* 30-36.

Emery, B. C., Lloyd, S. A., & Castleton, A. (1989, November). *Why women hit: A feminist perspective.* Paper presented at the annual conference of the National Conference on Family Relations, New Orleans.

Emery, R. E., & Laumann-Billings, L. (1998). An overview of the nature, causes, and consequences of abusive family relationships. *American Psychologist, 53,* 121-135.

Epidemiology of domestic violence. (1984, September 4). *Criminal Justice Newsletter, 16*(17), 4.

Erez, E., & Belknap, J. (1998). In their own words: Battered women's assessment of the criminal processing system's response. *Violence and Victims, 13,* 251-268.

Espinal, R., & Grasmuck, S. (1997). Gender, household and informal entrepreneurship in the Dominican Republic. *Journal of Comparative Family Studies, 28,* 103-128.

Estes, W. K., & Skinner, B. F. (1941). Some quantitative properties of anxiety. *Journal of Experimental Psychology, 29,* 390-400.

Ewing, C. P., & Aubrey, M. (1987). Battered women and public opinion: Some realities about myths. *Journal of Family Violence, 2,* 257-264.

Faludi, S. (1991). *Backlash.* New York: Crown.

Fantuzzo, J. W., DePaola, L. M., Lambert, L., Martino, T., Anderson, G., & Sutton, S. (1991). Effects of interparental violence on the psychological adjustment and competencies of young children. *Journal of Consulting and Clinical Psychology, 59,* 258-265.

Fawcett, G. M., Heise, L. L., Isita-Espejel, L., & Pick, S. (1999). Changing community responses to wife abuse. *American Psychologist, 54,* 41-49.

Feder, L. (1997). Domestic violence and police response in a pro-arrest jurisdiction. *Women & Criminal Justice, 8*(4), 79-97.

Feder, L. (1998). Police handling of domestic and nondomestic assault calls: Is there a case for discrimination? *Crime & Delinquency, 44,* 335-349.

Federal Bureau of Investigation. (1984). *Reporting handbook.* Washington, DC: Government Printing Office.

Federal Bureau of Investigation. (1989). *Uniform crime reports for the United States.* Washington, DC: Government Printing Office.

Federal court finds no protection against dismissal from employment due to spousal violence. (1996, February/March). *Domestic Violence Report, 1,* 7.

Feindler, E. L. (1988, August). *Cognitive-behavioral analysis of anger in abused women.* Paper presented at the annual meeting of the American Psychological Association, Atlanta.

Felix, A. C., III, & McCarthy, K. F. (1994). *An analysis of child fatalities, 1992.* Boston: Commonwealth of Massachusetts Department of Social Services.

Felson, R. B. (1992). "Kick 'em when they're down": Explanation of the relationship between stress and interpersonal aggression and violence. *Sociological Quarterly, 33,* 1-16.

Felson, R. B., & Messner, S. F. (1998). Disentangling the effects of gender and intimacy on victim precipitation in homicide. *Criminology, 36,* 405-423.

Ferguson, K. E. (1980). *Self, society, and womankind: The dialectic of liberation.* Westport, CT: Greenwood.

Ferraro, K. J. (1979). Hard love: Letting go of an abusive husband. *Frontiers, 4*(2), 16-18.

Ferraro, K. J. (1981). Battered women and the shelter movement. *Dissertation Abstracts International, 42,* 879A. (UMI No. 8115605)

Fields, M. (1978). *Battered women: Issues of public policy: A consultation sponsored by the United States Commission on Civil Rights.* Washington, DC: U.S. Commission on Civil Rights.

Fields-Meyer, T., & Benet, L. (1998, November 16). Speaking out. *People Weekly, 50*(18), 232, 234.

Fields-Meyer, T., Benet, L., Berestein, L., & Dodd, J. (1998, November 30). Upfront. *People Weekly, 50*(20), 66-68.

Fighting discrimination against battered victims. (1996, May). *Merritt Insurance Pro,* pp. 1-3.

Finkelhor, D. (1983). Common features of family abuse. In D. Finkelhor, R. J. Gelles, G. T. Hotaling, & M. A. Straus (Eds.), *The dark side of families* (pp. 17-30). Beverly Hills, CA: Sage.

Finkelhor, D. (1984). *Child sexual abuse: New theory and research.* New York: Free Press.

Finkelhor, D., & Yllö, K. (1982). Forced sex in marriage: A preliminary research report. *Crime & Delinquency, 82,* 459-478.

Finn, J. (1985). The stresses and coping behavior of battered women. *Social Casework: The Journal of Contemporary Social Work, 66,* 341-349.

Fitzpatrick, K. M., La Gory, M. E., & Ritchey, F. J. (1993). Criminal victimization among the homeless. *Justice Quarterly, 10,* 353-368.

Flanagan, T. J., & McGarrell, E. F. (1986). *Sourcebook of criminal justice statistics—1985* (NCJ No. 1008999). Washington, DC: Bureau of Justice Statistics.

Flanzer, J. P. (1993). Alcohol and other drugs are key causal agents of violence. In R. J. Gelles & D. R. Loseke (Eds.), *Current controversies on family violence* (pp. 171-181). Newbury Park, CA: Sage.

Flynn, C. P. (1990). Relationship violence by women: Issues and implications. *Family Relations, 39,* 194-198.

Flynn, C. P. (1996). Normative support for corporal punishment: Attitudes, correlates, and implications. *Aggression and Violent Behavior, 1,* 47-55.

Foa, E. B., Olasov, B., & Steketee, G. S. (1987, September). *Treatment of rape victims.* Paper presented at the conference State of the Art in Sexual Assault, Charleston, SC.

Follette, V. M., Polusny, M. A., Bechtle, A. E., & Naugle, A. E. (1996). Cumulative trauma: The impact of child sexual abuse, adult sexual assault, and spouse abuse. *Journal of Traumatic Stress, 9,* 25-35.

Follingstad, D. R. (1998, March). *Battered Woman Syndrome and Rape Trauma Syndrome: How exactly are they defined and what definitions can we actually state in court?* Paper presented at the American Psychology-Law Society 1998 Biennial Conference, Redondo Beach, CA.

Follingstad, D. R., Brennan, A. F., Hause, E. S., Polek, D. S., & Rutledge, L. L. (1991). Factors moderating physical and psychological symptoms of battered women. *Journal of Family Violence, 6,* 81-95.

Follingstad, D. R., Brondino, M. J., & Kleinfelter, K. J. (1996). Reputation and behavior of battered women who kill their partners: Do these variables negate self-defense? *Journal of Family Violence, 11,* 251-267.

Follingstad, D. R., Hause, E. S., Rutledge, L. L., & Polek, D. S. (1992). Effects of battered women's early responses on later abuse patterns. *Violence and Victims, 7,* 109-128.

Follingstad, D. R., Rutledge, L. L., Berg, B. J., Hause, E. S., & Polek, D. S. (1990). The role of emotional abuse in physically abusive relationships. *Journal of Family Violence, 5,* 107-120.

Fortune, M. (1987). *Keeping the faith.* San Francisco: Harper & Row.

Freud, A. (1942). *The ego and the mechanisms of defense.* New York: International Universities Press.

Frieze, I. H. (1979). Perceptions of battered wives. In I. H. Frieze, D. Bar-Tal, & J. S. Carroll (Eds.), *New approaches to social problems* (pp. 79-108). San Francisco: Jossey-Bass.

Frisch, M. B., & MacKenzie, C. J. (1991). A comparison of formerly and chronically battered women on cognitive and situational dimensions. *Psychotherapy, 28,* 339-344.

Fyfe, J. J., Klinger, D. A., & Flavin, J. M. (1997). Differential police treatment of male-on-female spousal violence. *Criminology, 35,* 455-473.

Gamache, D. J., Edleson, J. L., & Schock, M. D. (1988). Coordinated police, judicial and social service response to woman battering: A multi-baseline evaluation across communities. In G. T. Hotaling, D. Finkelhor, J. T. Kirkpatrick, & M. A. Straus (Eds.), *Coping with family violence: Research and policy perspectives* (pp. 193-209). Newbury Park, CA: Sage.

Garanzini, M. J. (1988). Troubled homes: Pastoral responses to violent and abusive families. *Pastoral Psychology, 36,* 218-229.

Gardner, R. A. (1987). *The parental alienation syndrome and the differentiation between fabricated and genuine child sex abuse.* Creskill, NJ: Creative Therapeutics.

Garner, J., & Clemmer, E. (1986). *Danger to police in domestic disturbances—A new look.* Washington, DC: National Institute of Justice.

Gartner, R. (1993). Methodological issues in cross-cultural large-survey research on violence. *Violence and Victims, 8,* 199-215.

Gartner, R., Baker, K., & Pampel, F. C. (1990). Gender stratification and the gender gap in homicide victimization. *Social Problems, 37,* 593-612.

Gauthier, D. K., & Bankston, W. B. (1997). Gender equality and the sex ratio of intimate killings. *Criminology, 35,* 577-600.

Gay, W. C. (1997). The reality of linguistic violence against women. In L. L. O'Toole & J. R. Schiffman (Eds.), *Gender violences: Interdisciplinary perspectives* (pp. 467-473). New York: New York University Press.

Geer, J., & Maisel, E. (1972). Evaluating the effects of the prediction-control confound. *Journal of Personality and Social Psychology, 23,* 314-319.

Geffner, R., & Pagelow, M. D. (1990). Victims of spouse abuse. In R. T. Ammerman & M. Hersen (Eds.), *Treatment of family violence: A sourcebook* (pp. 81-97). New York: Wiley.

Gellen, M. I., Hoffman, R. A., Jones, M., & Stone, M. (1984). Abused and nonabused women: MMPI profile differences. *Personnel and Guidance Journal, 62,* 601-604.

Gelles, R. J. (1995). *Domestic violence factoids* [On-line]. Available at http://www.mincava.umn.edu/papers/factoid.htm.

Gelles, R. J., & Harrop, J. W. (1989). Violence, battering, and psychological distress among women. *Journal of Interpersonal Violence, 4,* 400-420.

Gerow, J. R. (1989). *Psychology: An introduction* (2nd ed.). Glenville, IL: Scott, Foresman.

Gibbs, N. (1993, January 18). 'Til death do us part. *Time, 141*(2), 38, 40-45.

Gibson, J. W., & Gutierrez, L. (1991). A service program for safe-home children. *Families in Society, 72,* 554-562.

Gilbert, L., & Webster, P. (1982). *Bound by love, the sweet trap of daughterhood.* Boston: Beacon.

Gilligan, C. (1982). *In a different voice.* Cambridge, MA: Harvard University Press.

Giordano, P. C., Millhollin, T. J., Cernkovich, S. A., Pugh, M. D., & Rudolph, J. L. (1999). Delinquency, identity, and women's involvement in relationship violence. *Criminology, 37,* 17-37.

Gleason, W. J. (1995). Children of battered women: Developmental delays and behavioral dysfunction. *Violence and Victims, 10,* 153-160.

Goelman, D. M., Lehrman, F. L., & Valente, R. L. (Eds.). (1996). *The impact of domestic violence on your legal practice: A lawyer's handbook.* Chicago: American Bar Association. (No. 5480001)

Goelman, D. M., & Valente, R. L. (1997). *When will they ever learn? Education to end domestic violence: A law school report* (NCJ No. 168098). Washington, DC: U.S. Department of Justice, Office for Victims of Crime.

Goetting, A. (1991). Female victims of homicide: A portrait of their killers and the circumstances of their deaths. *Violence and Victims, 6,* 159-168.

Goldenson, R. M. (1984). *Longman dictionary of psychology and psychiatry.* New York: Longman.

Golding, J. M. (1999). Intimate partner violence as a risk factor for mental disorders: A meta-analysis. *Journal of Family Violence, 14,* 99-132.

Golding, J. M., Cooper, M. L., & George, L. K. (1997). Sexual assault history and health perceptions: Seven general populations studied. *Health Psychology, 16,* 417-425.

Goldner, V., Penn, P., Sheinberg, M., & Walker, G. (1990). Love and violence: Gender paradoxes in volatile attachments. *Family Process, 29,* 343-364.

Gondolf, E. W. (1988a). *Battered women as survivors: An alternative to treating learned helplessness.* Lexington, MA: Lexington Books.

Gondolf, E. W. (1988b). The effect of batterer counseling on shelter outcome. *Journal of Interpersonal Violence, 3,* 275-289.

Gondolf, E. W. (1995). Alcohol abuse, wife assault, and power needs. *Social Service Review, 18,* 274-284.

Gondolf, E. W. (1998a). *Assessing woman battering in mental health services.* Thousand Oaks, CA: Sage.

Gondolf, E. W. (1998b). Service contract and delivery of a shelter outreach project. *Journal of Family Violence, 13,* 131-145.

Gondolf, E. W. (1998c). The victims of court-ordered batterers. *Violence Against Women, 4,* 659-676.

Gondolf, E. W., Chang, Y. F., & Laporte, R. (1999). Capture-recapture analysis of batterer reassaults: An epidemiological innovation for batterer program evaluation. *Violence and Victims, 14,* 191-202.

Gondolf, E. W., Fisher, E., & McFerron, J. R. (1988). Racial differences among shelter residents: A comparison of Anglo, Black, and Hispanic battered woman. *Journal of Family Violence, 3,* 39-51.

Gondolf, E. W., & Shestakov, D. (1997). Spousal homicide in Russia. *Violence Against Women, 3,* 533-546.

Gonsiorek, J. C. (1988). Mental health issues of gay and lesbian adolescents. *Journal of Adolescent Health Care, 9,* 114-122.

Good, G. E. (1998). Men & masculinities: The good, the bad, and the ugly. *SPSMM Bulletin, 3*(4), 1-3.

Goodman, L. A. (1991). The prevalence of abuse among homeless and housed poor mothers: A comparison study. *American Journal of Orthospychiatry, 61,* 489-500.

Goodman, L. A., Bennett, L., & Dutton, M. A. (in press). Obstacles women face in prosecuting their batterers: The role of social support. *Journal of Interpersonal Violence.*

Goodman, L. A., Koss, M. P., Fitzgerald, L. F., Russo, N. F., & Puryear-Keita, G. P. (1993). Male violence against women. *American Psychologist, 48,* 1054-1058.

Goodwin, J. (1987). The etiology of combat-related post-traumatic stress disorders. In T. Williams (Ed.), *Post-traumatic stress disorders: A handbook for clinicians* (pp. 1-18). Cincinnati, OH: Disabled American Veterans.

Gordon, L. (1988). *Heroes of their own lives: The politics and history of family violence, Boston 1880-1960.* New York: Viking.

Gore-Felton, C., Gill, M., Koopman, C., & Spiegel, D. (1999). A review of acute stress reactions among victims of violence: Implications for early intervention. *Aggression and Violent Behavior, 4,* 203-306.

Gotlib, I. H., & Asarnow, R. F. (1979). Interpersonal and impersonal problem solving skills in mildly and clinically depressed university students. *Journal of Consulting and Clinical Psychology, 47,* 86-95.

Graham, D. L. R., Rawlings, E. I., Ihms, K., Latimer, D., Foliano, J., Thompson, A., Suttman, K., Farrington, M., & Hacker, R. (1995). A scale for identifying "Stockholm Syndrome" reactions in young dating women: Factor structure, reliability, and validity. *Violence and Victims, 10,* 3-22.

Graham, D. L. R., Rawlings, E. I., & Rigsby, R. (1994). *Loving to survive: Sexual terror, men's violence, and women's lives.* New York: New York University Press.

Graham, D. L. R., Rawlings, E. I., & Rimini, N. (1988). Survivors of terror: Battered women, hostages and the Stockholm Syndrome. In K. Yllö & M. Bograd (Eds.), *Feminist perspectives on wife abuse* (pp. 217-233). Newbury Park, CA: Sage.

Graham-Bermann, S. A. (1998). The impact of woman abuse on children's social development: Research and theoretical perspectives. In G. W. Holden, R. Geffner, & E. N. Jouriles (Eds.), *Children exposed to marital violence* (pp. 21-54). Washington, DC: American Psychological Association.

Graziano, A. M., Lindquist, C. M., Kunce, L. J., & Munjal, K. (1992). Physical punishment in childhood and current attitudes: An exploratory comparison of college students in the United States and India. *Journal of Interpersonal Violence, 7,* 147-155.

Green, B. L., Lindy, J., Grace, M., & Glese, G. (1989). Multiple diagnoses in post-traumatic stress disorder: The role of war stressors. *Journal of Nervous and Mental Disorders, 177,* 329-335.

Green, R. L. (1991). *MMPI-2/MMPI: An interpretive manual.* Boston: Allyn & Bacon.

Greene, E., Raitz, A., & Lindblad, H. (1989). Jurors' knowledge of battered women. *Journal of Family Violence, 4,* 105-125.

Greenfeld, L. A., & Minor-Harper, S. (Eds.). (1991). *Women in prison* (Special Report; NCJ No. 127991). Washington, DC: Bureau of Justice Statistics.

Greenfeld, L. A., Rand, M. R., Craven, D., Klaus, P. A., Perkins, C. A., Ringel, C., Warchol, G., Matson, C., & Fox, J. A. (1998, March). *Violence by intimates* (NCJ No. 167237). Washington, DC: Bureau of Justice Statistics.

Gruzinski, R. J., Brink, J. C., & Edleson, J. L. (1988). Support and education groups for children of battered women. *Child Welfare, 67,* 431-444.

Guns and dolls. (1990, May 28). *Newsweek, 115*(23), 58-62.

Gurley, D. (1989, January). *Understanding the mixed roles of social support and social obstruction in recovery from child abuse.* Paper presented at the Responses to Family Violence Research Conference, Purdue University, Lafayette, IN.

Haberfeld, Y., Semyonov, M., & Addi, A. (1998). A hierarchical linear model for estimating gender-based earnings differentials. *Work & Occupations, 25,* 97-112.

Hackler, J. (1991). The reduction of violent crime through economic equality for women. *Journal of Family Violence, 6,* 199-216.

Haddad, P., & Garralda, M. (1992). Hyperkinetic syndrome and disruptive early experiences. *British Journal of Psychiatry, 161,* 700-703.

Haj-Yahia, M. M. (1998a). Beliefs about wife beating among Palestinian women. *Violence Against Women, 4,* 533-558.

Haj-Yahia, M. M. (1998b). A patriarchal perspective of beliefs about wife-beating among Arab Palestinian men from the West Bank and Gaza Strip. *Journal of Family Issues, 19,* 595-621.

Hale, M. (1874). *The history of the pleas of the crown.* Philadelphia: Robert H. Small. (Original work published in 1736)

Halicka, M. (1995). Elder abuse and neglect in Poland. In J. I. Kosberg & J. L. Garcia (Eds.), *Elder abuse: International and cross-cultural perspectives* (pp. 157-169). Binghamton, NY: Haworth.

Halperin, J. M., Newcorn, J. H., Matier, K., Bedi, G., Hall, S., & Sharma, V. (1995). Impulsivity and the initiation of fights in children with disruptive behavioral disorders. *Journal of Child Psychology and Psychiatry, 36,* 1199-1211.

Hamberger, L. K. (1991, August). *Research concerning wife abuse: Implications for training physicians and criminal justice personnel.* Paper presented at the annual meeting of the American Psychological Association, San Francisco.

Hamberger, L. K., & Arnold, J. (1991). The impact of mandatory arrest on domestic violence perpetrator counseling services. *Family Violence Bulletin, 6*(1), 11-12.

Hamberger, L. K., & Hastings, J. E. (1991). Personality correlates of men who batter and nonviolent men: Some continuities and discontinuities. *Journal of Family Violence, 6,* 131-147.

Hamberger, L. K., Lohr, J. M., Bonge, D., & Tolin, D. F. (1997). An empirical classification of motivation for domestic violence. *Violence Against Women, 3,* 401-423.

Hambleton, B. B., Clark, G., Sumaya, C. V., Weissman, G., & Horner, J. (1997). HRSA's strategies to combat family violence. *Academic Medicine, 72*(Suppl. 1), S110-S115.

Hamby, S. L. (1996). The Dominance Scale: Preliminary psychometric properties. *Violence and Victims, 11,* 199-212.

Hampton, R. L., & Gelles, R. J. (1994). Violence toward Black women in a nationally representative sample of Black families. *Journal of Comparative Family Studies, 25,* 105-119.

Hanks, S. E. (1992). Translating theory into practice: A conceptual framework for clinical assessment, differential diagnosis, and multi-modal treatment of maritally violent individuals, couples, and families. In E. C. Viano (Ed.), *Intimate violence: Interdisciplinary perspectives* (pp. 157-176). Washington, DC: Hemisphere.

Hanneke, C. R., Shields, N. M., & McCall, G. J. (1986). Assessing the prevalence of marital rape. *Journal of Interpersonal Violence, 1,* 350-362.

Hansen, M., Harway, M., & Cervantes, N. (1991). Therapists' perceptions of severity in cases of family violence. *Violence and Victims, 6,* 225-235.

Hare-Mustin, R. T. (1986). The problem of gender in family therapy theory. *Family Process, 26,* 15-27.

Harlow, C. W. (1991). *Female victims of violent crimes* (NCJ No. 126826). Rockville, MD: Bureau of Justice Statistics.

Harris, M. B. (1991). Effects of sex of aggressor, sex of target, and relationship on evaluations of physical aggression. *Journal of Interpersonal Violence, 6,* 174-186.

Harrison, L. A., & Esqueda, C. W. (1999). Myths and stereotypes of actors in domestic violence: Implications for domestic violence culpability. *Aggression and Violent Behavior, 4,* 129-138.

Hart, S. N., & Brassard, M. R. (1990). Psychological maltreatment of children. In R. T. Ammerman & M. Hersen (Eds.), *Treatment of family violence: A sourcebook* (pp. 77-112). New York: Wiley.

Hartik, L. M. (1978). *Identification of personality characteristics and self-concept factors of battered women.* Unpublished doctoral dissertation, United States International University, San Diego, CA.

Hartmann, H. I. (1981). The family as the locus of gender, class and political struggle: The example of housework. *Signs: Journal of Women in Culture and Society, 6,* 366-393.

Harway, M. (1993). Battered women: Characteristics and causes. In M. Hansen & M. Harway (Eds.), *Battering and family therapy: A feminist perspective* (pp. 82-92). Newbury Park, CA: Sage.

Hastings, J. E., & Hamberger, L. K. (1988). Personality characteristics of spouse abusers: A controlled comparison. *Violence and Victims, 3,* 31-48.

Hathaway, J., Silverman, J., Brooks, D., Mucci, L., Tavares, B., Keenan, H., & Cordeiro, L. (1998, July). *Utilization of police, civil restraining orders and medical care services by female survivors of partner violence.* Paper presented at the Program Evaluation and Family Violence Research: An International Conference, Durham, NH.

Hathaway, S. R., & McKinley, J. C. (1967). *Minnesota Multiphasic Personality Inventory manual.* New York: Psychological Corporation.

Hazan, C., & Zeifman, D. (1994). Sex and the psychological tether. In K. Bartholomew & D. Perlman (Eds.), *Advances in personal relationships: Attachment processes in adulthood* (Vol. 5, pp. 151-177). London: Jessica Kingsley.

Healey, K. M. (1995). *Victim and witness intimidation: New developments and emerging responses* (NCJ No. 156555). Rockville, MD: U.S. Department of Justice.

Healey, K. M., & Smith, C. (1998). *Batterer programs: What criminal justice agencies need to know* (NCJ No. 171683). Washington, DC: National Institute of Health.

Healey, K. M., Smith, C., & O'Sullivan, C. (1998). *Batterer intervention: Program approaches and criminal justice strategies* (NCJ No. 168638). Washington, DC: National Institute of Justice.

Hebbert, T. B., Silverm, R. C., & Ellard, J. H. (1991). Coping with an abusive relationship: I. How and why do women stay? *Journal of Marriage and the Family, 53,* 311-325.

Heise, L. L. (1989). International dimensions of violence against women. *Response, 12*(1), 3-11.

Heise, L. L. (1996). Health workers: Potential allies in the battle against woman abuse in developing countries. *Journal of the American Medical Women's Association, 51,* 120-122.

Heise, L. L. (1998). Violence against women: An integrated, ecological framework. *Violence Against Women, 4,* 262-290.

Henderson, A. J. Z., Bartholomew, K., & Dutton, D. G. (1997). He loves me; he loves me not: Attachment and separation resolution of abused women. *Journal of Family Violence, 12,* 169-191.

Hendricks-Matthews, M. (1982). The battered woman: Is she ready for help? *Journal of Contemporary Social Work, 63,* 131-137.

Henning, K. R., & Klesges, L. M. (1999, July). *Evaluation of the Shelby County domestic violence court.* Paper presented at the 6th International Family Violence Conference, Durham, NH.

Henning, K. R., Leitenberg, H., Coffey, P., Turner, T., & Bennett, R. T. (1996). Long-term psychological and social impact of witnessing physical conflict between parents. *Journal of Interpersonal Violence, 11,* 35-51.

Herbert, T. B., Silver, R. C., & Ellard, J. H. (1991). Coping with an abusive relationship: How and why do women stay? *Journal of Marriage and the Family, 53,* 311-325.

Herek, G. M., Gillis, J. R., & Cogan, J. C. (1999). Psychological sequelae of hate-crime victimization among lesbian, gay, and bisexual adults. *Journal of Consulting and Clinical Psychology, 67,* 945-951.

Herman, J. L. (1992). *Trauma and recovery.* New York: Basic Books.

Herman, R. L., & Azrin, N. H. (1964). Punishment by noise in an alternative response situation. *Journal of the Experimental Analysis of Behavior, 7,* 16-26.

Herrnstein, R. J. (1970). On the law of effect. *Journal of the Experimental Analysis of Behavior, 13,* 243-266.

Heyman, R. E., & Neidig, P. H. (1999). A comparison of spousal aggression prevalence rates in U.S. army and civilian representative samples. *Journal of Consulting and Clinical Psychology, 67,* 239-242.

Hilton, Z. N. (1992). Battered women's concerns about their children witnessing wife assault. *Journal of Interpersonal Violence, 7,* 77-86.

Hiroto, D. S. (1974). Locus of control and learned helplessness. *Journal of Experimental Psychology, 102,* 187-193.

Hirschel, J. D., Dean, C. W., & Lumb, R. C. (1994). The relative contribution of domestic violence to assault and injury of police officers. *Justice Quarterly, 11,* 99-117.

Hirschel, J. D., Hutchison, I., & Dean, C. W. (1992). The failure of arrest to deter spouse abuse. *Journal of Research in Crime and Delinquency, 29,* 7-33.

Hirschel, J. D., Hutchison, I., Dean, C. W., Kelley, J. J., & Pesackis, C. E. (1991). *Charlotte spouse assault replication project: Final report* (Grant No. 89IJ-CK-K004). Washington, DC: Bureau of Justice Statistics.

Hirschel, J. D., Hutchison, I., Dean, C. W., & Mills, A. M. (1992). Review essay on the law enforcement response to spouse abuse: Past, present, and future. *Justice Quarterly, 9,* 247-283.

Hodson, C. A. (1982). Length of stay in a battering relationship: Test of a model. *Dissertation Abstracts International, 43,* 1983B. (UMI No. 8226470)

Hoff, L. (1990). *Battered women as survivors.* London: Sage.

Hoffman, K. L., Demo, D. H., & Edwards, J. N. (1994). Physical wife abuse in a non-Western society: An intergrated theoretical approach. *Journal of Marriage and the Family, 56,* 131-146.

Hofford, M., Bailey, C., Davis, J., & Hart, B. (1995). Family violence in child custody statutes: An analysis of state codes and legal practice. *Family Law Quarterly, 29,* 197-224.

Hofling, C. K., Brotzman, E., Darlymple, S., Graves, N., & Pierce, C. M. (1966). An experimental study in nurse-physician relationships. *Journal of Nervous and Mental Disease, 143,* 171-180.

Holden, G. W., Geffner, R., & Jouriles, E. N. (1998a). Appraisal and outlook. In G. W. Holden, R. Geffner, & E. N. Jouriles (Eds.), *Children exposed to marital violence* (pp. 409-421). Washington, DC: American Psychological Association.

Holden, G. W., Geffner, R., & Jouriles, E. N. (Eds.). (1998b). *Children exposed to marital violence.* Washington, DC: American Psychological Association.

Holiman, M. J., & Schilit, R. (1991). Aftercare for battered women: How to encourage the maintenance of change. *Psychotherapy, 28,* 345-353.

Holloway, M. (1994, August). Trends in women's health—A global view. *Scientific American,* pp. 76-83.

Holmes, W. M. (1993). Police arrests for domestic violence. *American Journal of Police, 12,* 101-125.

Holtzworth-Munroe, A. (1988). Causal attribution in marital violence: Theoretical and methodological issues. *Clinical Psychology Review, 8,* 331-344.

Holtzworth-Munroe, A., Smutzler, N., & Sandin, E. (1997). A brief review of the research on husband violence. Part II: The psychological effects of husband violence on battered women and their children. *Aggression and Violent Behavior, 2,* 179-213.

Holtzworth-Munroe, A., & Stuart, G. L. (1994). Typologies of male batterers: Three subtypes and the differences among them. *Psychological Bulletin, 116,* 476-497.

Holz, W. C., & Azrin, N. H. (1961). Discriminative properties of punishment. *Journal of the Experimental Analysis of Behavior, 4,* 225-232.

Home, A. M. (1994). Attributing responsibility and assessing gravity in wife abuse situations: A comparative study of police and social workers. *Journal of Social Service Research, 19,* 67-84.

Horne, S. (1999). Domestic violence in Russia. *American Psychologist, 54,* 55-61.

Horner, M. S. (1972). Toward an understanding of achievement-related conflicts in women. *Journal of Social Issues, 28,* 157-175.

Hornung, C. A., McCullough, B. C., & Sugimoto, T. (1981). Status relationships in marriage: Risk factors in spouse abuse. *Journal of Marriage and the Family, 43,* 675-692.

Horton, A. L., Wilkins, M. M., & Wright, W. (1988). Women who ended abuse: What religious leaders and religion did for these victims. In A. L. Horton & J. A. Williamson (Eds.), *Abuse and religion* (pp. 235-245). Lexington, MA: Lexington Books.

Hotaling, G. T., & Sugarman, D. B. (1986). An analysis of risk markers in husband to wife violence: The current state of knowledge. *Violence and Victims, 1,* 101-124.

Hotaling, G. T., & Sugarman, D. B. (1990). A risk marker analysis of assaulted wives. *Journal of Family Violence, 5,* 1-13.

Houskamp, B. M., & Foy, D. W. (1991). The assessment of post-traumatic stress disorder in battered women. *Journal of Interpersonal Violence, 6,* 367-375.

Hughes, H. M., Parkinson, D., & Vargo, M. (1989). Witnessing spouse abuse and experiencing physical abuse: A "double whammy"? *Journal of Family Violence, 4,* 197-209.

Huisman, K. A. (1996). Wife battering in Asian American communities. *Violence Against Women, 2,* 260-283.

Hull, C. L. (1952). *A behavior system.* New Haven, CT: Yale University Press.

Human Rights Watch. (1992). *Double jeopardy: Police abuse of women in Pakistan.* New York: Author.

Hunt, H. F., & Brady, J. V. (1955). Some effects of punishment and intercurrent anxiety on a simple operant. *Journal of Comparative and Physiological Psychology, 48,* 305-310.

Hutchison, I. W., & Hirschel, J. D. (1998). Abused women: Help-seeking strategies and police utilization. *Violence Against Women, 4,* 436-456.

Hwalek, M., Williamson, D., & Stahl, C. (1991). Community-based m-team roles: A job analysis. *Journal of Elder Abuse and Neglect, 3*(3), 45-71.

"I'm supposed to be safe . . . Oh my God." (1992, April 23). *Tribune Newspapers of Arizona,* p. A6.

Irvine, J. (1990). Lesbian battering: The search for shelter. In P. Elliott (Ed.), *Confronting lesbian battering* (pp. 25-30). St. Paul: Minnesota Coalition for Battered Women.

Jackson, S. M. (1998). Issues in the dating violence research: A review of the literature. *Aggression and Violent Behavior, 4,* 233-247.

Jacobson, N. S., Gottman, J. M., Gortner, E., Berns, S., & Shortt, J. W. (1996). Psychological factors in the longitudinal course of battering. *Violence and Victims, 11,* 625-629.

Jacobson, N. S., Gottman, J. M., Waltz, J., Rushe, R., Babcock, J. C., & Holtzworth-Munroe, A. (1994). Affect, verbal content and psychophysiology in the arguments of couples with a violent husband. *Journal of Consulting and Clinical Psychology, 62,* 982-988.

Jaffe, P. G., & Geffner, R. (1998). Child custody disputes and domestic violence: Critical issues for mental health, social service, and legal professionals. In G. W. Holden, R. Geffner, & E. N. Jouriles (Eds.), *Children exposed to marital violence* (pp. 371-396). Washington, DC: American Psychological Association.

Jaffe, P. G., Hastings, E., & Reitzel, D. (1992). Child witnesses of woman abuse: How can schools respond? *Response, 15*(2), 12-15.

Jaffe, P. G., Suderman, M., Reitzel, D., & Killip, S. M. (1992). An evaluation of a secondary school primary prevention program on violence in intimate relationships. *Violence and Victims, 7,* 129-146.

Jaffe, P. G., Wolfe, D. A., & Wilson, S. K. (1990). *Children of battered women.* Newbury Park, CA: Sage.

Jay, J. (1991, Nov-Dec). Terrible knowledge. *Family Therapy Networker,* pp. 18-29.

Jenkins, E. L. (1996). Homicide against women in the workplace. *Journal of the American Medical Women's Association, 51,* 118-119, 122.

Jerome, R., Grisby, L., Esselman, M., Klise, K., Free, C., Porterfield, E., Pierce, E., & Dagostino, M. (1998, August 17). Growing up gay. *People Weekly, 50*(5), 44-51.

Johns, S., & Hydle, I. (1995). Norway: Weakness in welfare. In J. I. Kosberg & J. L. Garcia (Eds.), *Elder abuse: International and cross-cultural perspectives* (pp. 139-156). Binghamton, NY: Haworth.

Johnson, B., Li, D., & Websdale, N. (1998). Florida mortality review project: Executive summary. In American Bar Association, *Legal interventions in family violence: Research findings and policy implications* (pp. 40-42; NCJ No. 171666). Washington, DC: U.S. Department of Justice.

Johnson, I. M. (1988). Wife abuse: Factors predictive of the decision-making process of battered women. *Dissertation Abstracts International, 48,* 3202A. (UMI No. 8803369)

Johnson, I. M. (1992). Economic, situational, and psychological correlates of the decision-making process of battered women. *Families in Society: The Journal of Contemporary Human Services, 73,* 168-176.

Johnson, J. M., & Bondurant, D. M. (1992). Revisiting the 1982 church response survey. *Studies in Symbolic Interaction, 13,* 287-293.

Johnson, L. D. (1998). Caught in the crossfire: Examining legislative and judicial response to the forgotten victims of domestic violence. *Law and Psychology Review, 22,* 271-286.

Johnston, M. P. (1995). Patriarchal terrorism and common couple violence: Two forms of violence against women. *Journal of Marriage and the Family, 57,* 283-294.

Joint Commission on Accreditation of Healthcare Organizations. (1992). *Accreditation manual for hospitals. Vol 1.* Oakbrook Terrace, IL: Author.

Josephs, R. A., Markus, H. R., & Tafarodi, R. W. (1992). Gender and self-esteem. *Journal of Personality and Social Psychology, 63,* 391-402.

Jouriles, E. N., & O'Leary, K. D. (1985). Interspousal reliability of reports of marital violence. *Journal of Consulting and Clinical Psychology, 53,* 419-421.

Julian, J., & Kornblum, W. (1983). *Social problems.* Englewood Cliffs, NJ: Prentice Hall.

Julian, T. W., & McKenry, P. C. (1993). Mediators of male violence toward female intimates. *Journal of Family Violence, 8,* 39-56.

Jurik, N. C., & Winn, R. (1990). Gender and homicide: A comparison of men and women who kill. *Violence and Victims, 5,* 227-242.

Justice, A., & Hirt, M. H. (1992, August). *Attachment styles of women with histories of abusive relationships.* Paper presented at the annual meeting of the American Psychological Association, Washington, DC.

Kaci, J. H. (1990). Issues of the 1990s. *Response, 13*(1), 4.

Kahn, M. W. (1980). Wife beating and cultural context: Prevalence in an aboriginal and islander community in Northern Australia. *American Journal of Community Psychology, 8,* 727-731.

Kalmuss, D. S. (1984). The intergenerational transmission of marital aggression. *Journal of Marriage and the Family, 46,* 11-19.

Kalmuss, D. S., & Straus, M. A. (1982). Wife's marital dependency and wife abuse. *Journal of Marriage and the Family, 44,* 277-286.

Kalu, W. J. (1993). Battered spouses as a social concern in work with families in two semi-rural communities in Nigeria. *Journal of Family Violence, 8,* 361-373.

Kamin, L. J. (1959). The delay-of-punishment gradient. *Journal of Comparative and Physiological Psychology, 52,* 44-51.

Kandel-Englander, E. (1992). Wife battering and violence outside the family. *Journal of Interpersonal Violence, 7,* 462-470.

Kann, M. E. (1998). Similarity and political patriarchy during the American founding. *Men and Masculinities, 1,* 193-219.

Karon, B. P., & Widener, A. J. (1997). Repressed memories and World War II: Lest we forget! *Professional Psychology: Research & Practice, 28,* 338-340.

Karsh, E. B. (1962). Effects of number of rewarded trials and intensity of punishment on running speed. *Journal of Comparative and Physiological Psychology, 55,* 44-51.

Kasian, M., & Painter, S. L. (1992). Frequency and severity of psychological abuse in a dating population. *Journal of Interpersonal Violence, 7,* 350-364.

Kaslow, N. J., Thompson, M. P., Meadows, L. A., Jacobs, D., Chance, S., Gibb, B., Bornstein, H., Hollins, L., Rashid, A., & Phillips, K. (1998). Factors that mediate and moderate the link between partner abuse and suicidal behavior in African American women. *Journal of Consulting and Clinical Psychology, 66,* 533-540.

Katz, J., Arias, I., Beach, S. R. H., & Roman, P. (1995). Excuses, excuses: Accounting for the effects of partner violence on marital satisfaction and stability. *Violence and Victims, 10,* 315-326.

Katz, R., & Wykes, T. (1985). The psychological difference between temporally predictable and unpredictable stressful events: Evidence for information control theories. *Journal of Personality and Social Psychology, 48,* 781-790.

Kaufman, G. K., & Straus, M. A. (1987). The "drunken bum" theory of wife beating. *Social Problems, 34,* 213-230.

Keilitz, S. L., Davis, C., & Eikeman, H. S. (1998, January). *Civil protection orders: Victims' views on effectiveness.* Washington, DC: National Institute of Justice.

Kemp, A., Green, B. L., Hovanitz, C., & Rawlings, E. I. (1995). Incidence and correlates of posttraumatic stress disorder in battered women: Shelter and community samples. *Journal of Interpersonal Violence, 10,* 43-55.

Kemp, A., Rawlings, E. I., & Green, B. L. (1991). Post-traumatic stress disorder (PTSD) in battered women: A shelter sample. *Journal of Traumatic Stress, 4,* 137-148.

Kesner, J. E., Julian, T., & McKenry, P. C. (1997). Application of attachment theory to male violence toward female intimates. *Journal of Family Violence, 12,* 211-228.

Kessler, R. C., McLeod, J. D., & Wethington, E. (1985). The costs of caring: A perspective on the relationship between sex and psychological distress. In I. G. Sarason & B. R. Sarason (Eds.), *Social support: Theory, research, and applications* (pp. 491-506). Dordrecht, Netherlands: Martinus Nijhoff.

Khan, F. I., Welch, T. L., & Zillmer, E. A. (1993). MMPI-2 profiles of battered women in transition. *Journal of Personality Assessment, 60,* 100-111.

Killcross, S., Robbins, T. W., & Everitt, B. J. (1997). Different types of fear-conditioned behaviour by separate nuclei within the amygdala. *Nature, 338,* 377-380.

Kilpatrick, K. L., Litt, M., & Williams, L. M. (1997). Post-traumatic stress disorder in child witnesses to domestic violence. *American Journal of Orthopsychiatry, 67,* 639-644.

Kim, K. I., & Cho, Y. G. (1992). Epidemiological survey of spousal abuse in Korea. In E. C. Viano (Ed.), *Intimate violence: An interdisciplinary perspective* (pp. 277-282). Bristol, PA: Taylor & Francis.

King, D. W., King, L. A., Foy, D. W., Keane, T. M., & Fairbank, J. A. (1999). Posttraumatic stress disorder in a national sample of female and male Vietnam veterans: Risk factors, war-zone stressors, and resilience-recovery variables. *Journal of Abnormal Psychology, 108,* 164-170.

Kingma, J. (1999). Repeat victimization of violence: A retrospective study from a hospital emergency department for the period 1971-1995. *Journal of Interpersonal Violence, 14,* 79-90.

Kirk, R. (1992). *Untold terror: Violence against women in Peru's armed conflict.* New York: Human Rights Watch.

Kirkwood, C. (1993). *Leaving abusive partners.* London: Sage.

Kishur, G. R. (1989). The male batterer: A multidimensional exploration of conjugal violence. *Dissertation Abstracts International, 49,* 2409A. (UMI No. 8814496)

Klee, J. B. (1944). The relation of frustration and motivation to the production of abnormal fixations in the rat. *Psychological Monographs, 56*(4, Serial No. 45).

Klein, C. F. (1995). Full faith and credit: Interstate enforcement of protection orders under the Violence Against Women Act of 1994. *Family Law Quarterly, 29,* 253-271.

Klein, E., Campbell, J. C., Soler, E., & Ghez, M. (1997). *Ending domestic violence.* Thousand Oaks, CA: Sage.

Klesges, L. M., Henning, K. R., Barnard, M., Ey, S., Patterson, S. M., & Alpert, B. S. (1999, July). *Adolescents' exposure to interparental conflict in their home environment: Relationships with blood pressure response.* Poster presentation at the 6th International Family Violence Research Conference, Durham, NH.

Knight, R. A., & Hatty, S. E. (1992). Violence against women in Australia's capital. In E. C. Viano (Ed.), *Intimate violence: An interdisciplinary perspective* (pp. 255-264). Bristol, PA: Taylor & Francis.

Kolbo, J. R. (1996). Risk and resilience among children exposed to family violence. *Violence and Victims, 11,* 113-128.

Koski, P. R., & Mangold, W. D. (1988). Gender effects in attitudes about family violence. *Journal of Family Violence, 3,* 225-237.

Koss, M. P. (1989). Hidden rape: Sexual aggression and victimization in a national sample of students in higher education. In M. A. Pirog-Good & J. E. Stets (Eds.), *Violence in dating relationships: Emerging social issues* (pp. 145-168). New York: Praeger.

Koss, M. P. (1990). The women's mental health research agenda. *American Psychologist, 45,* 374-380.

Koss, M. P., Gidyez, C. A., & Wisniewski, N. (1987). The scope of rape: Incidence and prevalence of sexual aggression in a national sample of higher education students. *Journal of Consulting and Clinical Psychology, 55,* 162-170.

Koss, M. P., Goodman, L. A., Browne, A., Fitzgerald, L. F., Puryear-Keita, G., & Russo, N. F. (1994). *Male violence against women at home, at work, and in the community.* Washington, DC: American Psychological Association.

Koss, M. P., Koss, P. G., & Woodruff, W. J. (1991a). Criminal victimization among primary care medical patients: Prevalence, incidence, and physician usage. *Behavioral Science and the Law, 9,* 85-86.

Koss, M. P., Koss, P., & Woodruff, W. J. (1991b). Deleterious effects of criminal victimization on women's health and medical utilization. *Archives of Internal Medicine, 151,* 342-357.

Kozu, J. (1999). Domestic violence in Japan. *American Psychologist, 54,* 50-54.

Krajewski, S. S. (1996). Results of a curriculum intervention with seventh graders regarding violence in relationships. *Journal of Family Violence, 11,* 93-112.

Kramer, T. L., & Green, B. L. (1991). Post-traumatic stress disorder as an early response to sexual assault. *Journal of Interpersonal Violence, 6,* 160-173.

Krishnan, S. P., Hilbert, J. C., VanLeeuwen, D., & Kolia, R. (1997). Documenting domestic violence among ethnically diverse populations: Results from a preliminary study. *Family and Community Health, 22*(3), 32-48.

Kuehl, S. J. (1991). Legal remedies for teen dating violence. In B. Levy (Ed.), *Dating violence: Young women in danger* (pp. 209-220). Seattle, WA: Seal Press.

Kuhl, A. F. (1985). Personality traits of abused women: Masochism myth refuted. *Victimology, 9,* 450-463.

Kuleshnyk, I. (1984). The Stockholm Syndrome: Toward an understanding. *Social Action and the Law, 10*(2), 37-42.

Kulka, R., Schlenger, W., Fairbank, J., Hough, R., Jordan, B., Marmar, C., & Weiss, D. (1990). *Trauma and the Vietnam war generation: Report and findings from the National Vietnam Veterans Readjustment Study.* New York: Brunner/Mazel.

Kury, H., & Ferdinand, T. (1997). The victim's experience and fear of crime. *International Review of Victimology, 5,* 93-140.

LaBell, L. S. (1979). Wife abuse: A sociological study of battered women and their mates. *Victimology: An International Journal, 4,* 257-267.

Labi, N. (1998, June 28). For the next generation, feminism is being sold as glitz and image. But what do girls really want? *Time, 151*(25), 60-61.

Landau, B. (1995). The Toronto forum on women abuse: The process and the outcome. *Family and Conciliation Courts Review, 33,* 63-78.

Landenburger, K. (1989). A process of entrapment in and recovery from an abusive relationship. *Issues in Mental Health Nursing, 10,* 209-227.

Laner, M. R. (1990). Violence or its precipitators: Which is more likely to be identified as a dating problem? *Deviant Behavior, 11,* 319-329.

Laner, M. R., & Thompson, J. (1982). Abuse and aggression in courting couples. *Deviant Behavior, 3,* 229-244.

Lang, D. (1974, November 25). A reporter at large: The bank drama. *New Yorker,* pp. 56-126.

Langan, P. A., & Dawson, J. M. (1995). *Spouse murder defendants in large urban counties* (NCJ No. 156831). Washington, DC: Bureau of Justice Statistics.

Langford, D. R. (1996). Predicting unpredictability: A model of women's processes of predicting battering men's violence. *Scholarly Inquiry for Nursing Practice: An International Journal, 10,* 371-385.

Langhinrichsen-Rohling, J., Neidig, P., & Thorn, G. (1995). Violent marriages: Gender differences in levels of current violence and past abuse. *Journal of Family Violence, 10,* 159-176.

Langley, P. A. (1991). Family violence: Toward a family-oriented public policy. *Families in Society: The Journal of Contemporary Human Services, 72,* 574-576.

Larkin, J., & Popaleni, K. (1994). Heterosexual courtship violence and sexual harassment: The private and public control of young women. *Feminism and Psychology, 4,* 213-237.

Launius, M. H., & Jensen, B. L. (1987). Interpersonal problem-solving skills in battered, counseling, and control women. *Journal of Family Violence, 2,* 151-162.

Launius, M. H., & Lindquist, C. U. (1988). Learned helplessness, external locus of control, and passivity in battered women. *Journal of Interpersonal Violence, 3,* 307-318.

LaViolette, A. L. (1991). *Battered women, power, and family systems therapy.* Garden Grove, CA: Newman.

Lazarus, R. S., & Folkman, S. (1984). *Stress, appraisal, and coping.* New York: Springer.

Learning to be assertive. (1992, May 22). *The Oprah Winfrey Show.* New York: Harpo Productions.

Lehnen, R. G., & Skogan, W. G. (1981). *The national crime survey: Working papers, Vol. 1, current and historical perspectives.* Washington, DC: U.S. Department of Justice.

Lemon, N. K. D. (1999). Cultural barriers to domestic violence protection. *Domestic Violence Report, 4,* 86, 94-96.

Lerner, G. (1986). *The creation of patriarchy.* New York: Oxford University Press.

Levant, R. F. (1995). *Masculinity reconstructed.* New York: Dutton.

Levenson, H. (1973). Activism and powerful others: Distinctions within the concept of internal-external control. *Journal of Personality Assessment, 38,* 377-383.

Levy, B. (1984). *Prevention skills for violence-free relationships.* Long Beach: Southern California Coalition for Battered Women.

Levy, B. (1990). Abusive teen dating relationships: An emerging issue for the '90s. *Response, 13*(1), 5.

Levy, B. (1993). *In love and in danger: A teen's guide to breaking free of abusive relationships.* Seattle, WA: Seal Press.

Levy, B. (1997, Winter/Spring). Common stereotypes contribute to invisibility of battered lesbians. *Update-Newsletter of the Southern California Coalition on Battered Women,* pp. 1, 6.

Levy, B., & Occhiuzzo Giggans, P. (1995). *What parents need to know about dating violence.* Seattle, WA: Seal Press.

Lie, G., & Gentlewarrior, S. (1991). Intimate violence in lesbian relationships: Discussion of survey findings and practical implications. *Journal of Social Service Research, 15,* 41-59.

Lie, G., Schlitt, R., Bush, J., Montagne, M., & Reyes, L. (1991). Lesbians in currently aggressive relationships: How frequently do they report aggressive past relationships? *Violence and Victims, 6,* 121-135.

Lipschitz, D. S., Kaplan, M. L., Sorkenn, J. B., Faedda, G. L., Chorney, P., & Asnis, G. M. (1996). Prevalence and characteristics of physical and sexual abuse among psychiatric outpatients. *Psychiatric Services, 47,* 189-191.

Lloyd, S. A. (1988, November). *Conflict and violence in marriage.* Paper presented at the annual meeting of the National Council on Family Relations, Philadelphia.

Lloyd, S. A. (1989, November). *The stability of physical aggression in marriage.* Paper presented at the annual meeting of the National Council on Family Relations, New Orleans.

Lloyd, S. A. (1991). The dark side of courtship: Violence and sexual exploitation. *Family Relations, 40,* 14-20.

Lloyd, S. A., & Taluc, N. (1999). The effects of male violence on female employment. *Violence Against Women, 5,* 370-392.

Loar, L. (1997, September). *Batterers and victims: When spousal and child abuse collide.* In R. Vaselle-Augenstein & M. Fraga (Chairs), Symposium conducted at the California Association of Batterers' Intervention Programs Semi-annual Conference, Oakland.

Loar, L., & Rathmann, C. (1994, Spring). A humane garden of children, plants, and animals grows in Sonoma County, California. *The Latham Letter,* pp. 6-9.

Lockhart, L. L., White, B. W., Causby, V., & Isaac, A. (1994). Letting out the secret: Violence in lesbian relationships. *Journal of Interpersonal Violence, 9,* 469-492.

Logan, F. A., & Wallace, W. C. (1981). *Fundamentals of learning and motivation* (3rd ed.). Dubuque, IA: William C. Brown.

Long, G. M., & McNamara, J. R. (1989). Paradoxical punishment as it relates to the battered woman syndrome. *Behavior Modification, 13,* 192-205.

Lorber, J., & Farrell, S. A. (Eds.). (1991). *The social construction of gender.* Newbury Park, CA: Sage.

Loren, W. (1994). Surviving domestic violence. *Violence UpDate, 4*(12), 3, 10.

Los Angeles Department of Probation. (1998, July). *Los Angeles Department of Probation approved batterers' programs.* Los Angeles: Author.

Lund, L. E. (1999). What happens when health practitioners report domestic violence injuries to the police? A study of the law enforcement response to injury reports. *Violence and Victims, 14,* 203-214.

Lupri, E., Grandin, E., & Brinkerhoff, M. B. (1994). Socioeconomic status and male violence in the Canadian home: A re-examination. *Canadian Journal of Sociology, 19,* 47-73.

Maccoby, E. E., & Jacklin, C. N. (1974). *The psychology of sex differences.* Stanford, CA: Stanford University Press.

MacEwen, K. E. (1994). Refining the intergenerational transmission hypothesis. *Journal of Interpersonal Violence, 9,* 350-365.

MacNair, R. R., & Elliott, T. R. (1992). Self-perceived problem-solving ability, stress appraisal, and coping over time. *Journal of Research in Personality, 26,* 150-164.

Maertz, K. F. (1990). Self-defeating beliefs of battered women (Doctoral dissertation, University of Alberta, Canada). *Dissertation Abstracts International, 51,* 5580B.

Magee, R., & Hampton, S. (1993). Family violence and the workplace: The role of employee assistance programs. *Family Violence and Sexual Assault Bulletin, 9*(1), 19-20.

Magen, R. H., Conroy, K., Hess, P. M., Panciera, A., & Simon, B. L. (1995, July). *Evaluation of a protocol to identify battered women during investigations of child abuse and neglect.* Paper presented at the 3rd International Family Violence Research Conference, Durham, NH.

Maguire, M., & Corbett, C. (1987). *The effects of crime and the work of victims' support schemes.* Gower, UK: Aldershot.

Maier, N. R. F. (1949). *Frustration: The study of behavior without a goal.* New York: McGraw-Hill.

Maier, N. R. F., Glazer, N. M., & Klee, J. B. (1940). Studies of abnormal behavior in the rat: III. The development of behavior fixations through frustration. *Journal of Experimental Psychology, 26,* 521-546.

Maier, S. F., & Seligman, M. E. P. (1976). Learned helplessness: Theory and evidence. *Journal of Experimental Psychology: General, 105,* 3-46.

Maier, S. F., Seligman, M. E. P., & Solomon, R. L. (1969). Pavlovian fear conditioning and learned helplessness. In B. A. Campbell & R. M. Church (Eds.), *Punishment and aversive behavior* (pp. 299-342). New York: Appleton-Century-Crofts.

Main, M., & George, C. (1985). Responses of abused and disadvantaged toddlers to distress in agemates: A study in a day care setting. *Developmental Psychology, 21,* 407-412.

Makepeace, J. M. (1986). Gender differences in courtship violence victimization. *Family Relations, 35,* 383-388.

Malloy, K. A. (1986). Psychological and demographic variables as predictors of women's decisions to leave abusive relationships. *Dissertation Abstracts International, 47,* 6963B. (UMI No. 8629940)

Marano, H. E. (1997, November/December). A new focus on family values. *Psychology Today, 30*(6), 52-55, 78.

Margolies, L., & Leeder, E. (1995). Violence at the door: Treatment of lesbian batterers. *Violence Against Women, 1,* 139-157.

Margolin, G. (1987). The multiple forms of aggressiveness between marital partners: How do we identify them? *Journal of Marital and Family Therapy, 13,* 77-84.

Margolin, G., John, R. S., & Foo, L. (1998). Interactive and unique risk factors for husbands' emotional and physical abuse of their wives. *Journal of Family Violence, 13,* 315-344.

Margolin, L., Moran, P. B., & Miller, M. (1989). Social approval for violations of sexual consent in marriage and dating. *Violence and Victims, 4,* 45-55.

Markward, M. J. (1996). Characteristics of sheltered women and intimates in sexually and nonsexually abusive relationships. *Family Therapy, 23,* 59-67.

Marshall, L. L. (1992). The Severity of Violence Against Men Scales. *Journal of Family Violence, 7,* 189-203.

Marshall, L. L. (1996). Psychological abuse of women: Six distinct clusters. *Journal of Family Violence, 11,* 379-409.

Marshall, L. L., & Rose, P. (1990). Premarital violence: The impact of family of origin violence, stress, and reciprocity. *Violence and Victims, 5,* 51-64.

Martin, A. D., & Hetrick, E. S. (1988). The stigmatization of the gay and lesbian adolescent. *Journal of Homosexuality, 15,* 163-183.

Martin, D. (1978). Battered women: Society's problem. In J. R. Chapman & M. Gates (Eds.), *The victimization of women* (pp. 111-141). Beverly Hills, CA: Sage.

Martin, M. E. (1997). Double your trouble: Dual arrest in family violence. *Journal of Family Violence, 12,* 139-157.

Martin, S. E. (1989). Research note: The response of the clergy to spouse abuse in a suburban county. *Violence and Victims, 4,* 217-225.

Maslow, A. H. (1970). *Motivation and personality* (2nd ed.). New York: Harper & Row.

Mason, L. D., with contributions by Otto, J. M. (2000). Protocol for culturally-oriented assessment. *Victimization of the Elderly and Disabled, 2,* 73-74.

Matlaw, J. R., & Spence, D. M. (1994). The hospital elder assessment team: A protocol for suspected cases of elder abuse and neglect. *Journal of Elder Abuse and Neglect, 6*(2), 23-37.

McCauley, J., Kern, D. E., Kolodner, K., Dill, L., Schroeder, A. F., DeChant, H., Ryder, J., Bass, E., & Derogotis, L. (1995). The "battering syndrome": Prevalence and clinical characteristics of domestic violence in primary care internal medicine practices. *Annals of Internal Medicine, 123,* 737-746.

McClennan, H., Joseph, S., & Lewis, C. A. (1994). Causal attributions for marital violence and emotional response by women seeking refuge. *Psychological Reports, 75,* 272-274.

McCloskey, L. A. (1996). Socioeconomic and coercive power within the family. *Gender & Society, 10,* 449-463.

McCloskey, L. A., Figueredo, A. J., & Koss, M. P. (1995). The effects of systemic family violence on children's mental health. *Child Development, 66,* 1239-1261.

McDonald, K. A. (1990). Battered wives, religion, & law: An interdisciplinary approach. *Yale Journal of Law and Feminism, 2,* 251-298.

McDowell, J., & Park, A. (1998, June 29). Feminism. *Time, 151*(25), 63.

McGee, C. (1998, July). *Children's and mothers' experiences of child protection services following domestic violence.* Paper presented at the meeting of Program Evaluation and Family Violence Research: An International Conference, Durham, NH.

McGreevy, P. (1997, July 19). LAPD called lax on violence by its own. *Los Angeles Daily News,* p. 3.

McGuire, P. A. (1999, April). Psychologists key in O.J. custody case. *APA Monitor, 30*(4), 21.

McKernan, M. G., & Shinnick-Gallagher, P. (1997). Fear conditioning induces lasting potentiation of synaptic currents in vitro. *Nature, 390,* 607-611.

McKibben, M. (1988). *Programming issues regarding older battered women.* Unpublished report, Wisconsin Bureau of Aging, Madison.

McLeer, S. V., & Anwar, R. (1989). A study of battered women presenting in an emergency department. *American Journal of Public Health, 79,* 65-66.

McMurray, A. (1997). Violence against ex-wives: Anger and advocacy. *Health Care for Women International, 18,* 543-556.

McNamara, J. R., Ertl, M. A., Marsh, S., & Walker, S. (1997). Short-term response to counseling and case management intervention in a domestic violence shelter. *Psychological Reports, 81,* 1243-1251.

McNeal, C., & Amato, P. R. (1998). Parents' marital violence: Long-term consequences for children. *Journal of Family Issues, 19,* 123-139.

McWhirter, P. T. (1999). La violencia privada. *American Psychologist, 54,* 37-40.

Mediation regulated for benefit of domestic violence victims. (1997, June/July). *Domestic Violence Report, 2,* 70.

Mercy, J. A., & Saltzman, L. E. (1989). Fatal violence among spouses in the United States, 1976-1985. *American Journal of Public Health, 79,* 65-66.

Merritt-Gray, M., & Wuest, J. (1995). Counteracting abuse and breaking free: The process of leaving revealed through women's voices. *Health Care for Women International, 16,* 399-412.

Messner, M. A. (1997). *Politics of masculinities.* Thousand Oaks, CA: Sage.

Meyer, M. K. (1998). Negotiating international norms: The inter-American commission of women and the convention on violence against women. *Aggressive Behavior, 24,* 135-146.

Mickelson, R. A. (1989). Why does Jane read and write so well? The anomaly of women's achievement. *Sociology of Education, 62,* 47-63.

Milgram, S. (1963). Behavioral studies of obedience. *Journal of Abnormal and Social Psychology, 67,* 371-378.

Miller, D. T., & Porter, C. A. (1983). Self-blame in victims of violence. *Journal of Social Issues, 39,* 139-152.

Miller, J. B. (1976). *Toward a new psychology of women.* Boston: Beacon.

Miller, N. E. (1959). Liberalization of basic S-R concepts: Extensions to conflict behavior, motivation, and social learning. In S. Koch (Ed.), *Psychology: A study of science* (Vol. 2, pp. 196-292). New York: McGraw-Hill.

Mills, L. G. (1998). Mandatory arrest and prosecution policies for domestic violence: A critical literature review and the case for more research to test victim empowerment approaches. *Criminal Justice and Behavior, 25,* 306-318.

Mills, T. (1985). The assault on the self: Stages in coping with battering husbands. *Qualitative Sociology, 8,* 103-123.

Mitchell, R. E., & Hodson, C. A. (1983). Coping with domestic violence: Social support and psychological health among battered women. *American Journal of Community Psychology, 11,* 629-654.

Mladjenovic, L., & Librien, V. (1993). Belgrade feminists 1992: Separation, guilt and identity crisis. *Feminist Review, 45,* 113-119.

Model police protocol on interstate orders. (1999, February/March). *Domestic Violence Report, 4,* 37.

Moffitt, T. E., & Caspi, A. (1999, July). *Findings about partner violence from the Dunedin multidisciplinary health and development study* (NCJ No. 170018). Washington, DC: National Institute of Justice.

Molidor, C., & Tolman, R. M. (1998). Gender and contextual factors in adolescent dating violence. *Violence Against Women, 4,* 180-194.

Mones, P. A. (1992). Battle cry for battered children. *California Lawyer, 12*(5), 58.

Monson, C. M., Byrd, G. R., & Langhinrichsen-Rohling, J. (1996). To have and to hold: Perceptions of marital rape. *Journal of Interpersonal Violence, 11,* 410-424.

Montgomery, C. (1994). Swimming upstream: The strengths of women who survive homelessness. *Advances in Nursing Science, 16*(3), 34-35.

Mookherjee, H. (1997). Marital status, gender, and perception of well-being. *Journal of Social Psychology, 137,* 95-105.

Morse, B. J. (1995). Beyond the Conflict Tactics Scale: Assessing gender differences in partner violence. *Violence and Victims, 10,* 251-272.

Morton, E., Runyan, C. W., Moracco, K. E., & Butts, J. (1998). Partner homicide-suicide involving female homicide victims: A population-based study in North Carolina, 1988-1992. *Violence and Victims, 13,* 91-106.

Morton, M. A. (1997). *Wife assault and the limits of leaving: The consequences of individualizing a social problem* [CD-ROM]. Abstract from: ProQuest File: Dissertation Abstracts Items: NN10285.

Moss, V. A., Pitula, C. R., Campbell, J. C., & Halstead, L. (1997). The experience of terminating an abusive relationship from an Anglo and African American perspective: A qualitative descriptive study. *Issues in Mental Health Nursing, 18,* 433-454.

Mowrer, O. H. (1947). On the dual nature of learning—A reinterpretation of "conditioning" and "problem solving." *Harvard Educational Review, 17,* 102-148.

Mrsevic, Z., & Hughes, D. M. (1997). Violence against women in Belgrade, Serbia: SOS hotline 1990-1993. *Violence Against Women, 3,* 101-128.

Muelleman, R. L., Lenaghan, P. A., & Pakieser, R. A. (1996). Battered women: Injury locations and types. *Annals of Emergency Medicine, 28,* 486-492.

Muldary, P. S. (1983). Attribution of causality of spouse assault. *Dissertation Abstracts International, 44,* 1249B. (UMI No. 8316576)

Murphy, C. M., & Meyer, S. L. (1991). Gender, power, and violence in marriage. *Behavior Therapist, 14,* 95-100.

Murty, K. S., & Roebuck, J. B. (1992). An analysis of crisis calls by battered women in the city of Atlanta. In E. C. Viano (Ed.), *Intimate violence: Interdisciplinary perspectives* (pp. 61-81). Bristol, PA: Taylor & Francis.

Myers, D. A. (1995). Eliminating the battering of women by men: Some considerations for behavior analysis. *Journal of Applied Behavior Analysis, 28,* 493-507.

Myers, J. E. B., Tikosh, M. A., & Paxson, M. A. (1992). Domestic violence prevention statutes. *Violence UpDate, 3*(4), 3, 5-9.

Nachman, S. (1991). Elder abuse and neglect substantiations: What they tell us about the problem. *Journal of Elder Abuse & Neglect, 3*(3), 19-43.

National Center on Women and Family Law. (1995). *Same-sex provisions of state domestic violence laws.* New York: Author. (Originally published in 1991)

National Center on Women and Family Law. (1994). *The effects of woman abuse on children: Psychological and legal authority* (2nd ed.). New York: Author.

National Council of Juvenile and Family Court Judges. (1994). *Model code on domestic and family violence.* Reno, NV: Author.

National Institute of Justice. (1999a). *Evaluation of policies, procedures and programs addressing violence against women.* Washington, DC: U.S. Department of Justice, Office of Justice Programs.

National Institute of Justice. (1999b). *Research on violence against Indian women.* Washington, DC: Author.

NCADV. (1997, Spring/Summer). NCADV reports on annual member survey. *Update, 3*(2), 10. (Newsletter of the California Coalition for Battered Women)

Nerenberg, L. (1996). *Older battered women.* Washington, DC: National Center on Elder Abuse.

Nerenberg, L., Hanna, S., Harshbarger, S., McKnight, R., McLaughlin, C., & Parkins, S. (1990). Linking systems and community services: The interdisciplinary team approach. *Journal of Elder Abuse and Neglect, 2*(1/2), 101-135.

Nerney, M. (1987). *Battered women and criminal justice.* New York: STEPS to End Family Violence. 104 East 107th Street, New York, NY, 10029.

Neufeld, J. A., McNamara, J. R., & Ertl, M. (1999). Incidence and prevalence of dating partner abuse and its relationship to dating practices. *Journal of Interpersonal Violence, 14,* 125-137.

New York Commission on Domestic Fatalities. (1998, December/January). *Domestic Violence Report, 3,* 27-30.

Newmark, L., Harrell, A., & Salem, P. (1995). Domestic violence and empowerment in custody and visitation cases. *Family and Conciliation Courts Review, 33,* 30-62.

Nezu, A. M., & Ronan, G. F. (1986). Social problem solving and depression: Deficits in generating alternatives and decision making. *Southern Psychologist, 2,* 63-71.

Nicole, J. (1997). *Hispanic immigrant women and domestic violence* [CD-ROM]. Abstract from: ProQuest File: Dissertation Abstracts Item: 1383003.

Nielsen, J. M., Endo, R. K., & Ellington, B. L. (1992). Social isolation and wife abuse: A research report. In E. C. Viano (Ed.), *Intimate violence: Interdisciplinary perspectives* (pp. 40-59). Bristol, PA: Taylor & Francis.

Nurius, P. S., Furrey, J., & Berliner, L. (1992). Coping capacity among women with abusive partners. *Violence and Victims, 7,* 229-243.

O'Brien, M., John, R. S., Margolin, G., & Erel, O. (1994). Reliability and diagnostic efficacy of parents' reports regarding children's exposure to marital aggression. *Violence and Victims, 9,* 45-62.

O'Keefe, M. (1994a). Adjustment of children from maritally violent homes. *Families in Society, 75,* 403-415.

O'Keefe, M. (1994b). Linking marital violence, mother-child/father-child aggression, and child behavior problems. *Journal of Family Violence, 9,* 63-78.

O'Keefe, M. (1994c). Racial/ethnic differences among battered women and their children. *Journal of Child and Family Studies, 3,* 283-305.

O'Keefe, M. (1997). Incarcerated battered women: A comparison of battered women who killed their abusers and those incarcerated for other offenses. *Journal of Family Violence, 12,* 1-19.

O'Keefe, M., & Treister, L. (1998). Victims of dating violence among high school students. *Violence Against Women, 4,* 195-223.

O'Leary, K. D. (1999). Psychological abuse: A variable deserving critical attention in domestic violence. *Violence and Victims, 14,* 1-23.

O'Leary, K. D. (in press). Conjoint therapy for partners who engage in physically aggressive behavior: Rationale and research. *Journal of Aggression, Maltreatment, & Trauma.*

O'Leary, K. D., Barling, J., Arias, I., Rosenbaum, A., Malone, J., & Tyree, A. (1989). Prevalence and stability of physical aggression between spouses: A longitudinal analysis. *Journal of Consulting and Clinical Psychology, 57,* 263-268.

O'Leary, K. D., Malone, J., & Tyree, A. (1994). Physical aggression in early marriage: Prerelationship and relationship effects. *Journal of Consulting and Clinical Psychology, 62,* 594-602.

O'Neal, M. F., & Dorn, P. W. (1998). Effects of time and an educational presentation on student attitudes toward wife beating. *Violence and Victims, 13,* 149-157.

Orava, T. A., McLeod, P. J., & Sharpe, D. (1996). Perceptions of control, depressive symptomatology, and self-esteem of women in transition from abusive relationships. *Journal of Family Violence, 11,* 167-186.

Orloff, L. E., & Kelly, N. (1995). A look at the Violence Against Women Act and gender-related political asylum. *Violence Against Women, 1,* 380-400.

Orlov, R. (1997, July 24). Violence may cost officers. *Los Angeles Daily News,* p. 4.

Osofsky, J. D. (1998). Children as invisible victims of domestic and community violence. In G. W. Holden, R. Geffner, & E. N. Jouriles (Eds.), *Children exposed to domestic violence* (pp. 95-117). Washington, DC: American Psychological Association.

Osthoff, S. (1992). Restoring justice: Clemency for battered women. *Response, 14*(2), 2-3.

Ostrom, B., & Kauder, N. (Eds.). (1997). *Examining the work of state courts, 1996: A national perspective from the Court Statistics Project (National Center for State Courts 1997).* Washington, DC: State Justice Institute and the Bureau of Justice Statistics.

O'Sullivan, C., & Carper, W. (1998, July). *Domestic violence during child visitation: Implications for judicial policies and support services.* Paper presented at the meeting of Program Evaluation and Family Research: An International Conference, Durham, NH.

O'Toole, L. L., & Schiffman, J. R. (Eds.). (1997). *Gender violence: Interdisciplinary perspectives.* New York: New York University Press.

Ott, B. J., Graham, D. L. R., & Rawlings, E. I. (1990, August). *Stockholm Syndrome in emotionally abused adult women.* Paper presented at the annual meeting of the American Psychological Association, Boston.

Overholser, J. C. (1993). Idiographic, quantitative assessment of self-esteem. *Personality and Individual Differences, 14,* 639-646.

Owens, D. M., & Straus, M. A. (1975). The social structure of violence in childhood and approval of violence as an adult. *Aggressive Behavior, 1,* 193-211.

Pagelow, M. D. (1981a). Factors affecting women's decisions to leave violent relationships. *Journal of Family Issues, 2,* 391-414.

Pagelow, M. D. (1981b). *Woman-battering: Victims and their experiences.* Beverly Hills, CA: Sage.

Pagelow, M. D. (1993). Response to Hamberger's comments. *Journal of Interpersonal Violence, 8,* 137-139.

Painter, S. L., & Dutton, D. G. (1985). Patterns of emotional bonding in battered women: Traumatic bonding. *International Journal of Women's Studies, 57,* 101-110.

Palmer, S. E., Brown, R. A., & Barrera, M. E. (1992). Group treatment program for abusive husbands: Long-term evaluation. *American Journal of Orthopsychiatry, 62,* 276-283.

Panel says battered women may have no choice but retaliation. (1987, August 3). *Criminal Justice Newsletter, 18*(15), 6-7.

Paquet, J., Damant, D., Beaudoin, G., & Proulx, S. (1998, July). *Domestic violence: Legal process and process of empowerment.* Paper presented at Program Evaluation and Family Violence Research: An International Conference, Durham, NH.

Parrot, A., & Bechhofer, L. (1991). *Acquaintance rape: The hidden crime.* New York: Wiley.

Pearson, J. (1997). Mediating when domestic violence is a factor: Policies and practices in court-based divorce mediation programs. *Mediation Quarterly, 14,* 319-335.

Pearson, J., & Griswold, E. A. (1997). A preliminary look at client experiences with the good clause exemption to child support cooperation requirements. *Domestic Violence Report, 2,* 65-66, 77-79.

Pearson, J., Thoennes, N., & Griswold, E. A. (1999). Child support and domestic violence: The victims speak out. *Violence Against Women, 5,* 427-448.

Pecora, P. J., Whitaker, J. K., Maluccio, A. N., Barth, R. P., & Plotnick, R. D. (1992). *The child welfare challenge: Policy, practice, and research.* Hawthorne, NY: Aldine.

Peled, E. (1993). Children who witness women battering: Concerns and dilemmas in the construction of a social problem. *Children and Youth Services Review, 15,* 43-52.

Pelletier-Brown, K. M. (1998). Battered women: Leaving abusive relationships. *Dissertation Abstracts International, 59*(7), 3351B. (UMI No. 9840224)

Pennebaker, J. W. (1991). Inhibition as the linchpin of health. In H. S. Friedman (Ed.), *Hostility coping and health* (pp. 127-140). Washington, DC: American Psychological Association.

Pennebaker, J. W., & Susman, J. R. (1988). Disclosure of traumas and psychosomatic process. *Social Stress and Medicine, 26,* 327-332.

Perilla, J. L., Bakeman, R., & Norris, F. H. (1994). Culture and domestic violence: The ecology of abused Latinas. *Violence and Victims, 9,* 325-339.

Perry, B. D. (1994). Neurobiological sequelae of childhood trauma: Post-traumatic stress disorders in children. In M. Murberg (Ed.), *Catecholamines in post-traumatic stress disorder: Emerging concepts* (pp. 253-276). Washington, DC: American Psychiatric Press.

Perry, B. D. (1996). *Maltreated children: Experience, brain development, and the next generation.* New York: Norton.

Perry, B. D. (1997). Incubated in terror: Neurodevelopmental factors in the cycle of violence. In J. D. Osofsky (Ed.), *Children, youth and violence: Searching for solutions* (pp. 124-149). New York: Guilford.

Petchers, M. K. (1995, July). *Child maltreatment among children in battered mothers' households.* Paper presented at the 4th International Family Violence Research Conference, Durham, NH.

Peterson, C., Maier, S. F., & Seligman, M. E. P. (1993). *Learned helplessness: A theory for the age of personal control.* New York: Oxford University Press.

Peterson, C., & Seligman, M. E. P. (1984). Causal explanations as a risk factor for depression: Theory and evidence. *Psychological Review, 91,* 347-374.

Petretic-Jackson, P. A., & Jackson, T. (1996). Mental health interventions with battered women. In A. R. Roberts (Ed.), *Helping battered women: New perspectives and remedies* (pp. 188-221). New York: Oxford University Press.

Pfouts, J. S. (1978). Violent families: Coping responses of abused wives. *Child Welfare, 57,* 101-111.

Phillips, A. L. (1993). *The battered woman's response to abuse: Familial, psychological, situational and relationship correlates.* Unpublished doctoral dissertation, University of Manitoba, Manitoba, Canada.

Pillemer, K. A., & Finkelhor, D. (1988). The prevalence of elder abuse: A random sample survey. *Gerontologist, 28,* 51-57.

Pillemer, K. A., & Finkelhor, D. (1989). Causes of elder abuse: Caregiver stress versus problem relatives. *American Journal of Orthopsychiatry, 59,* 179-187.

Pipher, M. (1994). *Reviving Ophelia.* New York: Ballantine.

Pleck, E. (1987). *Domestic tyranny.* New York: Oxford University Press.

Pollack, W. S. (1999). The sacrifice of Isaac: Toward a new psychology of boys and men. *SPSMM Bulletin, 4*(1), 7-14.

Poteat, G. M., Grossnickle, W. F., Cope, J. G., & Wynne, D. C. (1990). Psychometric properties of the wife abuse inventory. *Journal of Clinical Psychology, 48,* 828-834.

Power, C. (1998, August 3). When women are the enemy. *Newsweek, 132*(5), 37.

Prange, R. C. (1985). Battered women and why they return to the abusive situation: A study of attribution-style, multiple-dimensional locus of control and social-psychological factors. *Dissertation Abstracts International, 46,* 4026B. (UMI No. 8522840)

Prasad, B. D. (1994). Dowry-related violence: A content analysis of news in selected newspapers. *Journal of Comparative Family Studies, 25*(1), 71-89.

President announces crackdown on violence against children. (1998, October 1). *Criminal Justice Newsletter, 29*(19), 6-7.

Price, E. L., & Byers, E. S. (1999, July). *Risk factors for boys' psychologically abusive behaviour in dating relationships.* Paper presented at the 6th International Family Violence Conference, Durham, NH.

Procci, W. R. (1990). *Medical aspects of human sexuality.* New York: Cahners.

Ptacek, J. (1988). Why do men batter their wives? In K. Yllö & M. Bograd (Eds.), *Feminist perspectives on wife abuse* (pp. 133-157). Newbury Park, CA: Sage.

Quindlen, A. (1992, February 4). Editorial. *Long Beach Press Telegram,* p. 10.

Rabasca, L. (1999, February). Women addicts vulnerable to trauma. *APA Monitor, 30*(2), 32.

Radutsky, M. (1999, January 17). The war at home. In D. Hewitt (Producer), *60 minutes.* New York: Columbia Broadcasting System.

Ragg, D. M., Sultana, M., & Miller, D. (1999, July). *The Situational Appraisals Scales (SAS): Initial findings in the development of a measure of minimization for battered women.* Paper presented at the 6th International Family Violence Research Conference, Durham, NH.

Rand, M. R. (1997). *Violence-related injuries treated in hospital emergency departments* (NCJ No. 156921). Rockville, MD: U.S. Department of Justice.

Raphael, J. (1999). The family violence option: An early assessment. *Violence Against Women, 5,* 449-466.

Raphael, J., & Tolman, R. M. (1997). *Trapped by poverty/trapped by abuse: New evidence documents the relationship between domestic violence and welfare.* Ann Arbor: Taylor Institute and the University of Michigan.

Rausch, S. L., van der Kolk, B. A., Fisler, R. F., & Alpert, N. M. (1996). A symptom provocation study of posttraumatic stress disorder using positron emission tomography and script-driven imagery. *Archives of General Psychiatry, 53,* 380-387.

Rawlings, E. I., Allen, G., Graham, D. L. R., & Peters, J. (1994). Chinks in the prison wall: Applying Graham's Stockholm Syndrome theory in the treatment of battered women. In L. Vandecreek, S. Knapp, & T. Jackson (Eds.), *Innovations in clinical practice: A source book* (Vol. 13, pp. 401-417). Sarasota, FL: Professional Resource Press.

Renzetti, C. M. (1988). Violence in lesbian relationships. *Journal of Interpersonal Violence, 3,* 381-399.

Renzetti, C. M. (1989). Building a second closet: Third party responses to victims of lesbian partner abuse. *Family Relations, 38,* 157-163.

Renzetti, C. M. (1992). *Violent betrayal: Partner abuse in lesbian relationships.* Newbury Park, CA: Sage.

Rescorla, R. A., & Solomon, R. L. (1967). Two-process learning theory: Relations between Pavlovian conditioning and instrumental learning. *Psychological Review, 74,* 151-182.

Resnick, H. S., Kilpatrick, D. G., Dansky, B. S., Saunders, B. E., & Best, C. L. (1993). Prevalence of civilian trauma and posttraumatic stress disorder in a representative national sample of women. *Journal of Consulting and Clinical Psychology, 61,* 984-991.

Reyes, K. (1999, Spring). Domestic violence prevention for clergy proves slow-going. *Focus, 4,* 1-3.

Reyna, P. (1995, Fall). Underserved populations have critical needs. *Update: The Newsletter of the Southern California Coalition on Battered Women (SCCBW), 1*(5), 6.

Rhodes, N. R. (1992). Comparison of MMPI Psychopathic Deviate scores of battered and nonbattered women. *Journal of Family Violence, 7,* 297-307.

Rhodes, N. R., & McKenzie, E. B. (1998). Why do battered women stay?: Three decades of research. *Aggression and Violent Behavior, 3,* 391-406.

Riggs, D. S., Kilpatrick, D. G., & Resnick, H. S. (1992). Long-term psychological distress associated with marital rape and aggravated assault: A comparison to other crime victims. *Journal of Family Violence, 7,* 283-296.

Riggs, D. S., Murphy, C. M., & O'Leary, K. D. (1989). Intentional falsification in reports of interpartner aggression. *Journal of Interpersonal Violence, 4,* 220-232.

Rimonte, N. (1989). Domestic violence among Pacific Asians. In Asian Women United of California, *Making waves* (pp. 327-337). Boston: Beacon.

Rogan, M. T. (1997). Fear conditioning induces associative long-term potentiation in the amygdala. *Nature, 390,* 604-607.

Rogers, P., Krammer, L., Podesta, J. S., & Sellinger, M. (1998, August 31). Angry and hurt, but no quitter. *People Weekly, 50*(7), 61-62, 64.

Rogers, S. J. (1999). Wives' income and marital quality: Are there reciprocal effects? *Journal of Marriage and the Family, 61,* 123-132.

Rogge, R. D., & Bradbury, T. N. (1999). Till violence does us part: The differing roles of communication and aggression in predicting adverse marital outcomes. *Journal of Consulting and Clinical Psychology, 67,* 340-351.

Roiphe, A. (1986, September). Women who make sacrifices for their men. *Cosmopolitan, 201,* 308-313, 319.

Rosen, R. (1991, April 8). Women's rights are the same as human rights. *Los Angeles Times,* p. B5.

Rosenbaum, A., & O'Leary, K. D. (1981). Children: The unintended victims of marital violence. *American Journal of Orthopsychiatry, 51,* 692-699.

Rosenblum, L. A., & Harlow, H. F. (1963). Approach-avoidance conflict in the mother surrogate situation. *Psychological Reports, 12,* 83-85.

Ross, M., & Glisson, C. (1991). Bias in social work intervention with battered women. *Journal of Social Service Research, 14*(3/4), 79-105.

Rossman, B. B. R. (1994). Children in violent families: Current diagnostic and treatment considerations. *Family Violence and Sexual Assault Bulletin, 10*(3-4), 29-34.

Rossman, B. B. R. (1998). Descartes's error and posttraumatic stress disorder: Cognition and emotion in children who are exposed to parental violence. In G. W. Holden, R. Geffner, & E. N. Jouriles (Eds.), *Children exposed to marital violence* (pp. 223-256). Washington, DC: American Psychological Association.

Rossman, B. B. R., & Rosenberg, M. (1992). Family stress and functioning in children: The moderating effects of children's beliefs about their control over parental conflict. *Journal of Child Psychology and Psychiatry, 33,* 699-715.

Roth, J. A. (1994). *Psychoactive substances and violence.* Washington, DC: National Institute of Justice.

Rotheram-Bokes, M. J., Rosario, N., & Koopman, C. (1991). Minority youths at high risk: Gay males and runaways. In M. E. Colton & S. Gore (Eds.), *Adolescent stress: Causes and consequences* (pp. 181-200). New York: Aldine de Gruyter.

Rotter, J. B. (1954). *Social learning and clinical psychology.* Englewood Cliffs, NJ: Prentice Hall.

Rouse, L. P. (1988). Abuse in dating relationships: A comparison of blacks, whites, and Hispanics. *Journal of College Student Development, 29,* 312-319.

Rowe, B. R., & Lown, J. M. (1990). The economics of divorce and remarriage for rural Utah families. *Journal of Contemporary Law, 16,* 301-332.

Roy, M. (1977). *Battered women.* New York: Van Nostrand Reinhold.

Rozee-Koker, P., Wynne, C., & Mizrahi, K. (1989, April). *Workplace safety and fear of rape among professional women.* Paper presented at the annual meeting of the Western Psychological Association, Reno, NV.

Ruether, R. R. (1983). *Sexism and god-talk: Toward a feminist theology.* Boston: Beacon.

Rusbult, C. E., & Martz, J. M. (1995). Remaining in an abusive relationship: An investment model analysis of nonvoluntary dependence. *Personality and Social Psychology Bulletin, 21,* 558-571.

Russell, B., & Uhlemann, M. R. (1994). Women surviving an abusive relationship: Grief and the process of change. *Journal of Counseling and Development, 72,* 362-367.

Russell, D. E. H. (1983). The prevalence and incidence of forcible rape and attempted rape of females. *Victimology: An International Journal, 7,* 81-93.

Russell, M. N., Lipov, E., Phillips, N., & White, B. (1989). Psychological profiles of violent and nonviolent maritally distressed couples. *Psychotherapy, 26,* 81-87.

Saltzman, L. E., Mercy, J. A., Rosenberg, M. L., Elsea, W. R., Napper, G., Sikes, R. K., & Waxweiler, R. J. (1990). Magnitude and patterns of family and intimate assault in Atlanta, Georgia, 1984. *Violence and Victims, 5,* 3-17.

Sanders, B., & Moore, D. L. (1999). Childhood maltreatment and date rape. *Journal of Interpersonal Violence, 14,* 115-124.

Sandler, J., Davidson, R. S., Greene, W. E., & Holzschuh, R. D. (1966). Effects of punishment intensity on instrumental avoidance behavior. *Journal of Comparative and Physiological Psychology, 61,* 212-216.

Sansone, R. A., Wiederman, M. W., & Sansone, L. A. (1997). Health care utilization and history of trauma among women in a primary care setting. *Violence and Victims, 12,* 165-172.

Sapiente, A. A. (1988). Locus of control and causal attributions of maritally violent men. *Dissertation Abstracts International, 50,* 758B. (UMI No. 8822697)

Sappington, A. A., Pharr, R., Tunstall, A., & Rickert, E. (1997). Relationships among child abuse, date abuse, and psychological problems. *Journal of Clinical Psychology, 53,* 318-329.

Sato, R. A., & Heiby, E. M. (1992). Correlates of depressive symptoms among battered women. *Journal of Family Violence, 7,* 229-245.

Saunders, D. G. (1986). When battered women use violence: Husband-abuse or self-defense? *Violence and Victims, 1,* 47-60.

Saunders, D. G. (1988). Wife abuse, husband abuse, or mutual combat? A feminist perspective on the empirical findings. In K. Yllö & M. Bograd (Eds.), *Feminist perspectives on wife abuse* (pp. 99-113). Newbury Park, CA: Sage.

Saunders, D. G. (1989, November). *Who hits first and who hurts most? Evidence for the greater victimization of women in intimate relationships.* Paper presented at the annual meeting of the American Society of Criminology, Reno, NV.

Saunders, D. G. (1994). Posttraumatic stress symptom profiles of battered women: A comparison of survivors in two settings. *Violence and Victims, 9,* 31-44.

Saunders, D. G., Hamberger, L. K., & Hovey, M. (1993). Indicators of woman abuse based on a chart review at a family practice center. *Archives of Family Medicine, 2,* 537-543.

Saunders, D. G., & Size, P. B. (1986). Attitudes about woman abuse among police officers, victims, and victim advocates. *Journal of Interpersonal Violence, 1,* 25-42.

Schindehette, S. (1998, September 7). High infidelity. *People Weekly, 50*(8), 52-59.

Schneider, E. M. (1986). Describing and changing: Women's self-defense work and the problem of expert testimony on battering. *Women's Rights Law Reporter, 9*(3&4), 195-222.

Schneider, E. M., & Jordan, S. B. (1978). Representation of women who defend themselves in response to physical or sexual assault. *Family Law Review, 1,* 118-132.

Schornstein, S. L. (1997). *Domestic violence and health care: What every professional needs to know.* Thousand Oaks, CA: Sage.

Schuler, S. R., Hashmi, S. M., Riley, A. P., & Akhter, S. (1996). Credit programs, patriarchy and men's violence against women in rural Bangladesh. *Social Science & Medicine, 43,* 1729-1742.

Schuller, R. A., & Vidmar, N. (1992). Battered woman syndrome evidence in the courtroom: A review of the literature. *Law and Human Behavior, 16,* 273-291.

Schwartz, M. D. (1988). Marital status and woman abuse theory. *Journal of Family Violence, 3,* 239-248.

Schwartz, M. D., & DeKeseredy, W. S. (1993). The return of the "Battered Husband Syndrome" through typification of women as violent. *Crime, Law and Social Change, 20,* 249-265.

Scott, R. L., & Stone, D. A. (1986). MMPI measures of psychological disturbance in adolescent and adult victims of father-daughter incest. *Journal of Clinical Psychology, 42,* 251-259.

Sedlak, A. J. (1988a). The effects of personal experiences with couple violence on calling it "battering" and allocating blame. In G. T. Hotaling, D. Finkelhor, J. T. Kirkpatrick, & M. A. Straus (Eds.), *Coping with family violence* (pp. 31-59). Newbury Park, CA: Sage.

Sedlak, A. J. (1988b). Prevention of wife abuse. In V. B. Van Hasselt, R. L. Morrison, A. S. Bellack, & M. Hersen (Eds.), *Handbook of family violence* (pp. 319-358). New York: Plenum.

Seligman, M. E. P. (1968). Chronic fear produced by unpredictable electric shock. *Journal of Comparative and Physiological Psychology, 66,* 402-411.

Seligman, M. E. P. (1975). *Helplessness: On depression, development and death.* San Francisco: Freeman.

Seligman, M. E. P., & Meyer, B. (1970). Chronic fear and ulcers in rats as a function of the unpredictability of safety. *Journal of Comparative and Physiological Psychology, 73,* 202-207.

Selye, H. (1946). The General Adaptation Syndrome. *Journal of Clinical Endocrinology, 6,* 117-230.

Sex abuse: Identifying survivors in adulthood. (1990, December 3). *Behavior Today, 21*(49), 3-4.

Shainess, N. (1979). Vulnerability to violence: Masochism as process. *American Journal of Psychotherapy, 33,* 174-189.

Sharps, P. W., Campbell, J. C., McFarlane, J., Sachs, C., & Xu, X. (1998, October). *Missed opportunities for prevention of femicide by health care providers.* Paper presented at the 4th International Conference on Children Exposed to Family Violence, San Diego, CA.

Shepard, M., & Pence, E. (1988). The effect of battering on the employment status of women. *Affilia, 3*(2), 55-61.

Shepherd, J. (1990). Victims of personal violence: The relevance of Symonds' model of psychological response and loss theory. *British Journal of Social Work, 20,* 309-332.

Sheriff won't contest domestic violence law. (1996, December 29). *Los Angeles Daily News,* p. 16.

Sherman, L. W. (1992). *Policing domestic violence: Experiments and dilemmas.* New York: Free Press.

Sherman, L. W., Schmidt, J. D., Rogan, D. P., Gartin, P. R., Cohn, E. G., Collins, D. J., & Bacich, A. R. (1991). From initial deterrence to long-term escalation: Short-custody arrest for poverty ghetto domestic violence. *Criminology, 29,* 821-850.

Shir, J. S. (1999). Battered women's perceptions and expectations of their current and ideal marital relationship. *Journal of Family Violence, 14,* 71-82.

Sidman, M. (1953). Two temporal parameters of the maintenance of avoidance behavior by the white rat. *Journal of Comparative and Physiological Psychology, 46,* 253-261.

Sierra, L. (1997, December). Representing battered women charged with crimes for failing to protect their children from abusive partners. *Double-Time, 5*(1 & 2), 1, 4-7.

Sigler, R. T., & Lamb, D. (1995, June). Community-based alternatives to prison: How the public and court personnel view them. *Federal Probation,* pp. 3-9.

Silverman, J. G., & Williamson, G. W. (1997). Social ecology and entitlements involved in battering by heterosexual males: Contributions of family and peers. *Violence and Victims, 12,* 147-164.

Silvern, L., Karyl, J., Waelde, L., Hodges, W. F., Starek, J., Heidt, E., & Min, K. (1995). Retrospective reports of parental partner abuse: Relationships to depression, trauma symptoms and self-esteem among college students. *Journal of Family Violence, 10,* 177-202.

Silverstein, L. B. (1996). Fathering is a feminist issue. *Psychology of Women Quarterly, 20,* 3-37.

Singer, W. (1995). Development and plasticity of cortical processing architectures. *Science, 270,* 758-764.

Sirles, E. A., Lipchik, E., & Kowalski, K. (1993). A consumer's perspective on domestic violence intervention. *Journal of Family Violence, 8,* 267-276.

Skinner, B. F. (1938). *The behavior of organisms.* New York: Appleton-Century-Crofts.

Sleutel, M. R. (1998). Women's experiences of abuse: A review of qualitative research. *Issues in Mental Health Nursing, 19,* 525-539.

Small, M. A., & Tetreault, P. A. (1990). Social psychology, "marital rape exemptions," and privacy. *Behavioral Sciences and the Law, 8,* 141-149.

Smith, C. (1988). *Status discrepancies and husband-to-wife violence.* Durham: University of New Hampshire, Family Violence Research Program.

Smith, J. P., & Williams, J. G. (1992). From abusive household to dating violence. *Journal of Family Violence, 7,* 153-165.

Smith, M. D. (1990). Patriarchal ideology and wife beating: A test of a feminist hypothesis. *Violence and Victims, 5,* 257-273.

Smith, P. H., Danis, M., & Helmick, L. (1998). Changing the health care response to battered women: A health education approach. *Family & Community Health, 20*(4), 1-18.

Smith, S. (1984). The battered woman: A consequence of female development. *Women & Therapy, 3*(2), 3-9.

Snodgrass, S. E. (1990, August). *Sex role stereotypes are alive and well.* Paper presented at the annual meeting of the American Psychological Association, Boston.

Solomon, R. L., Kamin, L. J., & Wynne, L. C. (1953). Traumatic avoidance learning: The outcomes of several extinction procedures with dogs. *Journal of Abnormal and Social Psychology, 48,* 291-302.

Somer, E., & Braunstein, A. (1999). Are children exposed to interparental violence being psychologically maltreated? *Aggression and Violent Behavior, 4,* 449-456.

Sorensen, E., Goldman, J., Ward, M., Albanese, I., Graves, L., & Chamberlain, C. (1995). Judicial decision-making in contested custody cases: The influence of reported child abuse, spouse abuse, and parental substance abuse. *Child Abuse & Neglect, 19,* 251-260.

Sorenson, S. B., & Telles, C. A. (1991). Self-reports of spousal violence in a Mexican-American and non-Hispanic white population. *Violence and Victims, 6,* 3-15.

Sparr, L. E. (1996). Mental defense and posttraumatic stress disorder: Assessment of criminal intent. *Journal of Traumatic Stress, 9,* 405-425.

Spence, K. W. (1956). *Behavior theory and conditioning.* New Haven, CT: Yale University Press.

Sponsors introduce new draft of victims' constitutional amendment. (1998, March 17). *Criminal Justice Newsletter, 29*(6), 1-2.

Stacey, W. A., & Shupe, A. (1983). *The family secret.* Boston: Beacon.

Stahly, G., Ousler, A., & Tanako, J. (1988, April). *Family violence and child custody: A survey of battered women.* Paper presented at the annual meeting of the Western Psychological Association, San Francisco.

Stanko, E. A. (1988). Fear of crime and the myth of the safe home: A feminist critique of criminology. In K. Yllö & M. Bograd (Eds.), *Feminist perspectives on wife abuse* (pp. 75-88). Newbury Park, CA: Sage.

Stanton, E. C., Anthony, S. B., & Gage, M. J. (Eds.). (1889). *History of women suffrage: Vol. 1: 1848-1861.* New York: Fowler & Wells. (Originally published in 1881)

Star, B. (1980). Patterns in family violence. *Social Casework: The Journal of Contemporary Social Work, 61,* 339-346.

Stark, E. (1993). Mandatory arrest of batterers: A reply to critics. *American Behavioral Scientist, 36,* 651-680.

Stark, E., Flitcraft, A., Zuckerman, D., Gray, A., Robinson, J., & Frazier, W. (1981). *Wife assault in the medical setting: An introduction for health personnel* (Monograph Series No. 7). Washington, DC: Department of Health and Human Services, National Clearinghouse on Domestic Violence.

Steiner, J. (1966). *Treblinka.* New York: New American Library.

Steinmetz, S. K. (1977). The battered husband syndrome. *Victimology: An International Journal, 2*(3-4), 499-509.

STEPS to End Family Violence. (1987). *Battered women and criminal justice.* New York: Author.

Sternberg, K. J., Lamb, M. E., Greenbaum, C., Cicchetti, D., Dawud, S., Cortes, R. M., Krispin, O., & Lorey, F. (1993). Effects of domestic violence on children's behavior problems and depression. *Developmental Psychology, 29,* 44-52.

Stets, J. E. (1990). Verbal and physical aggression in marriage. *Journal of Marriage and the Family, 52,* 501-514.

Stets, J. E., & Straus, M. A. (1989). The marriage license as a hitting license: A comparison of assaults in dating, cohabiting, and married couples. In M. A. Pirog-Good & J. E. Stets (Eds.), *Violence in dating relationships: Emerging social issues* (pp. 33-52). New York: Praeger.

Stets, J. E., & Straus, M. A. (1990). Gender differences in reporting marital violence and its medical and psychological consequences. In M. A. Straus & R. J. Gelles (Eds.), *Physical violence in American families: Risk factors and adaptations to violence in 8,145 families* (pp. 151-166). New Brunswick, NJ: Transaction Books.

Stone, A. E., & Fialk, R. J. (1999, December/January). Backlash against the abused victim in custody disputes. *Domestic Violence Report, 4,* 26-27.

Straus, M. A. (1979). Measuring intrafamily conflict and aggression: The Conflict Tactics Scale (CTS). *Journal of Marriage and the Family, 41,* 75-88.

Straus, M. A. (1983). Ordinary violence, child abuse and wife beating: What do they have in common? In D. Finkelhor, R. J. Gelles, G. T. Hotaling, & M. A. Straus (Eds.), *The dark side of families: Current family violence research* (pp. 213-234). Beverly Hills, CA: Sage.

Straus, M. A. (1987). The costs of family violence. *Public Health Reports, 102,* 638-641.

Straus, M. A. (1991a). *Children as witness to marital violence: A risk factor for life long problems among a nationally representative sample of American men and women.* Paper presented at the Ross Roundtable on Children and Violence, Washington, DC.

Straus, M. A. (1991b). *Incidence and chronicity of assaults by wives on husbands: Implications for primary prevention of wife-beating.* Unpublished manuscript, University of New Hampshire, Durham.

Straus, M. A. (1993). Physical assaults by wives—A major social problem. In R. J. Gelles & D. R. Loseke (Eds.), *Current controversies on family violence* (pp. 67-87). Newbury Park, CA: Sage.

Straus, M. A. (1997). Physical assaults by women partners: A major social problem. In M. R. Walsh (Ed.), *Women, men, and gender: Ongoing debates* (pp. 210-221). New Haven, CT: Yale University Press.

Straus, M. A., & Gelles, R. J. (1986). Societal change and change in family violence from 1975 to 1985 as revealed by two national surveys. *Journal of Marriage and the Family, 48,* 465-479.

Straus, M. A., & Gelles, R. J. (1990). *Physical violence in American families: Risk factors and adaptations to violence in 8,145 families.* New Brunswick, NJ: Transaction Books.

Straus, M. A., Gelles, R. J., & Steinmetz, S. K. (1980). *Behind closed doors: Violence in the American family.* Garden City, NY: Doubleday.

Straus, M. A., & Smith, C. (1990). Family patterns of primary prevention of family violence. In M. A. Straus & R. J. Gelles (Eds.), *Physical violence in American families: Risk factors and adaptations to violence in 8,145 families* (pp. 507-526). New Brunswick, NJ: Transaction Books.

Straus, M. A., & Sweet, S. (1992). Verbal/symbolic aggression in couples: Incidence rates and relationships to personal characteristics. *Journal of Marriage and the Family, 58,* 825-841.

Straus, R. B. (1995). Supervised visitation and family violence. *Family Law Quarterly, 29,* 229-252.

Strentz, T. (1979, April). Law enforcement policy and ego defenses of the hostage. *FBI Law Enforcement Bulletin,* pp. 2-12.

Strube, M. J., & Barbour, L. S. (1983). The decision to leave an abusive relationship: Economic dependence and psychological commitment. *Journal of Marriage and the Family, 45,* 785-793.

Strube, M. J., & Barbour, L. S. (1984). Factors related to the decision to leave an abusive relationship. *Journal of Marriage and the Family, 46,* 837-844.

Stubbing, E. (1990). Police who think family homicide is preventable are pointing the way. *Response, 13*(1), 8.

Stuckless, N. (1998). *The influence of anger, perceived injustice, revenge, and time on the quality of life of survivor-victim* [CD-ROM]. Abstract from: ProQuest File: Dissertation Abstracts Item: NN20428.

Suarez, K. E. (1994). Teenage dating violence: The need for expanded awareness and legislation. *California Law Review, 82,* 423-471.

Sue, D. W., & Sue, D. (1990). *Counseling the culturally different* (2nd ed.). New York: Wiley.

Sugarman, D. B., & Hotaling, G. T. (1991). Dating violence: A review of contextual and risk factors. In B. Levy (Ed.), *Dating violence—Young women in danger* (pp. 100-118). Seattle, WA: Seal Press.

Suh, E. K., & Abel, E. M. (1990). The impact of spousal violence on the children of the abuse. *Journal of Individual Social Work, 4,* 27-34.

Sullivan, C. M. (1991a). Battered women as active helpseekers. *Violence UpDate, 1*(12), 1, 8, 10-11.

Sullivan, C. M. (1991b). The provision of advocacy services to women leaving abusive partners. *Journal of Interpersonal Violence, 6,* 41-54.

Sullivan, C. M., Basta, J., Tan, C., & Davidson, W. S., II. (1992). After the crisis: A needs assessment of women leaving a domestic violence shelter. *Violence and Victims, 7,* 271-280.

Sullivan, C. M., & Bybee, D. I. (1999). Reducing violence using community-based advocacy for women with abusive partners. *Journal of Consulting and Clinical Psychology, 67,* 43-53.

Sullivan, C. M., Rumptz, M. H., Campbell, R., Eby, K., & Davidson, W. S., II. (1996). Retaining participants in longitudinal community research: A comprehensive protocol. *Journal of Applied Behavioral Science, 32,* 262-276.

Sullivan, C. M., Tan, C., Basta, J., Rumptz, M., & Davidson, W. S., II. (1992). An advocacy intervention program for women with abusive partners: Initial evaluation. *American Journal of Community Psychology, 30,* 309-332.

Sullivan, J. P., & Mosher, D. L. (1990). Acceptance of guided imagery of marital rape as a function of macho personality. *Violence and Victims, 5,* 275-286.

Sutliff, J. A. (1995). *Avoidance coping strategies and symptomatology of victims of violence* [CD-ROM]. Abstract from: Proquest File: Dissertation Abstracts Item: 9518035.

Swann, W. B., Jr., & Read, S. J. (1981). Acquiring self-knowledge: The search for feedback that fits. *Personality and Social Psychology, 41,* 1119-1128.

Swenson, S. V. (1984). Effects of sex-role stereotypes and androgynous alternatives in mental health judgments of psychotherapists. *Psychological Reports, 54,* 475-481.

Syers, M., & Edleson, J. L. (1992). The combined effects of coordinated criminal justice intervention in woman abuse. *Journal of Interpersonal Violence, 7,* 490-502.

Symonds, A. (1979). Violence against women—The myth of masochism. *American Journal of Psychotherapy, 23,* 161-173.

Szinovacz, M. E. (1983). Using couple data as a methodological tool: The case of marital violence. *Journal of Marriage and the Family, 45,* 633-644.

Tan, C., Basta, J., Sullivan, C. M., & Davidson, W. S. (1995). The role of social support in the lives of women exiting domestic violence shelters. *Journal of Interpersonal Violence, 10,* 437-451.

Tang, C. S. (1999). Wife abuse in Hong Kong Chinese families: A community survey. *Journal of Family Violence, 14,* 173-191.

Tatara, T., & Kuzmeskus, L. M. (1997). *Summaries of statistical data on elder abuse in domestic settings for FY 95 and FY 96.* Washington, DC: National Center on Elder Abuse.

Tavris, C. (1992, February). *The mismeasure of woman.* Presentation given at the national conference of the Association of Women in Psychology, Long Beach, CA.

The battered woman: Breaking the cycle of abuse. (1989, June 15). *Emergency Medicine, 15,* 104-115.

Theodore, R. M. (1992). The relationship between locus of control and level of violence in married couples. In E. C. Viano (Ed.), *Intimate violence: Interdisciplinary perspectives* (pp. 37-48). Bristol, PA: Taylor & Francis.

Thoenen, H. (1995). Neurotrophins and neuronal plasticity. *Science, 270,* 593-598.

Thoits, P. A. (1982). Conceptual, methodological, and theoretical problems in studying practical implications. *Journal of Personality and Social Psychology, 52,* 813-832.

Thompson, C. (1989). Breaking through walls of isolation: A model for churches in helping victims of violence. *Pastoral Psychology, 38,* 35-38.

Thompson, K. D. (1995). *Officially reported characteristics of spouse abuse victims seeking assistance in Utah, 1992* [CD-ROM]. Abstract from: ProQuest File: Dissertation Abstracts Item: 1358266.

Thorne-Finch, R. (1992). *Ending the silence: The origins and treatment of male violence against women.* Toronto: University of Toronto Press.

Three deputies get domestic violence convictions sealed. (1997, May 1). *Los Angeles Daily News,* p. 6.

Tierney, K. J. (1982). The battered women movement and the creation of the wife beating problem. *Social Problems, 29,* 207-220.

Tinsley, C. A., Critelli, J. W., & Ee, J. S. (1992, August). *The perception of sexual aggression: One act, two realities.* Paper presented at the annual meeting of the American Psychological Association, Washington, DC.

Tjaden, P., & Thoennes, N. (1998, November). *Prevalence, incidence, and consequences of violence against women: Findings from the National Violence Against Women survey* (NCJ No. 172837). Washington, DC: National Institute of Justice.

Tjaden, P., Thoennes, N., & Allison, C. J. (1999, July). *Comparing violence over the life-span in samples of same-sex and opposite-sex cohabitants.* Paper presented at the 6th International Family Violence Research Conference, Durham, NH.

Tolman, R. M. (1999). Guest editor's introduction. *Violence Against Women, 5,* 355-369.

Tomkins, A. J., Mohamed, S., Steinman, M., Macolini, R. M., Kenning, M. K., & Afrank, J. (1994). The plight of children who witness woman battering: Psychological knowledge and policy implications. *Law and Psychology Review, 18,* 137-187.

Tomz, J. E., & McGillis, D. (1997). *Serving crime victims and witnesses* (2nd ed.; NCJ No. 163174). Washington, DC: U.S. Department of Justice.

Tontodonato, P., & Crew, B. K. (1992). Dating violence, social learning theory, and gender: A multivariate analysis. *Violence and Victims, 7,* 3-14.

Toufexis, A. (1987, December 21). Home is where the hurt is: Wife beating among the well-to-do no longer a secret. *Time,* p. 68.

Tran, C. G. (1997). *Domestic violence among Vietnamese refugee women: Prevalence, abuse characteristics, psychiatric symptoms, and psychosocial factors* [CD-ROM]. Abstract from: ProQuest File: Dissertation Abstracts Item: 9713666.

Trimpey, M. L. (1989). Self-esteem and anxiety: Key issues in an abused women's support group. *Issues in Mental Health Nursing, 10,* 297-308.

Trute, B. (1998). Going beyond gender specific treatments in wife battering: Pro-feminist couple and family therapy. *Aggression and Violent Behavior, 3,* 1-5.

Tsesis, A. V. (1996). Preventing homelessness by empowering battered women through vocational opportunities. *Domestic Violence Report, 1*(5), 3, 12-13.

Tucker, N. (1999, April 14). Zimbabwe women stripped of rights. *Long Beach (CA) Press-Telegram,* pp. A13-A14.

Tuel, B. D., & Russell, R. K. (1998). Self-esteem and depression in battered women: A comparison of lesbian and heterosexual survivors. *Violence Against Women, 4,* 344-362.

Turkat, I. D. (1995). Divorce related malicious mother syndrome. *Journal of Family Violence, 10,* 253-264.

Turkat, I. D. (1999). Divorce-related malicious parent syndrome. *Journal of Family Violence, 14,* 95-97.

Turque, B., Murr, A., Miller, M., Foote, D., Fleming, C., Biddle, N. A., Starr, M., & Namuth, T. (1994, June 27). He could run . . . but he couldn't hide. *Newsweek, 123*(26), 12-27.

Tutty, L. M. (1996). Post-shelter services: The efficacy of follow-up programs for abused women. *Research on Social Work Practice, 6,* 425-441.

Tutty, L. M., Weaver, C., & Rothery, M. A. (1999). Residents' views of the efficacy of shelter services for assaulted women. *Violence Against Women, 5,* 898-925.

Two New York lower court welfare-related confidentiality decisions troubling for battered women. (1999, February/March). *Domestic Violence Report, 4,* 41.

Ulrich, R. E., Wolff, P. C., & Azrin, N. H. (1964). Shock as an elicitor of intra- and inter-species fighting behavior. *Animal Behavior, 12,* 14-15.

The Urban Institute. (1998). *Evaluation of the STOP formula grants to combat violence against women.* Washington, DC: Author.

U.S. Bureau of the Census. (1997). *Current population survey [Poverty statistics on population groups].* Washington, DC: Author.

U.S. Department of Justice. (1983). *Report to the nation on crime and justice: The data.* Washington, DC: Author.

U.S. Department of Justice. (1992). *Sourcebook of criminal justice statistics 1991* (NCJ No. 137369). Washington, DC: Author.

U.S. Department of Justice. (1996, May). *The validity and use of evidence concerning battering and its effects in criminal trials* (NCJ No. 160972). Washington, DC: Author.

U.S. Department of Justice, Bureau of Justice Statistics. (1994). *Violence between intimates* (NCJ No. 149259). Washington, DC: Author.

Valencia, A., & Van Hoorn, J. (1999). La Isla Pacifico: A haven for battered Mexican American women. *American Psychologist, 54,* 62-63.

Varvaro, F. F. (1991). Using a grief response assessment questionnaire in a support group to assist battered women in their recovery. *Response, 13*(4), 17-20.

Vaughn, D. (1987, July). The long goodbye. *Psychology Today,* pp. 37-38, 42.

Vazquez, C. I. (1996). Spousal abuse and violence against women: The significance of understanding attachment. *Annals of the New York Academy of Sciences, 789,* 119-128.

Victim agencies struggle with domestic violence and DUI cases. (1992, June 15). *Criminal Justice Newsletter, 23*(19), 5-7.

Vinton, L. (1991). Abused older women: Battered women or abused elders? *Journal of Women and Aging, 3,* 5-19.

Vinton, L. (1992). Battered women's shelters and older women: The Florida experience. *Journal of Family Violence, 7,* 63-72.

Vinton, L. (1998). A nationwide survey of domestic violence shelters' programming for older women. *Violence Against Women, 4,* 559-571.

Vinton, L., Altholz, J. A., & Lobell, T. (1997). A five-year follow-up study of domestic violence programming for battered older women. *Journal of Women and Aging, 9,* 3-15.

Violence and women offenders. (1990). *Response, 13*(1), 7.

Virginia Coalition for the Homeless. (1995). *1995 shelter provider survey.* Richmond: Author.

Vitanzas, S., Vogel, L. C., & Marshall, L. L. (1995). Distress and symptoms of post-traumatic stress disorder in abused women. *Violence and Victims, 10,* 23-34.

Vivian, D., & Langhinrichsen-Rohling, J. (1994). Are bi-directionally violent couples mutually victimized? A gender-sensitive comparison. *Violence and Victims, 9,* 107-124.

Waaland, P., & Keeley, S. (1985). Police decision making in wife abuse: The impact of legal and extralegal factors. *Law and Human Behavior, 9,* 355-366.

Waldman, S. (1992, May 4). Deadbeat dads. *Newsweek, 119*(5), 46-52.

Waldner-Haugrud, L. K. (1999). Sexual coercion in lesbian and gay relationships: A review and critique. *Aggression and Violent Behavior, 4,* 139-149.

Waldner-Haugrud, L. K., Gratch, L. V., & Magruder, B. (1997). Victimization and perpetration rates of violence in gay and lesbian relationships: Gender issues explored. *Violence and Victims, 12,* 173-184.

Walker, L. E. (1977). Battered women and learned helplessness. *Victimology: An International Journal, 2,* 525-534.

Walker, L. E. (1979). *The battered woman.* New York: Harper & Row.

Walker, L. E. (1983). The battered woman syndrome study. In D. Finkelhor, R. J. Gelles, G. T. Hotaling, & M. A. Straus (Eds.), *The dark side of families* (pp. 31-48). Beverly Hills, CA: Sage.

Walker, L. E. (1984). *The battered woman syndrome.* New York: Springer.

Walker, L. E. (1985a). Psychological impact of the criminalization of domestic violence on victims. *Victimology: An International Journal, 10,* 281-300.

Walker, L. E. (1985b, June 7). *Psychology of battered women.* Symposium conducted at the Laguna Human Options Conference, Laguna Beach, CA.

Walker, L. E. (1999). Psychology and domestic violence. *American Psychologist, 54,* 21-29.

Walker, L. E., & Browne, A. (1985). Gender and victimization by intimates. *Journal of Personality, 53,* 179-194.

Warchol, G. (1998). *Workplace violence, 1992-1996* (NCJ No. 168634). Washington, DC: Bureau of Justice Statistics.

Warren v. State, 255 Ga. 151, 336 S.E.2d 221 (1985).

Watson, J. B., & Raynor, R. (1920). Conditioned emotional reactions. *Journal of Experimental Psychology, 3,* 1-14.

Wauchope, B. A. (1988). *Help-seeking decisions of battered women: A test of learned helplessness and two stress theories.* Durham: University of New Hampshire, Family Violence Research Program.

Waxman, L., & Trupin, R. (1997). *A status report on hunger and homelessness in America's cities: 1997.* Washington, DC: U.S. Conference of Mayors. (1620 Eye St., NW, 4th floor, Washington, DC, 20006-4005)

Weaver, T. L., & Clum, G. A. (1995). Psychological distress associated with interpersonal violence: A meta-analysis. *Clinical Psychology Review, 15,* 115-140.

Websdale, N. (1995a). An ethnographic assessment of the policing of domestic violence in rural eastern Kentucky. *Social Justice, 22,* 102-122.

Websdale, N. (1995b). Rural woman abuse: The voices of Kentucky women. *Violence Against Women, 1,* 309-338.

Wessel, L., & Campbell, J. C. (1997). Providing sanctuary for battered women: Nicaragua's casas de la mujer. *Issues in Mental Health Nursing, 18,* 455-476.

West, C., & Zimmerman, D. H. (1987). Doing gender. *Gender & Society, 1,* 125-151.

Westrupt, D., & Fremouw, W. J. (1998). Stalking behavior: A literature review and suggested functional analytic assessment technology. *Aggression and Violence Behavior, 1,* 255-274.

Wetzel, L., & Ross, M. A. (1983). Psychological and social ramification of battering: Observations leading to a counseling methodology for victims of domestic violence. *Personnel and Guidance Journal, 61,* 423-428.

Whatley, M. A. (1993). For better or worse: The case of marital rape. *Violence and Victims, 8,* 29-39.

Whipple, V. (1987). Counseling battered women from fundamentalist churches. *Journal of Marital and Family Therapy, 13,* 251-258.

White, J. W., & Koss, M. P. (1991). Courtship violence: Incidence in a national sample of higher education students. *Violence and Victims, 6,* 247-256.

Wife rape: Ignored by providers, more devastating to victims. (1997, October/November). *Domestic Violence Report, 3,* 1, 6, 14.

Willet, S. L., & Barnett, O. W. (1987, April). *Relational consequences of wife beating for violent husbands.* Paper presented at the annual meeting of the Western Psychological Association, Long Beach, CA.

Williams, C. J. (1999, May 27). In Kosovo, rape seen as awful death. *Los Angeles Times,* pp. A1, A18-A19.

Williams, K. R., & Hawkins, R. (1989). The meaning of arrest for wife assault. *Criminology, 1,* 163-181.

Wilson, K., Vercella, R., Brems, C., Benning, D., & Renfro, N. (1992). Levels of learned helplessness in abused women. *Women and Therapy, 13*(4), 53-67.

Wilson, M. I., & Daly, M. (1992). Who kills whom in spouse killings? On the exceptional sex ratio of spousal homicides in the United States. *Criminology, 30,* 189-215.

Wilson, M. N., Baglioni, A. J., Jr., & Downing, D. (1989). Analyzing factors influencing readmission to a battered women's shelter. *Journal of Family Violence, 4,* 275-284.

Wilson, M. N., & Daly, M. (1993). Spousal homicide risk and estrangement. *Violence and Victims, 8,* 3-16.

Wilt, S., Illman, S., & Field, M. B. (1997). *Female homicide victims in New York City 1990-1994.* New York: Department of Health Inquiry Prevention Program.

Winner, K. (1996). *Divorced from justice: The abuse of women and children by divorce lawyers and judges.* New York: HarperCollins.

Wirtz, P. W., & Harrell, A. V. (1987). Effects of postassault exposure to attack-similar stimuli on long-term recovery of victims. *Journal of Consulting and Clinical Psychology, 55,* 10-16.

Witwer, M. B., & Crawford, C. A. (1995). *A coordinated approach to reducing family violence: Conference highlights* (NCJ No. 155184). Washington, DC: U.S. Department of Justice.

Wolfe, D. A., Werkerle, C., Gough, R., Reitzel-Jaffee, D., Grasley, C., Pittman, A. L., Lefebvre, L., & Stumpf, J. (1996). *The youth relationship manual: A group approach with adolescents for the prevention of woman abuse and promotion of healthy relationships.* Thousand Oaks, CA: Sage.

Wong, R. R. (1995). Divorce mediation among Asian Americans. *Family and Conciliation Courts Review, 33,* 110-128.

Wood, A. D., & McHugh, M. C. (1994). Woman battering: The response of the clergy. *Pastoral Psychology, 42,* 185-196.

Wood, P. B., Gove, W. R., Wilson, J. A., & Cochran, J. K. (1997). Nonsocial reinforcement and habitual criminal conduct: An extension of learning theory. *Criminology, 35,* 335-366.

Woods, S. J. (1999). Normative beliefs regarding the maintenance of intimate relationships among abused and nonabused women. *Journal of Interpersonal Violence, 14,* 479-491.

Worth, D. M., Matthews, P. A., & Coleman, W. R. (1990). Sex role, group affiliation, family background, and courtship violence in college students. *Journal of College Student Development, 31,* 250-254.

Wuest, J., & Merritt-Gray, M. (1999). Not going back: Sustaining the separation in the process of leaving abusive relationships. *Violence Against Women, 5,* 110-133.

Wurtele, S. K., & Miller-Perrin, C. L. (1992). *Preventing child sexual abuse: Sharing the responsibility.* Lincoln: University of Nebraska Press.

Wyatt, G. E., Guthrie, G. E., & Notgrass, C. M. (1992). Differential effects of women's child sexual abuse and subsequent sexual revictimization. *Journal of Consulting and Clinical Psychology, 60,* 167-173.

Yegidis, B. L., & Renzy, R. B. (1994). Battered women's experiences with a preferred arrest policy. *Affilia, 9,* 60-70.

Yllö, K. A. (1993). Through a feminist lens: Gender, power, and violence. In R. J. Gelles & D. R. Loseke (Eds.), *Current controversies on family violence* (pp. 47-62). Newbury Park, CA: Sage.

Yoshihama, M., & Sorenson, S. B. (1994). Physical, sexual, and emotional abuse by male intimates: Experiences of women in Japan. *Violence and Victims, 9,* 63-77.

Youngstrom, N. (1992). Laws to aid battered women backfire. *APA Monitor, 23*(2), 45.

Zlotnick, C. K., Kohn, R., Peterson, J., & Pearlstein, T. (1998). Partner physical victimization in a national sample of American families. *Journal of Interpersonal Violence, 13,* 156-166.

Zorza, J. (1991). Woman battering: A major cause of homelessness. *Clearinghouse Review, 61,* 421-429.
Zorza, J. (1994). Woman battering: High costs and the state of the law. *Clearinghouse Review, 28,* 383-395.
Zorza, J. (1995). Recognizing and protecting the privacy and confidentiality needs of battered women. *Family Law Quarterly, 29,* 273-311.
Zorza, J. (1997). Recent cases. *Domestic Violence Report, 2,* 90.
Zorza, J. (1998). Our clients may affect us: Vicarious traumatization. *Domestic Violence Report,* 2(2), 21-22, 26.
Zorza, J. (1999a, February/March). California appellate court seizes on Simpson's custody case to give domestic violence greater importance. *Domestic Violence Report, 4,* 33-34, 40.
Zorza, J. (1999b, December/January). Dual victim treatment helps preschoolers and mothers dramatically. *Domestic Violence Report, 4,* 20.
Zorza, J., & Schoenberg, L. (1995). *Improving the health care response to domestic violence through protocols and policies.* Washington, DC: National Center on Women and Family Law.
Zorza, R., & Klemperer, J. (1999, April/May). The Internet-based domestic court preparation project: Using the Internet to overcome barriers to justice. *Domestic Violence Report, 4,* 49-50, 59-60.

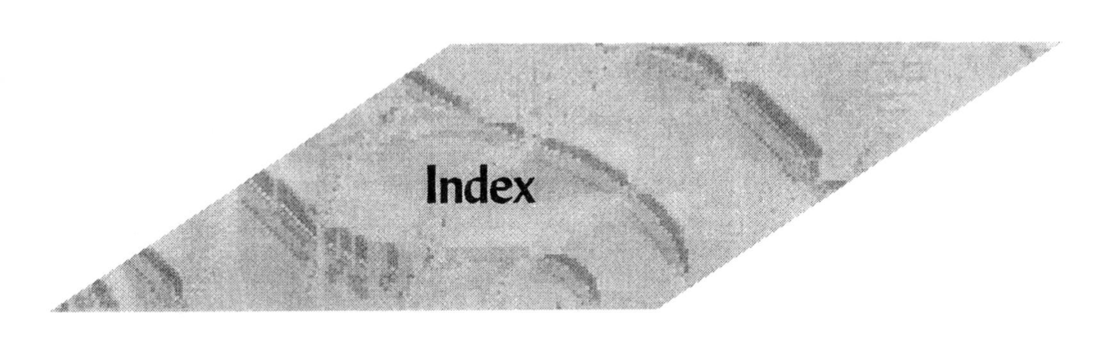

Index

About the Authors

Alyce D. LaViolette has worked with battered women since 1978, first as an advocate at WomenShelter in Long Beach, California, and then in private practice. In 1979, she founded Alternatives to Violence, one of the first programs in the country for spouse abusers. She has developed training programs for the Los Angeles and California State Departments of Probation and for the Orange County Department of Children and Family Services. She is a frequently requested conference and keynote speaker and also serves as an expert witness.

Ms. LaViolette has published articles, coauthored a parenting curriculum for domestically violent families, and written a pamphlet on battered women and therapy. She is a founding member and cochair of both the Association of Batterers' Intervention Programs and the California Association of Batterers' Intervention Programs. She has been a member, advisory board member, and trainer for the Statewide California Coalition on Battered Women since 1978. She has received numerous awards for her work, including the Humanitarian Award from the Los Angeles Commission on Assaults Against Women, the I Am Foundation's Community Service Award, and proclamations from Los Angeles County and the State of California.

Ola W. Barnett is Professor Emerita of Psychology at Pepperdine University, Malibu, California. She received her doctorate at the University of California, Los Angeles, specializing in learning. Her major research and publication areas have been the characteristics of interpersonally violent men, the assessment of marital violence, and battered women. She remains active in the field of family violence, conducting research in the areas of marital and dating violence and the effectiveness of shelter programs. She is the recipient of the Charles B. Luckman Distinguished Teaching Fellows Award. She coauthored (with Cindy L. Miller-Perrin and Robin D. Perrin) the best-selling text *Family Violence Across the Lifespan* (Sage, 1997).